D1879988

HUMAN RESOURCE MANAGEMENT

HUMAN RESOURCE MANAGEMENT

Kumar Pranit

genNEXT Publication

Human Resource Management (PB)

Rs. 150

© Kumar Pranit

ISBN: 978-93-80222-08-0

All rights reserved. No Part of this book may be reproduced in any manner without written permission.

Published in 2010 in India by
Gennext Publication
23 Main Ansari Road, Darya Ganj,
New Delhi-110002
E-Mail:GenNextpublication@hotmail.com
Phone: 23282060

Printed at: Chawla Offset Press, Delhi

Contents

Preface

Human resource management is the planned and logical approach to the management of an organization's most treasured assets; the people working there who individually and collectively contribute to the achievement of the objectives of the business. Human resources are the most unique and precious possessions of an organization. The productive management of an organization's human resources is a dynamic and challenging job. The scarceness of gifted resources and the rising expectations of the contemporary worker have further changed the complexity of the human resource function.

This textbook examines the various HR processes that are related to attracting, managing, motivating, and developing employees for the welfare of the business organization. It discusses the matters in HR management in the altering environment and suggests best possible waysof managing human resources.

This textbook presents practical simple tools and concepts of Human resource management for students as well as managers. It presents the essentials of Human resource management in a lucid style.

Detailed chapters are included on various topics of Human resource management. Each chapter gives real world examples and relevant Human resource management principles in a straightforward manner.

This volume is an essential addition to any student and business manager library; especially anyone needed to make important, informed decisions in the presence of scarce resources. A valuable source of knowledge for all students, teachers, consultants and lay person who are interested in gaining knowledge of Human resource management.

The well-written materials ensure that students are able to understand all topics clearly. Author is confident that this book will be a handy tool for the students learning Human resource management. Sincere feedback, suggestions and comments are always welcome

1

Introduction

Human resource management (HRM) is the basis of all management activity, but it is not the basis of all business activity. A business may depend fundamentally on having a unique product, or on obtaining the necessary funding. The basis of management is always the same: getting the people of the business to make things happen in a productive way, so that the business prospers and the people thrive.

HR MANAGEMENT FOR THE TWENTY-FIRST CENTURY

Businesses are diverse. Prisons, restaurants, oil companies, corner shops, fire brigades, churches, hotel chains, hospitals, schools, newspapers, charities, doctors' and dentists' surgeries, professional sports teams, airlines, barristers' chambers and universities are all businesses in the sense that they have overall corporate missions to deliver and these have to be achieved within financial constraints. They all need to have their human resources managed, no matter how much some of the resourceful humans may resent aspects of the management process which limit their individual freedom of action.

Managing resourceful humans requires a constant balancing between meeting the human aspirations of the people and meeting the strategic and financial needs of the business. At times the balance can shift too far in one direction. Through the 1960s and 1970s the human aspirations of senior people in companies and public sector operations tended to produce large staffs, with heavyweight bureaucracies and stagnant businesses. One consultancy in the 1970s produced monthly comparative data measuring company success in terms of profitability and the number of employees – the more the better. At the same time the aspirations of employees lower down in the bureaucracy tended to maintain the status quo and a concentration on employee benefits that had scant relevance to business effectiveness. By the end of the twentieth century financial imperatives had generated huge reactions to this in the general direction of 'downsizing' or reducing the number of people employed to create businesses that were lean, fit and flexible. Hierarchies were 'delayered' to reduce numbers of staff and many functions were 'outsourced', so as to simplify the operation of the business, concentrating on core expertise at the expense of peripheral activities, which were then bought in as needed from consultants or specialist suppliers. Reducing headcount became a fashionable criterion for success. By the beginning of the twenty-first century the problems of the scales being tipped so considerably towards rationalisation were beginning to show. Businesses became more than slim; some became anorexic. Cost cutting achieved impressive short-tem results, but it cannot be repeated year after year without impairing the basic viability of the business. Steadily the number of problem cases mounted. In Britain there was great public discussion about problems with the national rail network and the shortage of skilled staff to carry out maintenance and repairs or lack of trained guards.

THE NATURE OF HUMAN RESOURCE MANAGEMENT

HR managers need to be particularly aware of the risks associated with cost cutting, as they may be the greatest culprits. The British National Health Service has long been criticised for inefficient use of resources, so large numbers of managers and administrators have been recruited to make things more efficient. Many of these new recruits are HR people who may be perceived by health professionals as creating inefficient and costly controls at the expense of employing more health professionals. We are not suggesting that these criticisms are necessarily justified, but there are undoubtedly situations in which the criticisms are justified.

There is now a move towards redressing that balance in search for an equilibrium between the needs for financial viability and success in the marketplace on the one hand and the need to maximise human capital on the other.

BUSINESSES, ORGANIZATIONS AND HUMAN RESOURCE MANAGEMENT

Most books on management and the academic study of management use the term 'organization' as the classifier: organizational behaviour, organizational psychology, organizational sociology and organization theory are standard terms because they focus on the interaction between the organization as an entity and its people or with the surrounding society. So far we have used the word 'business'. We will not stick to this throughout the book, but we have used it to underline the fact that HR people are concerned with the management of resourceful humans not employed within the organization as well as those who are. The above criticism of NASA's complacency was because they had lost the sense of ownership and responsibility for a human capital input simply because the people were employed by a different organization. HR people have to be involved in the effective management of all the people of the business, not only those who are directly employed within the organization itself. We need to remember that organization is a process as well as an entity.

We use the word 'organization' to describe an entity when we are describing the place where we work ('my organization'), a particular business enterprise ('Shell is an international organization') or as a general term to describe undertakings ('over 200 organizations were represented at the conference'). Organization as a process describes how something is done ('the organization of the conference was very efficient'; 'the project failed due to poor organization'). Think of examples of HR work which are organization as a process.

Human resource managers administer the contract of employment, which is the legal basis of the employment relationship, but within that framework they also administer a psychological contract for performance. To have a viable business the employer obviously requires those who do its work to produce an appropriate and effective performance and the performance may come from employees, but is just as likely to come from non-employees. A business which seeks to be as lean and flexible as it can needs to reduce long-term cost commitments and focus its efforts on the activities which are the basis of its competitive advantage. It may be wise to buy in standard business services, as well as expertise, from specialist providers. Performance standards can be unambiguously agreed and monitored (although they rarely are), while the contract can be ended a great deal more easily than is the case with a department full of employees.

We refer to a contract for performance because both parties have an interest in performance. The employer needs it from the employee, but an employee also has a psychological need to perform, to do well and to fulfil personal needs that for many can best be met in the employment context. Schoolteachers cannot satisfy their desire to teach without a school to provide premises, equipment and pupils. A research chemist can do little without a well-equipped laboratory and qualified colleagues; very few coach drivers can earn their living unless someone else provides the coach.

DEFINING HUMAN RESOURCE MANAGEMENT

The term 'human resource management' is not easy to define. This is because it is commonly used in two different ways. On the one hand it is used generically to describe the body of management activities covered in books such as this. Used in this way HRM is really no more than a more modern and supposedly imposing name for what has long been labelled 'personnel management'. On the other hand, the term is equally widely used to denote a particular approach to the management of people which is clearly distinct from 'personnel management'. Used in this way 'HRM' signifies more than an updating of the label; it also suggests a distinctive philosophy towards carrying out people-oriented organizational activities: one which is held to serve the modern business more effectively than 'traditional' personnel management. We explore the substance of these two meanings of human resource management in the following paragraphs, referring to the first as 'HRM mark 1' and the second as 'HRM mark 2'.

HRM Mark 1: The Generic Term

The role of the human resource functions is explained by identifying the key objectives to be achieved. Four objectives form the foundation of all HR activity.

STAFFING OBJECTIVES

Human resource managers are first concerned with ensuring that the business is appropriately staffed and thus able to draw on the human resources it needs. This involves designing organization structures, identifying under what type of contract different groups of employees (or subcontractors) will work, before recruiting, selecting and developing the people required to fill the roles: the right people, with the right skills to provide their services when needed. There is a need to compete effectively in the employment market by recruiting and retaining the best, affordable workforce that is available. This involves developing employment packages that are sufficiently attractive to maintain the required employee skills levels and, where necessary, disposing of those judged no longer to have a role to play in the organization.

PERFORMANCE OBJECTIVES

Once the required workforce is in place, human resource managers seek to ensure that people are well motivated and committed so as to maximise their performance in their different roles. Training and development has a role to play, as do reward systems to maximise effort and focus attention on performance targets. In many organizations, particularly where trade unions play a significant role, human resource managers negotiate improved performance with the workforce. The achievement of performance objectives also requires HR specialists to assist in disciplining employees effectively and equitably where individual conduct and/or performance standards are unsatisfactory. Welfare functions can also assist performance by providing constructive assistance to people whose performance has fallen short of their potential because of illness or difficult personal circumstances. Last but not least, there is the range of employee involvement initiatives to raise levels of commitment and to engage employees in developing new ideas.

CHANGE MANAGEMENT OBJECTIVES

A third set of core objectives in nearly every business relates to the role played by the HR function in effectively managing change. Frequently change does not come along in readily defined episodes precipitated by some external factor. Instead it is endemic and well-nigh continuous, generated as much by a continual need to innovate as from definable environmental pressures. Change comes in different forms. Sometimes it is merely structural, requiring reorganization of activities or the introduction of new people into particular roles. At other times cultural change is sought in order to alter attitudes, philosophies or long-present organizational norms. In any of these scenarios the HR function can play a central role. Key activities include the recruitment and/or development of people with the necessary leadership skills to drive the change process, the employment of change agents to encourage acceptance of change and the construction of reward systems which underpin the change process. Timely and effective employee involvement is also crucial because 'people support what they help to create'.

ADMINISTRATION OBJECTIVES

The fourth type of objective is less directly related to achieving competitive advantage, but is focused on underpinning the achievement of the other forms of objective. In part it is simply carried out in order to facilitate an organization's smooth running. Hence there is a need to maintain accurate and comprehensive data on individual employees, a record of their achievement in terms of performance, their attendance and training records, their terms and conditions of employment and their personal details. However, there is also a legal aspect to much administrative activity, meaning that it is done because the business is required by law to comply. Of particular significance is the requirement that payment is administered professionally and lawfully, with itemised monthly pay statements being provided for all employees. There is also the need to make arrangements for the deduction of taxation and national insurance, for the payment of pension fund contributions and to be on top of the complexities associated with Statutory Sick Pay and Statutory Maternity Pay, as well as maternity and paternity leave. Additional legal requirements relate to the monitoring of health and safety systems and the issuing of contracts to new employees. Accurate record keeping is central to ensuring compliance with a variety of newer legal obligations such as the National Minimum Wage and the Working Time Regulations. Each of the four types of HR objective is important and necessary for organizations in different ways. However, at certain times one or more can assume greater importance than the others.

DELIVERING HRM OBJECTIVES

The larger the organization, the more scope there is to employ people to specialise in particular areas of HRM. Some, for example, employ employee relations specialists to look after the collective relationship between management and employees. Where there is a strong tradition of collective bargaining, the role is focused on the achievement of satisfactory outcomes from ongoing negotiations. Increasingly, however, employee relations specialists are required to provide advice about legal developments, to manage consultation arrangements and to preside over employee involvement initiatives.

Another common area of specialisation is in the field of training and development. Although much of this is now undertaken by external providers, there is still a role for in-house trainers, particularly in management development. Increasingly the term 'consultant' is used instead of 'officer' or 'manager' to describe the training specialist's role, indicating a shift towards a situation in which line managers determine the training they want rather than the training section providing a standardised portfolio of courses. The other major specialist roles are in the fields of recruitment and selection, health, safety and welfare, compensation and benefits and human resource planning.

In addition to the people who have specialist roles there are many other people who are employed as human resources or personnel generalists. Working alone or in small teams, they carry out the range of HR activities and seek to achieve all the objectives outlined above. In larger businesses generalists either look after all personnel matters in a particular division or are employed at a senior level to develop policy and take responsibility for HR issues across the organization as a whole. In more junior roles, human resource administrators and assistants undertake many of the administrative tasks mentioned earlier. The wide range of elective subjects which can now be chosen by those seeking qualification through the Institute's examinations has made it as relevant to those seeking a specialist career as to those who prefer to remain in generalist roles. However, many smaller businesses do not need, or cannot afford, HR managers at all. They may use consultants or the advisory services of university departments. They may use their bank's computer to process the payroll, but there is still a human resource dimension to their managers' activities.

HRM Mark 2: A Distinctive Approach to the Management of People

The second meaning commonly accorded to the term 'human resource management' denotes a particular way of carrying out the range of activities discussed above. Under this definition, a 'human resource management approach' is something qualitatively different from a 'personnel management approach'. Commentators disagree, however, about how fundamental a shift is signified by a movement from personnel management to human resource management. For some, particularly those whose focus of interest is on the management of collective relationships at work, the rise of HRM in the last two decades of the twentieth century represents something new and very different from the dominant personnel management approach in earlier years. A particular theme in their work is the contention that personnel management is essentially workforce centred, while HRM is resource centred. Personnel specialists direct their efforts mainly at the organization's employees; finding and training them, arranging for them to be paid, explaining management's expectations, justifying management's actions, satisfying employees' work-related needs, dealing with their problems and seeking to modify management action that could produce an unwelcome employee response. The people who work in the organization are the starting point, and they are a resource that is relatively inflexible in comparison with other resources, like cash and materials.

Although indisputably a management function, personnel management is not totally identified with management interests. Just as sales representatives have to understand and articulate the aspirations of the customers, personnel managers seek to understand and articulate the aspirations and views of the workforce. There is always some degree of being in between management and the employees, mediating the needs of each to the other.

HRM, by contrast, is directed mainly at management needs for human resources (not necessarily employees) to be provided and deployed. Demand rather than supply is the focus of the activity. There is greater emphasis on planning, monitoring and control, rather than mediation. Problem solving is undertaken with other members of management on human resource issues rather than directly with employees or their representatives. It is totally identified with management interests, being a general management activity, and is relatively distant from the workforce as a whole. David Guest emphasises the differences between the two approaches in his model illustrating 'stereotypes of personnel management and human resource management'.

Personnel Human Resource Management

	Personnel Management	***Human Resource Management***
Time and planning perspective	Short term, reactive, ad hoc, marginal	Long term, proactive, strategic, integrated
Psychological contract	Compliance	Commitment
Control systems	External controls	Self-control
Employee relations perspective	Pluralist, collective, low trust	Unitarist, individual, high trust
Preferred structures/ systems	Bureaucratic/ mechanistic, centralised, formal defined roles	Organic, devolved, flexible roles
Roles	Specialist/ professional	Largely integrated into line management
Evaluation criteria	Cost minimisation	Maximum utilisation (human asset accounting)

An alternative point of view, while recognising the differences, downplays the significance of a break between personnel and human resources management. Such a conclusion is readily reached when the focus of analysis is on what HR/personnel managers actually do, rather than on the more profound developments in the specific field of collective employee relations. Legge concludes that there is very little difference in fact between the two, but that there are some differences that are important; first, that human resource management concentrates more on what is done to managers than on what is done by managers to other employees; second, that there is a more proactive role for line managers; and, third, that there is a top management responsibility for managing culture – all factors to which we return later in the book. From this perspective, human resource management can simply be seen as the most recent mutation in a long line of developments that have characterised personnel management practice as it evolved during the last century. HRM is therefore the latest new dimension to be added to a role which has developed in different directions at different stages in its history. Below we identify four distinct stages in the historical development of the personnel management function. HRM, as described above, is a fifth.

THE EVOLUTION OF PERSONNEL AND HR MANAGEMENT

SOCIAL JUSTICE

The origins of personnel management lie in the nineteenth century, deriving from the work of social reformers such as Lord Shaftesbury and Robert Owen. Their criticisms of the free enterprise system and the hardship created by the exploitation of workers by factory owners enabled the first personnel managers to be appointed and provided the first frame of reference in which they worked: to ameliorate the lot of the workers. Such concerns are not obsolete. There are still regular reports of employees being exploited by employers flouting the law, and the problem of organizational distance between decision makers and those putting decisions into practice remains a source of alienation from work.

In the late nineteenth and early twentieth centuries some of the larger employers with a paternalist outlook began to appoint welfare officers to manage a series of new initiatives designed to make life less harsh for their employees. Prominent examples were the progressive schemes of unemployment benefit, sick pay and subsidised housing provided by the Quaker family firms of Cadbury and Rowntree, and the Lever Brothers' soap business. While the motives were ostensibly charitable, there was and remains a business as well as an ethical case for paying serious attention to the welfare of employees. This is based on the contention that it improves commitment on the part of staff and leads potential employees to compare the organization favourably vis-à-vis competitors. The result is higher productivity, a longer-serving workforce and a bigger pool of applicants for each job. It has also been argued that a commitment to welfare reduces the scope for the development of adversarial industrial relations. The more conspicuous welfare initiatives promoted by employers today include employee assistance schemes, childcare facilities and health-screening programmes.

HUMANE BUREAUCRACY

The second phase marked the beginnings of a move away from a sole focus on welfare towards the meeting of various other organizational objectives. Personnel managers began to gain responsibilities in the areas of staffing, training and organization design. Influenced by social scientists such as F.W. Taylor and Henri Fayol personnel specialists started to look at management and administrative processes analytically, working out how organizational structures could be designed and labour deployed so as to maximise efficiency. The humane bureaucracy stage in the development of personnel thinking was also influenced by the Human Relations School, which sought to ameliorate the potential for industrial conflict and dehumanisation present in too rigid an application of these scientific management approaches. Following the ideas of thinkers such as Elton Mayo, the fostering of social relationships in the workplace and employee morale thus became equally important objectives for personnel professionals seeking to raise productivity levels.

NEGOTIATED CONSENT

Personnel managers next added expertise in bargaining to their repertoire of skills. In the period of full employment following the Second World War labour became a scarce resource. This led to a growth in trade union membership and to what Allan Flanders, the leading industrial relations analyst of the 1960s, called 'the challenge from below'. Personnel specialists managed the new collective institutions such as joint consultation committees, joint production committees and suggestion schemes set up in order to accommodate the new realities. In the industries that were nationalised in the 1940s, employers were placed under a statutory duty to negotiate with unions representing employees. To help achieve this, the government encouraged the appointment of personnel officers and set up the first specialist courses for them in the universities.

ORGANIZATION

The late 1960s saw a switch in focus among personnel specialists, away from dealing principally with the rank-and-file employee on behalf of management, towards dealing with management itself and the integration of managerial activity. This phase was characterised by the development of career paths and of opportunities within organizations for personal growth. This too remains a concern of personnel specialists today, with a significant portion of time and resources being devoted to the recruitment, development and retention of an elite core of people with specialist expertise on whom the business depends for its future. Personnel specialists developed techniques of manpower or workforce planning. This is basically a quantitative activity, boosted by the advent of information technology, which involves forecasting the likely need for employees with different skills in the future.

A PHILOSOPHY OF HUMAN RESOURCE MANAGEMENT

The philosophy of human resource management that is the basis of this book has been only slightly modified since it was first put forward in 1979. Despite all the changes in the labour market and in the government approach to the economy, this seems to be the most realistic and constructive approach, based on the earlier ideas of Enid Mumford and McCarthy and Ellis. The original was: Personnel management is most realistically seen as a series of activities enabling working man and his employing organization to reach agreement about the nature and objectives of the employment relationship between them, and then to fulfil those agreements.

Human resource management is a series of activities which: first enables working people and the organization which uses their skills to agree about the objectives and nature of their working relationship and, secondly, ensures that the agreement is fulfiled.

This remains our philosophy. Only by satisfying the needs of the individual contributor will the business obtain the commitment to organizational objectives that is needed for organizational success, and only by contributing to organizational success will individuals be able to satisfy their personal employment needs. It is when employer and employee – or business and supplier of skills – accept that mutuality and reciprocal dependence that human resource management is exciting, centre stage and productive of business success. Where the employer is concerned with employees only as factors of production, personnel management is boring and a cost that will always be trimmed. Where employees have no trust in their employer and adopt an entirely instrumental orientation to their work, they will be fed up and will make ineffectual the work of any HR function.

Human resource managers are like managers in every other part of the organization. They have to make things happen rather than wait for things to happen, and to make things happen not only do they need to have the right approach; they also have to know their stuff.

DEBATES IN HRM

The world in which human resource managers exist and with which they interact is continually changing, generating new issues and conundrums to consider. While in most cases managers have a fair degree of choice about how to deal with new ideas and new sets of circumstances, the choices themselves are often difficult. Our final task in this opening chapter is to introduce readers to a number of these issues in general terms.

In one way or another all the major debates that occupy HR professionals, analysts and commentators concern the appropriate response to the major trends which are evolving in our business environment. But people differ in their analysis of the extent and nature of these developments and this colours their ideas about whether or not radical change in the way that people are managed is or is not appropriate. Here we can usefully distinguish between three separate fields of debate.

The first is concerned with understanding and conceptualising the nature of current responses. How are organizations dealing with the issues that they face in terms of the management of their people? Are they developing new approaches that differ fundamentally from those that have been established for some time or are we witnessing a more steady, considered evolution of practice?

The second field of debate concerns what HR managers should be doing. Are new or radical changes in policy and practice necessary? Or is the correct response to environmental developments the further refinement of more familiar approaches? Further debate concerns the extent to which the answer to these questions is broadly the same for all employing organizations or whether it differs quite profoundly from industry to industry or firm to firm.

A third debate is oriented towards longer-term future developments. Many believe and have argued persuasively that we are currently witnessing changes in our business environment which are as fundamental and significant as those which accompanied the industrial revolution two hundred years ago. They further argue that the world of work which will emerge in future decades will be wholly different in major respects from that we currently inhabit. It follows that those organizations which 'see the future' most clearly and change accordingly stand to gain most. But are these predictions really accurate? Could the analysis on which they are built be faulty in key respects?

Of course it is also possible to ask rather different kinds of questions about the HR practices that are being, will be or should be developed, which in turn lead us to engage in various types of debate. Some, for example, focus exclusively on the requirements of the organization and the search for competitive advantage. What can the HR function do which will maximise organizational growth, effectiveness and efficiency? However, many also like to think more broadly and to concern themselves with the impact of employment practice on the workforce and on society in more general terms. Hence we also engage in debates that are essentially ethical in nature or which have a prominent ethical dimension.

KEY ENVIRONMENTAL DEVELOPMENTS

The major trends in our contemporary business environment are well understood, well documented and uncontroversial. People differ, though, in their understanding of the speed of change and of the extent to which all organizations are or will be affected. As far as product markets are concerned the big trend is towards ever more intense competitive pressures, leading some to argue that we are now entering the era of hyper-competition. This is being driven by two major developments, the significance of which has increased considerably in recent years.

First, we are witnessing moves towards the globalisation of economic activity on a scale that has not been experienced before in human history. More and more the markets for the goods and products we sell are international, which means of course that competition for those markets as well as our established ones is also increasingly becoming international. Large organizations that were able to dominate national markets a decade or two ago (many owned and operated by governments) are now mainly privately owned and faced with vastly more competition from similar organizations based all over the world. This has led to consolidation through the construction of global corporations and strategic alliances whose focus in terms of people management is also international.

The second major antecedent of hyper-competition is technology, which moves forward at an ever-accelerating pace year by year. Developments in information technology, energy production, chemical engineering, laser technology, transportation and biotechnology are in the process of revolutionising the way that many industries operate. It is partly the sheer pace of change and the need for organizations to stay ahead of this very fast-moving game which drives increased competition. Being the first to develop and make efficient use of new technologies is the means by which many organizations maintain their competitive position and can thus grow and prosper.

But IT, and in particular the growth of e-business, is significant too because it has the potential vastly to increase the number of competitors that any one organization faces. This is because it makes it much easier for customers and potential customers to compare what your organization can offer in terms of price and quality with what others can offer.

What does this mean in practical terms from the point of view of the HR manager? First, it means that practices continually have to be developed which have the effect of enhancing an organization's competitive position. Ways need to be found of improving quality and of bringing to market attractive new products and services, while at the same time ensuring that the organization remains competitive in terms of its cost base. Second, it means that a good deal of volatility is the norm and that change, often of a profound nature, is something that people working in organizations must expect and be ready for. So a capacity for organizational flexibility has become central to the achievement and maintenance of competitive advantage. Third, there are direct practical outcomes. For example, HR managers have to learn how to manage an international workforce effectively and how best to attract, retain and develop and motivate people with those relatively scarce skills that are essential if an organization is effectively to harness and deploy evolving technologies.

For the HR manager, however, unlike colleagues in other areas of management, responding to product market developments is only part of what is needed. Other major environmental trends are equally important and must also be understood and built into decision making. There are two areas which are particularly important:

- Labour market trends
- The evolution of employment regulation

Developments in the labour market are significant partly in terms of the numbers of people and skills available, and partly in terms of attitudes towards work and the workplace. Major developments appear to be occurring in both these areas. Many industries, for example, have found themselves facing skills shortages in recent years. The impact varies from country to country depending on relative economic prosperity, but most organizations in the India have seen a tightening of their key labour markets in recent years. Unemployment levels have remained low, while demographic trends have created a situation in which more older people are retiring than younger people are entering the job market. There are all kinds of implications. For a start, employers are having to make themselves more attractive to employees than has been necessary in recent years. No longer can they simply assume that people will seek work with them or seek to remain employed with them. In a tight labour market individuals have more choice about where and when they work, and do not need to put up with a working environment in which they are unhappy. If they do not like their jobs there are more opportunities for them to look elsewhere. So organizations are increasingly required to compete with one another in labour markets as well as in product markets. This has implications for policy in all areas of HRM, but particularly in the areas of reward, employee development and recruitment.

Labour market conditions along with other social trends serve to shape the attitudes of people towards their work. In order to mobilise and motivate a workforce, HR managers must be aware of how these are changing and to respond effectively. One of the most significant trends in recent years, for example, has been a reduced interest on the part of employees in joining trade unions and taking part in their activities. A more individualistic attitude now prevails in the majority of workplaces, people focusing on themselves and their own career development rather than standing in solidarity with fellow workers. Another well-documented trend is the increased desire for employees to achieve a better balance between their home and work lives and their increased willingness to seek out employers who can provide this.

The growth in the extent and complexity of employment regulation is a third area which HR managers are obliged to grasp and the elements of which they must implement in their organizations. Prior to 1970, with one or two exceptions, there was no statutory regulation of the employment relationship in the India. An individual's terms and conditions of employment were those that were stated in the contract of employment and in any collective agreements. The law did not intervene beyond providing some basic health and safety protection, the right to modest redundancy payments and a general requirement on employers and employees to honour the contractual terms agreed when the employment began. Since 1970 this situation has wholly changed. The individual contract of employment remains significant and can be enforced in court if necessary, but there has been added to this a whole range of statutory rights which employers are obliged to honour. The most significant are in the fields of health and safety, equal pay, unlawful discrimination and unfair dismissal. Much recent new law such as that on working time, family-friendly rights, consultation and discrimination on grounds of sexual orientation and belief has an Indian origin, and a great deal more can be expected in the years ahead.

Debates about how HR managers are and should be responding to these various trends form the focus of much of what follows in this book. Below we briefly set out the main contours of three specific debates that have a general relevance to many of the topic areas we discuss later,

THE PSYCHOLOGICAL CONTRACT

According to many, one consequence of these evolving environmental pressures is a significant and fundamental change in what has become known as 'the psychological contract'. This refers to the expectations that employees have about the role that they play and to what the employer is prepared to give them in return. Whereas a legal contract of employment sets out terms and conditions of employment, remuneration arrangements and the basic rules which are to govern the employment relationship, the psychological contract concerns broad expectations about what each party thinks it will gain from the relationship. By its nature the psychological contract is not a written document. Rather, it exists entirely within people's heads. But this has not prevented researchers from seeking to pin it down and to track the extent to which we are witnessing ongoing change in established psychological contracts. While people disagree about the extent to which this change has in fact occurred, there is general agreement about the phenomenon itself and the notion that an 'old' psychological contract to which generations of employees have become accustomed is being superseded to some extent by a 'new' psychological contract which reflects the needs of the present business environment.

A switch from the 'old' approach to the 'new' involves employers giving less job security and receiving less loyalty from employees in return. Instead, employees are given developmental opportunities and are expected to give the employer flexibility. The whole perception of the employment relationship on both sides is thus radically different. Moreover, moving from old psychological contracts towards new ones is a problematic process that involves managers 'breaching' the established deal. This is likely to lead to dissatisfaction on the part of employees who are affected and to some form of collective industrial action in unionised settings.

The big question is how far has a change of this nature actually occurred? Are we really witnessing a slow decline in the old psychological contract and its replacement by the new one, or have reports of its death been exaggerated?

On this issue there is a great deal of disagreement. Many researchers claim to have found evidence of substantial change in many industries, particularly as regards reduced employee loyalty. Yet others, notably Guest and Conway in their many studies have found relatively little evidence of any change in the state of the psychological contract. Their findings suggest that while some change has occurred in the public sector, perceptions closer to the 'old' psychological contract remain a great deal more common than those associated with the 'new' approach.

It is difficult to reach firm conclusions about why these very marked differences of opinion exist. It is possible that the old psychological contract remains intact for most people, but that a significant minority, particularly managers and some public sector workers, have had to adjust to profound change. It is also possible that organizations have tried to move away from the old approach towards the new one, but have found it difficult to take their employees with them and have thus sought other methods of increasing their competitiveness. A third possibility, suggested by Atkinson , is that the differences in the conclusions people reach about this issue derive from the methodologies they adopt when studying it. She argues that large-scale studies which involve sending questionnaires to employees have tended to report little change in the state of the psychological contract, while smaller-scale studies based on interviews with managers and trade union officials tend to report the opposite.

BEST PRACTICE VS. BEST FIT

The debate between best practice and best fit is an interesting one of general significance which has consequences across the field of HRM. As well as being a managerial issue it concerns one of the most significant academic controversies in the HR field at present. At root it is about whether or not there is an identifiable 'best way' of carrying out HR activities which is universally applicable. It is best understood as a debate between two schools of thought, although in practice it is quite possible to take a central position which sees validity in both the basic positions.

Adherents of a best practice perspective argue that there are certain HR practices and approaches to their operation which will invariably help an organization in achieving competitive advantage. There is therefore a clear link between HR activity and business performance, but the effect will only be maximised if the 'right' HR policies are pursued. A great deal of evidence has been published in recent years, using various methodologies, which appears to back up the best practice case. While there are differences of opinion on questions of detail, all strongly suggest that the same basic bundle of human resource practices or general human resource management orientation tends to enhance business performance in all organizations irrespective of the particular product market strategy being pursued. According to David Guest this occurs through a variety of mechanisms:

Human resource practices exercise their positive impact by:

(i) Ensuring and enhancing the competence of employees,

(ii) By tapping their motivation and commitment, and

(iii) By designing work to encourage the fullest contribution from employees.

Borrowing from elements of expectancy theory, the model implies that all three elements should be present to ensure the best outcome. Positive employee behaviour should in turn impact upon establishment level outcomes such as low absence, quit rates and wastage, as well as high quality and productivity.

The main elements of the 'best practice bundle' that these and other writers identify are those which have long been considered as examples of good practice in the HRM field. They include the use of the more advanced selection methods, a serious commitment to employee involvement, substantial investment in training and development, the use of individualised reward systems and harmonised terms and conditions of employment as between different groups of employees.

The alternative 'best fit' school also identifies a link between human resource management practice and the achievement of competitive advantage. Here, however, there is no belief in the existence of universal solutions. Instead, all is contingent on the particular circumstances of each organization. What is needed is HR policies and practices which 'fit' and are thus appropriate to the situation of individual employers. What is appropriate (or 'best') for one will not necessarily be right for another. Key variables include the size of the establishment, the dominant product market strategy being pursued and the nature of the labour markets in which the organization competes. It is thus argued that a small organization which principally achieves competitive advantage through innovation and which competes in very tight labour markets should have in place rather different HR policies than those of a large firm which produces low-cost goods and faces no difficulty in attracting staff. In order to maximise competitive advantage, the first requires informality combined with sophisticated human resource practices, while the latter needs more bureaucratic systems combined with a 'low cost – no frills' set of HR practices.

The best fit or contingency perspective originated in the work of Joan Woodward and her colleagues at Imperial College in the 1950s. In recent years it has been developed and applied to contemporary conditions by academics such as Randall Schuler and Susan Jackson, John Purcell and Ed Lawler. In addition, a number of influential models have been produced which seek to categorise organizational contingencies and suggest what mix of HR practices is appropriate in each case. To a great extent the jury is still out on these questions. Proponents of both the 'best practice' and 'best fit' perspectives can draw on bodies of empirical evidence to back up their respective positions and so the debate continues.

THE FUTURE OF WORK

Debates about what will happen in the future are inevitably speculative and impossible to prove one way or the other, but a great deal of attention and government research funding is currently being devoted to this issue. It matters a great deal from a public policy point of view because judgements about employers' human resource needs in the future must determine decisions about education and training now. Government actions in the fields of economic policy, employment legislation and immigration are also affected.

A good starting point is the work of influential writers such as Charles Handy, William Bridges and Jeremy Rifkin. In different ways they have argued that the product market forces identified above will lead in future decades to the emergence of a world of work which is very different in many respects from that which most in western industrialised countries currently experience. Both the type of work we do and the nature of our contractual arrangements will, it is argued, change profoundly as we complete our journey out of the industrial era and into a new post-industrial age.

The first consequence will be a marked shift towards what is described as knowledge work. In the future, it is claimed, most people will be employed, in one way or another, to carry out tasks which involve the generation, interpretation, processing or application of knowledge. Automation and the availability of cheaper labour in developing countries will see further declines in much manufacturing activity, requiring the western economies to create wealth from the exploitation of scientific and technological advances. It follows that many more people will be employed for their specialist knowledge and that far fewer routine jobs will exist than is currently the case. Demand for professional and technical people will increase, while demand for manual and lower-skilled workers will decrease. It also means that competitive advantage from an employer's perspective will derive from the capacity to create and deploy knowledge more effectively than others can.

The second major claim that is made is that the 'job' as we have come to know it will become rarer and rarer. In the future many fewer people will occupy defined jobs in organizations. Instead we will tend increasingly to work on a self-employed basis carrying out specific, time-limited projects for organizations. This is inevitable, so the argument goes, in a highly volatile business climate. Organizations simply will not be able to offer long-term guarantees of work and so will be forced to stop offering contracts of employment in the way that they currently do. The future is therefore bleak for people who want job security, but bright for those who are happy working for many employers and periodically re-educating themselves for a new type of career.

In many respects these arguments are persuasive. They are based on a rational analysis of likely developments in the business environment as globalisation and technological advances further evolve. They remain, however, highly controversial and are increasingly subject to challenge by researchers who argue that change on this kind of scale is not currently happening and will not happen in the near future.

A prominent critic of the views expressed by the predictors of radical change is Peter Nolan, who argues that the case is often overstated to a considerable degree: Change is evident, to be sure, but the shifts in the patterns and rhythms of work are not linear, pre-determined by technology or, as some writers have uncritically assumed, driven by universal trends in market globalisation.

Instead, according to Nolan and his colleagues, we are witnessing the resolute continuation of established approaches and some reversal of trends that began to develop in the 1980s and 1990s but which have since petered out. Job tenure in the India, for example, has risen significantly in recent years while the proportion of people employed on fixed-term contracts and a self-employed basis has fallen. While we are seeing a slow growth in the proportion of people employed in professional and scientific roles (from 34 per cent to 37 per cent in the 1990s), there is no fall occurring in the number of manual jobs. At the same time the proportion of people employed in relatively low-skilled jobs in the service sector is growing quickly. Critics of Handy and the other futurologists have thus identified a gap between a rhetoric which emphasises fundamental change and a reality which gives little support to the view that we are in the process of shaping a 'new world of work'.

These different conceptions of the future may well derive from a preference for a focus on different types of environmental development. A reading of the major contemporary product market trends can easily lead to predictions of radical change. The twin forces of technological advance and globalisation do indeed point to a transformation of many aspects of our lives. But trends in employment are equally determined by developments in the labour market and regulatory environments. These suggest a strong preference on the part of both employees and law makers for a continuation of traditional approaches towards employment.

2

Function of HR Management

Human resource management (HRM) is the most precious and coherent approach to the management of any establishment's most valued assets - the individuals working there who individually and jointly lead to the achievement of the objectives of the business. The terms "human resource management" and "human resources" (HR) have largely substituted the term "personnel management" as a description of the processes needed in managing individuals in organizations. Human Resource management is evolving rapidly. Human resource management is both an academic theory and a business practice that addresses the theoretical and practical techniques of managing manpower.

Its features include:

- Personnel administration
- Personnel management
- Manpower management
- Industrial management

But these conventional expressions are becoming rarer for the theoretical discipline. Occasionally even industrial relations and employee relations are confusingly listed as synonyms, though these typically refer to the relationship between management and workers and the behaviour of workers in the establishment. The theoretical discipline is based mainly on the assumption that employees are individuals with varying aims and needs, and therefore ought to not be thought of as fundamental business resources, such as trucks and filing cabinets. The field takes a positive view of workers, assuming that almost all wish to add to the enterprise productively, and that the main obstacles to their endeavours are want of knowledge, insufficient training, and failures of process.

Human Resource Management is seen by practitioners in the field as a modern view of workplace management than the conventional approach. Its proficiencies force the managers of an enterprise to express their aims with specificity in order that they can be understood and undertaken by the work-force, and to provide the resources demanded for them to successfully attain their assignments. Therefore, Human Resource Management techniques, when the right way practiced, are expressive of the aims and operating practices of the enterprise overall. Human Resource Management is also seen by many to have a key role in risk reduction inside organizations.

Synonyms such as personnel management are frequently used in a more qualified sense to describe activities that are necessary in the recruiting of manpower, providing its members with payroll and gains, and administrating their work-life needs.

STAFFING: A MANAGEMENT FUNCTION

After an establishment's structural design is in place, it necessitates individuals with the right skills, knowledge, and abilities to fill in that structure. Individuals are an establishment's most significant resource, because individuals either produce or undermine an establishment's reputation for quality in both products and service. Additionally, an establishment must respond to change effectively in order to remain competitive. The right staff can carry an establishment through a period of change and ensure its future success. Because of the implication of employing and maintaining a committed and competent staff, effectual human resource management is essential to the success of all organizations.

Human resource management (HRM), or *staffing,* is the management function devoted to gaining, training, appraising, and compensating employees. In effect, all managers are human resource managers, though human resource specialists may perform some of these activities in large organizations. Solid Human Resource Management practices can mould a company's manpower into a prompted and committed team capable of managing change effectively and accomplishing the organizational objectives.

Realizing the fundamental principles of Human Resource Management can help any manager lead more effectively. Every manager ought to realize the following three principles:

- All managers are human resource managers.

- Employees are much more significant assets than buildings or equipments good employees give a company the competitive edge.
- Human resource management is a coping with process; it must match the needs of the establishment with the needs of the employee.

LAWS AND REGULATIONS

Laws and regulations at the federal, state, and local levels regulate how organizations carry on staffing. Many laws were established, which banished most discriminatory employing practices. Three sensitive areas of legal concern that managers must abide by with are equal opportunity, affirmative action, and sexual harassment, described in the following sections. These fields, as well as other laws, impact all human resource practices.

Equal Opportunity

Individuals are saved from illegal discrimination, which occurs when individuals who share a certain characteristic, such as race, age, or gender, are discriminated against because of that characteristic. Individuals who have the assigned characteristics are called the *protected class.* Laws have keyed out the following characteristics for protection:

- Age (people over 40)
- Gender (women, comprising those who are pregnant)
- People with disabilities (physical and mental)
- Military experience
- Caste
- Religion (special beliefs and practices)

The main goal of the laws is to ensure that everyone has an equal opportunity of getting a task or being promoted at work.

The Industrial Employment Act of 1946

Classification ought to be made as per the Standing Orders. Where there are no Standing Orders or service rules applicable to employees, then classification can be made either based on trade tests or any other test which is reasonable and in accordance with the Model Standing

Orders. In general, the workers are classified as:

- apprentice/trainee;
- casual;
- temporary;
- badli/substitute;
- probationer;
- permanent; and
- fixed period employees

Factories Act of 1948

The main aim of the Factories Act is:

- To regulate working conditions in factories.
- To ensure that fundamental minimum necessities for the safety, health and welfare of the factory workers are provided.
- To regulate of working hours, leave, holidays, overtime and employment of children, women and young persons.

This act applies to all factories letting in Government factories. A "factory" as defined in the Act means any premises admitting the precincts:

- Where ten or more workers are employed on any day of the preceding 12 months and a manufacturing process is carried on with the aid of electric power; and
- Where 20 or more workers are employed on any day of the preceding 12 months and a manufacturing process is conducted without the aid of electric power.

The obligations of the employers are, basically speaking, the rights of the employees to claim the minimal health and safety measures and welfare amenities as provided for in the Act, observance of working hours, holidays, overtime, annual leave and special protection against risky processes and dangerous contents, to obtain data relating to workers' health and safety at work from the occupier, to get trained by or through the occupier, in respect of workers' health and safety, to represent to the Inspector directly or although a representative in the matter of inadequate provision for protection of health or safety in the factory, not to pay any fee or charge for the facilities or appliances rendered by the employer and to claim wages for or in lieu of allowable leave under the provisions of the Payment of Wages Act.

Payment of Wages Act, 1936

Under the Payment of Wages Act, 1936 the following are the common responsibilities of the employer:

- Every employer is mainly accountable for payment of wages to employees. The employer ought to fix the wage period (which may be per day, per week or per month) but in no case it ought to exceed one month;
- Every employer ought to make well-timed payment of wages. If the employment of any person is being terminated, those wages ought to be paid within two days of the date of termination; and
- The employer ought to pay the wages in cash, i.e., in current coins or currency notes. Nevertheless wages may also be paid either by cheque or by crediting in employee's bank account after obtaining written consent.

Minimum Wages Act, 1948

The employer is bound to pay to every employee employed by him wages at a rate not less than the minimum rates of wages fixed for that class of employees without making any deduction (except as permitted under the Payment of Wages Act). The employees are entitled to the minimum wages at all times and under all considerations.

Workmen's Compensation Act, 1923

The employer must pay compensation for an accident suffered by an employee during the course of employment and in accordance with the Act. The employer must submit a statement to the Commissioner (within 30 days of receiving the notice) giving the considerations attending the death of a worker as result of an accident and indicating whether the employer is liable to deposit any compensation for the same. It ought to also submit an accident report to the Commissioner within seven days of the accident.

Employees Provident Funds and Miscellaneous Provisions Act, 1952

The employer must pay its and the employees' contributions and administrative charges as required under the Act and schemes. Financial difficulty is no excuse for non-payment. The contribution has to be made regardless of the fact whether wages are paid to the employee due to lockout, strike, or other related reason. Employer must furnish the requirement returns to the Provident Funds Commissioner.

DETERMINING HR NEEDS

Staffing is an ongoing process that commences with finding the right individuals through proper planning, recruiting, and selecting. But staffing does not end once employees are hired; management must keep and foster its individuals via training, appraising, compensating, and implementing employment decisions that decide such things as promotions, transfers, and layoffs.

Selecting the Best Person

The first step in the staffing process demands human resource planning. Human resource planning begins with a task analysis in which descriptions of all jobs (tasks) and the qualifications demanded for each position are developed. A task description is a written statement of what a jobholder does, how it is done, and why it is done. It normally impersonates task content, environment, and conditions of employment. The task specification states the minimum satisfactory qualifications an incumbent must possess to execute a given task successfully. It identifies the knowledge, skills, and powers demanded to do the task effectively.

Task analysis is then complied by a human resource inventory, which catalogues qualifications and interests. Next, a human resource guess is developed to predict the establishment's future needs for jobs and individuals based on its strategic plans and normal attrition. The forecast is then equated to the inventory to determine whether the establishment's staffing needs will be met with being personnel or whether managers will have to recruit new employees or terminate existent ones.

Having the right individuals on staff is essential to the success of an establishment. Numerous selection devices help employers predict which applicants will be successful if hired. These devices aim to be not only valid, but also reliable. *Validity* is proof that the relationship between the selection device and some relevant task criterion exists. *Reliability* is an indicant that the device measures the same thing consistently. For instance, it would be appropriate to give a keyboarding test to a candidate applying for a task as an administrative assistant. Nonetheless, it would not be valid to give a keyboarding test to a candidate for a task as a physical education teacher. If a keyboarding test is given to the same individual on two distinguish occasions, the results ought to be similar. To be effectual predictors, a selection device must have an acceptable level of consistency.

Recruiting

Recruitment makes up all the activities an establishment may use to attract a pool of viable candidates. Effectual recruiting is more and more important today for numerous reasons:

- The employment rate has in general declined each year through the 1990s. Experts refer to the current enrolling position as one of "evaporated employee resources."
- Many experts believe that today's Generation X employees (those born between 1963 and 1981) are less inclined to build long-term employment relationships than were their predecessors. Therefore, finding the right motivators for attracting, employing, and retaining qualified personnel may be more complicated than in former years.

Keep in mind that recruiting strategies differ among organizations. Though one may instantly think of campus recruiting as a typical recruiting activity, many organizations use internal recruiting, or promote-from-within policies, to fill their high-level positions. Open positions are posted, and current employees are given preferences when these positions become available. Internal recruitment is less costly than an external search. It also gives higher employee commitment, development, and satisfaction because it offers chances for career progress to employees rather than outsiders.

If internal sources don't create an acceptable candidate, many external recruiting strategies are uncommitted, comprising the following:

- Employee referrals
- Employment agencies (private, public, or temporary agencies)
- Executive recruiters (occasionally called head-hunters)
- Internet employment sites
- Internship programs

- Newspaper advertising
- Unions

But there's more to entering than just attracting employees; managers need to be able to weed out the top candidates. Once a manger has a consortium of applicants, the selection process can start out.

Application forms

For almost all employers, the application form is the first step in the selection process. Application forms provide a record of salient information about applicants for positions, and also furnish data for personnel research. Interviewers may use replies from the application for follow-up questions during an interview. These forms range from requests for fundamental information, such as names, addresses, and telephone numbers, to comprehensive personal history profiles detailing applicants' education, task experience skills, and achievements.

For example, employers ought to not ask whether an applicant rents or owns his or his own home, because an applicant's response may adversely affect his or his chances at the task. Minorities and women may be less likely to own a home, and home ownership is probably unrelated to task performance. Alternatively, asking about the CPA exam for an accounting position is set aside, even if only one-half of all female or minority applicants have taken the exam versus nine-tenths of male appliers.

A quick test for disparate affect suggested by the Uniform Selection Guidelines is the four-fifths rules. In general, a disparate impact is presumed when the proportions of protected class applicants who are actually hired is less that 80 percent (four-fifths) of the proportion of the majority group applicants selected. For instance, assume that an employer has 100 white male applicants for an entry-level task and hires one-half of them, for a selection ratio of 1:2, or 50 percent (50/100). The four-fifths rule doesn't mean that the employers must hire four-fifths, or 40 protected class members. Rather, the rule means that the employer's selection ratio of protected class-applicants ought to be at least four-fifths of that of the absolute majority groups.

Testing

Testing is some other method of selecting competent future employees. Though testing use has ebbed and flowed during the past two decades, current studies reveal that more than 80 percent of employers use testing as part of their selection process. Again, these tests must be valid and reliable, or serious EEO questions may be raised about the use of them. As a result, a manager necessitates to make sure that the test measures only task-relevant dimensions of applicants.

Most tests focus on specific task-related abilities and skills, such as math or motor skills. Typical types of exams constitute the following:

- **Integrity tests** measurement elements such as dependability, carefulness, responsibility, and honesty. These tests are used to learn about the attitudes of applicants toward a variety of task-related subjects. Since the passage of the Employee Polygraph Protection Act in 1988, polygraph (lie detector) tests have been effectively banned in employment situations. In their place, attitude tests are being used to evaluate attitudes about honesty and, presumably, on-the-task behaviours.
- **Personality tests** measurement personality or temperament. These tests are among the least reliable. Personality tests are debatable and not very valid, because little or no relationship exists between personality and performance.
- **Knowledge tests** are more authentic than personality tests because they measure an applicant's comprehension or knowledge of a subject. A math test for an accountant and a weather test for a pilot are examples. Human relations specialists must be able to demonstrate that the test reflects the knowledge needed to perform the task. For example, a teacher hired to teach math ought to not be given a keyboarding test.
- **Performance simulation tests** are altering in popularity. Based on task analysis data, they more easily meet the requirement of task relatedness than written tests. Performance simulation tests are made up of real task behaviours. The best-known performance simulation test is known as work sampling, and other credible simulation processes are performed at judgment centres.
- An *assessment* is a selection skill that examines candidates' dealing of simulated task situations and evaluates a candidate's potentiality by observing his or his performance in experiential activities designed to assume daily work.
    - ☐ **Assessment centres,** where work sampling is

frequently completed, utilize line executives, supervisors, or trained psychologists to assess candidates as they go through exercises that simulate real problems that these candidates would confront on their jobs. Activities may constitute interviews, problem-solving exercises, group discussions, and business-decision games. Assessment centres have consistently demonstrated results that accurately predict later task performance in managerial places.

- **Work sampling** is an effort to produce a illumination replica of a task, giving applicants the chance to demonstrate that they possess the essential talents by actually doing the tasks.

Interviews

Another widely used selection proficiency is the *interview,* a formal, in-depth conversation conducted to evaluate an applicant's acceptability. In general, the interviewer seeks to answer three broad questions:

1. Can the applicant do the task?
2. Will the applicant do the task?
3. How does the applicant compare with others who are being considered for the task?

Interviews are famous because of their flexibility. They can be adapted to unskilled, skilled, managerial, and staff employees. They also allow a two-way exchange of information where interviewers can learn about the applicant and the applicant can learn about the employer. Interviews do have some shortcomings, nevertheless. The most noticeable flaws are in the areas of reliability and validity. Good reliability means that the interpretation of the interview results doesn't vary from interviewer to interviewer. Reliability is meliorated when identical questions are asked. The validity of interviews is frequently questionable because few departments use standardized interviews.

Managers can boost the dependability and robustness of selection interviews by planning the interviews, establishing rapport, closing the interview with time for questions, and reviewing the interview as soon as possible after its decision.

Other selection techniques

Reference checking and health exams are two other significant selection techniques that help in the staffing decision.

- **Reference checking** allows employers to verify information rendered by the candidate. Nonetheless, obtaining information about potential candidates is frequently difficult because of privacy laws and employer business concern about defamation lawsuits.

- **Health exams** key out health problems that increase absenteeism and accidents, as well as discovering diseases that may be unknown to the applicant.

ORIENTATION AND TRAINING PROGRAMS

Once employees are selected, they must be ready to do their jobs, which is when orientation and training come in. Orientation means allowing for new employees with fundamental information about the employer. Training programs are used to ensure that the new employee has the fundamental knowledge required to perform the task satisfactorily. Orientation and training programs are significant elements in the processes of developing committed and flexible high-potential manpower and socializing new employees. Additionally, these programs can save employers money, providing big returns to an establishment, because an establishment that invests money to train its employees results in both the employees and the establishment relishing the dividends.

Orientation

Orientation programs not only amend the rate at which employees are able to perform their jobs but also help employees satisfy their personal desires to feel they are part of the establishment's social fabric. The HR department generally orients newcomers to broad organizational issues and fringe benefits. Supervisors complete the orientation process by introducing new employees to co-workers and others involved in the task. A buddy or wise man (mentor) may be assigned to uphold the process.

Training needs

Merely employing and placing employees in jobs doesn't assure their success. In fact, even tenured employees may need training, because of changes in the business environment. Here are some changes that may indicate that current employees need training:

- Introduction of new equipment or processes

- A change in the employee's task responsibilities
- A drop in an employee's productivity or in the quality of output
- An increase in safety violations or accidents
- An increased number of questions
- Complaints by customers or co-workers

Once managers decide that their employees need training, these managers necessitate to develop clear training aims that outline anticipated results. These managers must also be able to distinctly communicate these aims to employees. Keep in mind that training is only one response to a performance problem. If the problem is want of motivation, a poorly designed task, or an extraneous condition (such as a family problem), training isn't likely to offer much help.

Types of training

After particular training aims have been demonstrated, training sessions ought to be scheduled to provide the employee an opportunity to meet his or his aims. The following are typical training programs provided by employers:

- **Basic literacy training:** Organizations more and more necessitate to provide fundamental literacy training in the areas of reading and math skills to their employees.
- **Technical training:** New technology and structural designs have increased the demand to upgrade and improve employees' technical skills in both white-collar and blue-collar jobs.
- **Interpersonal skills training:** To the highest degree employees belong to a work team, and their work performance depends on their abilities to in effect interact with their co-workers. Interpersonal skills training help employees build communication skills.
- **Problem-solving training:** Today's employees frequently work as members of self-managed teams who are accountable for solving their own problems. Problem-solving training has become a fundamental part of almost every organizational effort to introduce self-managed teams or implement Total Quality Management (TQM).
- **Diversity training:** As one of the fastest growing areas of

training, diversity training increases awareness and builds cultural sensitivity skills. Awareness training tries to produce a discernment of the need for, and meaning of, managing and evaluating diversity. Skill-building training educates employees about specific cultural conflicts in the workplace.

Training methods

Most training takes place on the task due to the simplicity and lower cost of on-the-task training method acting. Two popular types of on-the-task training constitute the following:

- **Task rotation:** By allotting individuals to dissimilar jobs or tasks to different individuals on an irregular basis, leaders can add variety and expose individuals to the dependence that one task has on others. Task rotation can help stimulate individuals to higher levels of contributions, renew individual's interest and enthusiasm, and promote them to work more as a team.
- **Mentoring programs:** A fresh employee frequently learns his or his task under the direction of a seasoned old hand. In the trades, this type of training generally is called an apprenticeship. In white-collar jobs, it is called a coaching or mentoring relationship. In each, the new employee works under the observation of an experienced worker.

Occasionally, training aims cannot be conformed to through on-the-task training; the employer needs to look to other resources. *Off-the-task training* can rely on outside consultants, local college faculty, or in-house personnel. The more popular off-the-task training methods are classroom lectures, videos, and simulation exercises. Thanks to new technologies, employers can now facilitate some training, such as tutorials, on the employees' own computers, reducing the overall costs. Irrespective of the method selected, effectual training ought to be individualized. Some individuals absorb selective information better when they read about it, others learn best by observation, and still others learn better when they hear the information. These different learning styles aren't contradictory. When training is designed around the preferred learning style of an employee, the benefits of training are maximized because employees are able to hold more of what they learn.

Additionally to training, employers ought to extend development plans, which include a series of steps that can help employees acquire skills to reach long-term aims, such as a task promotion. Training, alternatively, is quick and specific to a present task.

EVALUATING EMPLOYEE PERFORMANCE

Employee performance ought to be assessed regularly. Employees want feedback—they want to know what their supervisors think about their work. Regular performance evaluations not only provide feedback to employees, but also provide employees with a chance to correct deficiencies. Evaluations or reviews also help in making key personnel decisions, such as the following:

- Justifying promotions, transfers, and terminations
- Identifying training needs
- Providing feedback to employees on their performance
- Determining necessary pay adjustments

Most organizations employ employee evaluation systems; one such system is known as a performance appraisal. A performance appraisal is a formal, structured system designed to evaluate the real task performance of an employee against designated performance standards. Though performance appraisals systems vary by organizations, all employee evaluations ought to have the following three components:

- Specific, task-related criteria against which performance can be equated
- A rating scale that lets employees know how well they're meeting the criteria
- Objective methods, forms, and processes to determine the rating

Customarily, an employee's immediate boss conducts his or his performance appraisal. Notwithstanding, some organizations use other devices, such as peer evaluations, self-appraisals, and even customer evaluations, for conducting this significant task. The latest approach to performance evaluation is the use of 360-degree feedback. The *360-degree feedback appraisal* provides performance feedback from the full circle of daily contacts that an employee may have. This method acting of performance appraisal fits well into organizations that have introduced teams, employee involvement, and Total Quality Management programs.

MAKING EMPLOYMENT DECISIONS

Employment decisions go outside determining which employees are due for raises. Through regular, objective performance appraisals, managers assume information to make and implement decisions about promotions, transfers, demotions, separations, and compensation. In most organizations, outstanding employees are acknowledged for their hard work and outstanding performances, and offered promotions. A promotion broadly speaking means rewarding an employee's efforts by moving that person to a task with increased authority and responsibility.

Downsizing has led numerous firms to rely on lateral moves or transfers instead of promoting employees. A lateral move can act as an opportunity for future vertical advancement because it can broaden an employee's experiences and add skills. Alternatively, occasionally employees' performances signal that they are not adapting well to their jobs and may need fewer duties. One option is a demotion, or reassignment to a lower rank or less prestigious position. Demotions aren't a popular skill because of the stigma accompanied this move. A thought is that demotions ought to be used as punishment for inefficient performance.

The departure of an employee from an establishment is denoted as separation. Separation may be voluntary or involuntary. Resignations and retirements are voluntary separations. Involuntary separations are layoffs and/or firings. Recently, the rash of downsizing all through the country has resulted in many layoffs. Occasionally, nonetheless, an employee must be terminated because of poor performance. Dismissal or firing of employees ought to occur only on the basis of just cause and only after all sensible steps to rehabilitate the employee have failed. In some cases, such as gross insubordination or theft, immediate discharge is necessitated.

COMPENSATING EMPLOYEES

Employee compensation concerns to all work-related payments, comprising wages, commissions, insurance, and time off. Wages and salaries are the most obvious forms of compensation and are based on task evaluations that determine the relative values of jobs to the establishment. Under the hourly wage system, employees are paid a determined amount for each hour they work. The system is in general used for lower skilled occupations. Salaried employees receive a fixed sum per week or month, irrespective how many hours they work. Most professional positions are salaried; the reality is that these employees normally work in excessiveness of a "minimum" 40-hour workweek.

Some businesses are compensated through incentive pay programs. Salespeople normally receive commissions based upon the quantities of goods they sell. Some sales compensation plans contain elements of both a salary and commission. A production worker's pay may be based upon some combination of an hourly wage and an incentive for each "piece" he or he makes. Some employees are offered merit awards as an honour for sustained superior performance.

Employee benefits are adds on to wages or pay. Some benefits, such as unemployment and worker's compensation, are legally mandated. Other benefits are optional and help build employee loyalty to an establishment, comprising the following:

- Bonuses (incentive money paid to employees additionally to their regular compensation)
- Employee discounts
- Health insurance
- Pension plans
- Profit-sharing (money from a portion of the company profits used to supplement regular compensation)
- Stock options (a plan that permits employees to buy shares of stock in the employee's firm at or below the present market value)
- Vacation, sick, and personal days

A top management executive is given benefits unequalled to his or her status. Additional executive benefits are termed perquisites (perks).

RELATIONS WITH OUTSIDE FACTORS

The Employment Relations Act was brought in the year 2000 to provide the framework for regulating relationships between employers and employees. The Act recognises "that employment relationships must be built on good faith behaviour" (Section 3(a)(i)) and the "inherent inequality of bargaining power in employment relationships" (Section 3(a)(ii)).

The Department of Labour has carried on research into the operation of the personal grievance provisions of the Act, including a long term and short term series of projects.

Long term research programme

- a survey of businesses, with 852 respondents, of which 130 had experienced challenges during the previous 12 months;
- a survey of public sector organizations, with 130 respondents of which 40 had experienced quarrels during the previous 12 months;
- case studies of 15 challenges

Short term research programme

- a survey of mediations carried out over a one month period,
- a review of Employment Relations Authority determinations over the same period
- a series of focus groups

Consequences from the long term research programme provided the basic source for the findings presented in this report, with additional information from the short term research programme used where pertinent. Nevertheless, a formal, external solution pathway can be started by either party. Once an employee or employer applied for mediation or an Employment Relations Authority hearing, there was little chance for the problem solution to go forward down an informal path.

In the case studies, pure misconduct cases tended to follow a more certain path - an internal disciplinary meeting, attended by the employee with a representative, followed by a warning, dismissal, or resignation. In contrast, performance and relationship issues (in particular) tended to be more complex. Employers seemed to be less clear about how to resolve these issues. As a result, the problem frequently continued for a longer time. This was aggravated where employers or employees went "fishing" for additional issues, which increased the level of tension and made the trouble more difficult to resolve.

For both employers and employees, the interests involved impacted on their choices regarding the path of the employment relationship problem. For employees, the stakes included whether the employee had found a new task, the impact on their families, or the hope to clear their name. For employers, the stakes included their assessment of the costs of the solution pathway, the effect of publicity on their reputation, or whether the problem would produce a case law within their organization.

Employers frequently assert that process is more important than substance. Nevertheless, in hearings on employment disputes, matters of substance and process aren't always easy (or appropriate) to disentangle. For example, if an employee "wins" because the Authority finds that the employer failed to investigate alleged misconduct, the employer is likely to see this as "process trumping substance" while the employee may conceive that their claim on the substance would have prevailed had an investigation taken place.

Though the Act doesn't explicitly discern between substantive and procedural unfairness, the Authority can and does modify awards as per its assessment of the merits. For instance, the review of Authority determinations found two examples where the Authority found that discharges were unacceptable in process terms, but awarded nothing to the employees because of their contributory behaviour. In around one quarter of all cases examined the Authority reduced or rejected awards on the base of contributory conduct.

WELFARE AND SECURITY MEASURES

Welfare constitutes anything that is done for the comfort and improvement of employees and is provided over and above the wages. Welfare helps in keeping the morale and motivation of the employees high so as to retain the employees for longer duration. The welfare measures need not be in monetary terms only but in any kind/forms. Employee welfare lets in monitoring of working conditions, creation of industrial harmony through infrastructure for health, industrial relations and insurance against disease, accident and unemployment for the workers and their families.

Employee welfare means all those activities of employer which are directed towards providing the employees with certain facilities and services additionally to wages or salaries.

Employee welfare has the following objectives:

1. To render better life and health to the workers.
2. To make the workers happy and satisfied.
3. To relieve workers from industrial fatigue and to improve intellectual, cultural and material conditions of living of the workers.

The fundamental features of employee welfare measures are as follows:

1. Employee welfare comprises numerous facilities, services and amenities provided to workers for improving their health, efficiency, economic improvement and social status.
2. Welfare measures are additionally to regular wages and other economic gains available to workers due to legal provisions and collective bargaining.
3. Employee welfare schemes are flexible and invariably changing. New welfare measures are added to the existing ones from time to time.
4. Welfare measures may be introduced by the employers, government, employees or by any social or charitable agency.
5. The purpose of employee welfare is to bring about the growth of the whole personality of the workers to make a better manpower.

The very logic behind providing welfare schemes is to produce efficient, healthy, loyal and satisfied labour force for the establishment. The intention of providing such facilities is to make their work life better and also to raise their standard of living. The important benefits of welfare measures can be summarized as follows:

- They provide better physical and mental health to workers and therefore promote a healthy work environment.
- Facilities like housing schemes, medical benefits, and education and recreation facilities for workers' families help in raising their standards of living. This makes workers to pay more attention towards work and therefore increases their productivity.
- Employers get stable labour force by providing welfare facilities. Workers take active interest in their jobs and work with a feeling of involvement and participation.
- Employee welfare measures increase the productivity of establishment and promote healthy industrial relations thereby maintaining industrial peace.
- The social evils prevalent among the labours such as substance abuse, etc are reduced to a greater extent by the welfare policies.

Note: For detailed information related to this chapter reader can visit site of United Technologies. United Technologies (UTC) provides technology products and services to the building systems and aerospace industries. The company provides helicopters, elevators, air conditioning equipment, hydrogen fuel cells, life support systems, aerospace products and aftermarket services, and fire and security protection services. The company primarily operates in the US. It is headquartered in Hartford, Connecticut and employs 223,100 people. utc.com

3

Strategic Human Resource Management

There is a strong lobby propounding the view that human resources are the source of competitive advantage for the business, rather than, say, access to capital or use of technology. It is therefore logical to suggest that attention needs to be paid to the nature of this resource and its management as this will impact on human resource behaviour and performance and consequently the performance of the organization. Indeed Boxall and Steeneveld argue that there is no need to prove the relationship between firm performance and labour management as it is self-evident that the quality of human resource management is a critical influence on the performance of the firm. It is not, therefore, surprising that the rhetoric of strategic human resource management has been readily adopted, especially as a strategic approach is considered to be one of the characteristics of HRM as opposed to personnel management, which is seen as operational. If, as Boxall and Purcell suggest, HR is strategic to business success, then HR needs to be a strategic player and the role of business strategist will be a key role for HR specialists in the future.

STRATEGIC HUMAN RESOURCE MANAGEMENT AND HUMAN RESOURCE STRATEGY

Our understanding of HR strategy has changed considerably since strategy first became the subject of great attention. We have moved from viewing strategy as a physical document to seeing it as an incremental process, affected by political influences and generating learning. Tyson's definition of human resource strategy is a useful starting point, although somewhat limited, as will be seen from our later discussion.

The intentions of the corporation both explicit and covert, toward the management of its employees, expressed through philosophies, policies and practices.

This definition is helpful because research on human resource strategy in the early 1980s tended to focus on seeking an HR strategy document in order to determine whether there was a strategic approach to HR and what that approach was. This was rather like searching for the Holy Grail. Not surprisingly few complete HR strategies were found and HR specialists berated themselves for having failed in this critical area. Gradually the thinking changed to encompass a view that HR strategy need not be written on a piece of paper or need not, indeed, be explicit, as the Tyson quotation illustrates. Further developments in thinking began to accept the idea that strategies are neither finished, nor complete, but rather incremental and piecemeal. There is compelling evidence to suggest that strategic HR tends to be issue based rather than the formulation of a complete and integrated strategy. Strategic thinking, strategic decision making and a strategic orientation were gradually understood as much more realistic expectations.

In parallel with this thinking there were developments in the general strategy literature which viewed strategy as a process which was not necessarily rational and top down, but a political and evolutionary process. Mintzberg argues that strategy is 'formed' rather than 'formulated' and that any intended strategy is changed by events, opportunities, the actions of employees and so on – so that the realised strategy is different from the initial vision. Strategy, Mintzberg argues, can only be identified in retrospect and, as Boxall and Purcell suggest, is best seen in the ultimate behaviour of the organization. Wrapped up in this view is also the idea that strategy is not necessarily determined by top management alone but can be influenced 'bottom up', as ideas are tried and tested in one part of the organization and gradually adopted in a wholesale manner if they are seen to be applicable and successful.

This leads on to the concept of strategy as learning both in content and in process, which is supported by the notion of strategy as a process of change. Literature draws out the need to sense changes in the environment, develop a resultant strategy and turn this strategy into action. While the HR function has often found itself excluded from the strategy formation process, HR strategy has more often been seen in terms of the implementation of organizational strategies. However, implementation of HR strategy has been weak, at best. Among the qualities of the most successful organizations is the ability to turn strategy into action quickly, in other words to implement the chosen strategy, and Guest maintained that the capability to implement strategic plans is an important feature of successful HRM. However, a lack of attention to the implementation of HR strategy has been identified, and the information that does exist suggests that this is a problematic area. Legge maintained that the evidence of implementation of HR strategies was patchy and sometimes contradictory, and Skinner and Mabey found that responsibility for implementation was unclear, with only 54 per cent of respondents, in organizations with an HR director, perceiving that the HR function played a major part in implementation. In their research Kane and Palmer found that the existence of an HR strategy was only a minor influence on the HR policies and procedures that were used. Frameworks such as the HR scorecard are aimed, at least in part, at facilitating the management and implementation of HR architecture 'the sum of the HR function, the broader HR system, and the resulting employee behaviors' as a strategic asset.

THE LINK BETWEEN BUSINESS AND HR STRATEGY

The nature, desirability and feasibility of the link between business strategy and HR strategy is a consistent theme which runs through the strategy literature, although, as we shall discuss later, some theories suggest that implementing 'best practice' in HRM is even more important than this. Figure below is a simple model that is useful in visualising different ways in which this relationship may be played out and has relevance for the newer conceptions of strategy based on the resource-based view of the firm, as well as earlier conceptions.

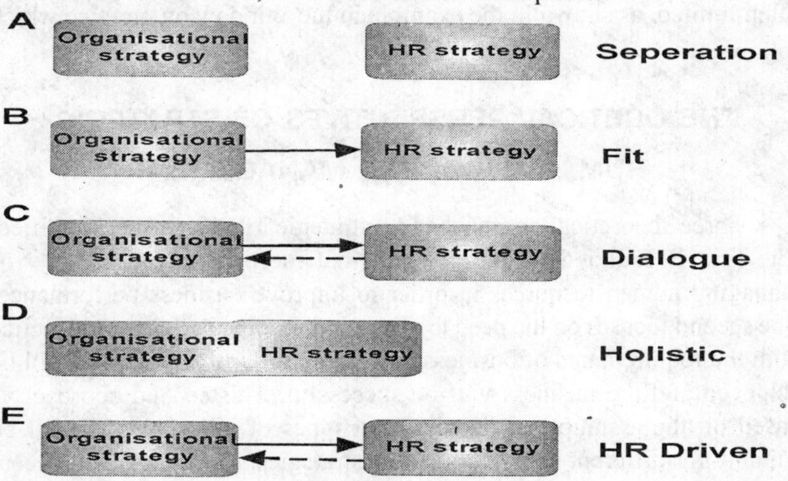

Fig : Potential Relationships between Organizational Strategy and HR Strategy

In the separation model (A) there is no relationship at all, if indeed organizational and human resource strategy does exist in an explicit form in the organization. This is a typical picture of twenty years ago, but it still exists today, particularly in smaller organizations.

The fit model (B) represents a growing recognition of the importance of people in the achievement of organizational strategy. Employees are seen as key in the implementation of the declared organizational strategy, and human resource strategy is designed to fit with this.

This whole approach depends on a view of strategy formulation as a logical rational process, which remains a widely held view. The relationship in the fit model is exemplified by organizations which cascade their business objectives down from the senior management team through functions, through departments, through teams and so on. Functions, for example, have to propose a functional strategy which enables the organizational strategy to be achieved. Departments have to propose a strategy which enables the functional strategy to be achieved, and so on. In this way the HR function (as with any other) is required to respond to organizational strategy by defining a strategy which meets organizational demands.

The dialogue model (C) takes the relationship one step further, as it recognises the need for two-way communication and some debate. What is demanded in the organization's strategy may not be viewed as feasible and alternative possibilities need to be reviewed. The debate, however, is often limited, as shown in the example in the Window on practice which follows.

THE ORETICAL PERSPECTIVES OF STRATEGIC HUMAN RESOURCE MANAGEMENT

Three theoretical approaches to strategic HRM can be identified. The first is founded on the concept that there is 'one best way' of managing human resources in order to improve business performance. The second focuses on the need to align employment policies and practice with the requirements of business strategy in order that the latter will be achieved and the business will be successful. This second approach is based on the assumption that different types of HR strategies will be suitable for different types of business strategies. Thirdly, a more recent approach to strategic HRM is derived from the resource-based view of the firm, and the perceived value of human capital. This view focuses on the quality of the human resources available to the organization and their ability to learn and adapt more quickly than their competitors. Supporters of this perspective challenge the need to secure a mechanistic fit with business strategy and focus instead on long-term sustainability and survival of the organization via the pool of human capital.

UNIVERSALIST APPROACH

The perspective of the universalist approach is derived from the conception of human resource management as 'best practice'. In other words it is based on the premise that one model of labour management – a high-commitment model – is related to high organizational performance in all contexts, irrespective of the particular competitive strategy of the organization. An expression of this approach can be seen in Guest's theory of HRM, which is a prescriptive model based on four HR policy goals: strategic integration, commitment, flexibility and quality. These policy goals are related to HRM policies which are expected to produce desirable organizational outcomes.

Guest describes the four policy goals as follows:

- *Strategic integration* – ensuring that HRM is fully integrated into strategic planning, that HRM policies are coherent, that line managers use HRM practices as part of their everyday work.
- *Commitment* – ensuring that employees feel bound to the organization and are committed to high performance via their behaviour.
- *Flexibility* – ensuring an adaptable organization structure, and functional flexibility based on multiskilling.
- *Quality* – ensuring a high quality of goods and services through high-quality, flexible employees.

Guest sees these goals as a package – all need to be achieved to create the desired organizational outcomes which are high job performance, problem solving, change, innovation and cost effectiveness; and low employee turnover, absence and grievances.

Clarity of goals gives a certain attractiveness to this model – but this is where the problems also lie. Whipp questions the extent to which such a shift is possible, and Purcell sees the goals as unattainable. The goals are also an expression of human resource management, as opposed to personnel management, and as such bring us back to the debate about what human resource management really is and the inherent contradictions in the approach. Ogbonna and Whipp argue that internal consistency within such a model is extremely difficult to achieve because of such contradictions (for example the tension between flexibility and commitment). Because the prescriptive approach brings with it a set of values, it suggests that there is only one best way and this is it.

Pfeffer and Becker and Gerhart are well-known exponents of this view. While there is some support for this perspective, there remains some debate as to which particular human resource practices will stimulate high commitment.

Falling somewhere between the universalist approach and the fit approach is the Harvard model of HRM. This model, produced by Beer et al., is analytical rather than prescriptive. The model recognises the different stakeholder interests that impact on employee behaviour and performance, and also gives greater emphasis to factors in the environment that will help to shape human resource strategic choices – identified in the Situational factors box. Poole also notes that the model has potential for international or other comparative analysis, as it takes into account different sets of philosophies and assumptions which may be operating.

Although Beer et al.'s model is primarily analytical, there are prescriptive elements leading to some potential confusion. The prescription in Beer et al.'s model is found in the HR outcomes box, where specific outcomes are identified as universally desirable.

FIT OR CONTINGENCY APPROACH

The fit or contingency approach is based on two critical forms of fit. The first is external fit (sometimes referred to as vertical integration) – that HR strategy fits with the demands of business strategy; the second is internal fit (sometimes referred to as horizontal integration) -- that all HR policies and activities fit together so that they make a coherent whole, are mutually reinforcing and are applied consistently.

The strength of this model is that it provides a simple framework to show how selection, appraisal, development and reward can be mutually geared to produce the required type of employee performance. For example, if an organization required cooperative team behaviour with mutual sharing of information and support, the broad implications would be:

- *Selection*: successful experience of teamwork and sociable, cooperative personality; rather than an independent thinker who likes working alone.

- *Appraisal*: based on contribution to the team, and support of others; rather than individual outstanding performance.
- *Reward*: based on team performance and contribution; rather than individual performance and individual effort.

There is little doubt that this type of internal fit is valuable. However, questions have been raised over the model's simplistic response to organization strategy. The question 'what if it is not possible to produce a human resource response that enables the required employee behaviour and performance?' is never addressed. So, for example, the distance between now and future performance requirements, the strengths, weaknesses and potential of the workforce, the motivation of the workforce and employee relations issues are not considered.

This model has been criticised because of its dependence on a rational strategy formulation rather than on an emergent strategy formation approach; and because of the nature of the one-way relationship with organizational strategy. It has also been criticised owing to its unitarist assumptions, as no recognition is made for employee interests and their choice of whether or not to change their behaviour.

Taking this model and the notion of fit one step further, human resource strategy has been conceived in terms of generating specific employee behaviours. In the ideal form of this there would be analysis of the types of employee behaviour required to fulfil a predetermined business strategy, and then an identification of human resource policies and practices which would bring about and reinforce this behaviour. A very good example of this is found in Schuler and Jackson. They used the three generic business strategies defined by Porter and for each identified employee role behaviour and HRM policies required.

Similar analyses can be found for other approaches to business strategy, for example in relation to the Boston matrix and the developmental stage of the organization. Some human resource strategies describe the behaviour of all employees, but others have concentrated on the behaviour of Chief Executives and senior managers; Miles and Snow, for example, align appropriate managerial characteristics to three generic strategies of prospector, defender and analyser. The rationale behind this matching process is that if managerial attributes and skills are aligned to the organizational strategy, then a higher level of organizational performance will result. There is little empirical evidence to validate this link, but work by Thomas and Ramaswamy does provide some support. They used statistical analysis to investigate if there was a match between manager attributes and skills in organizations with either a defender or a prospector strategy in 269 of the Fortune 500 companies in the United States. They found an overall statistical relationship between manager attributes and strategy. Taking the analysis a step further they then compared 30 organizations which were misaligned with 30 which were aligned and found that performance in the aligned companies (whether prospector or defender) was statistically superior. While this work can be criticised, it does provide an indication of further research which can be developed to aid our understanding of the issues. Sanz-Valle et al. found some partial support for the Schuler and Jackson model in terms of the link between business strategy and HR practices, but they did not investigate the implications of this link for organizational performance. The types of strategies described above are generic, and there is more concentration in some organizations on tailoring the approach to the particular needs of the specific organization.

Many human resource strategies aim not just to target behaviour, but through behaviour change to effect a movement in the culture of the organization. The target is, therefore, to change the common view of 'the way we do things around here' and to attempt to manipulate the beliefs and values of employees. There is much debate as to whether this is achievable.

We have previously recounted some of the concerns expressed about Fombrun et al.'s specific model; however, there is further criticism of the fit or matching perspective as a whole. Grundy claims that the idea of fit seems naive and simplistic. Ogbonna and Whipp argue that much literature assumes that fit can be targeted, observed and measured and there is an underlying assumption of stability. Given that most companies may have to change radically in response to the environment, any degree of fit previously achieved will be disturbed. Thus, they contend that fit is a theoretical ideal which can rarely be achieved in practice. Boxall criticises: the typologies of competitive advantage that are used, arguing that there is evidence that high-performing firms are good 'all rounders'; the fact that strategy is a given and no account is made of how it is formed or by whom; the assumption that employees will behave as requested; and the aim for consistency, as it has been shown that firms use different strategies for different sections of their workforce.

RESOURCE-BASED APPROACH

The resource-based view of the firm has stimulated attempts to create a resource-based model of strategic HRM. The resource-based view of the firm is concerned with the relationships between internal resources (of which human resources are one), strategy and firm performance. It focuses on the promotion of sustained competitive advantage through the development of human capital rather than merely aligning human resources to current strategic goals. Human resources can provide competitive advantage for the business, as long as they are unique and cannot be copied or substituted for by competing organizations. The focus is not just on the behaviour of the human resources (as with the fit approach), but on the skills, knowledge, attitudes and competencies which underpin this, and which have a more sustained impact on long-term survival than current behaviour (although this is still regarded as important). Briggs and Keogh maintain that business excellence is not just about 'best practice' or 'leapfrogging the competition', but about the intellectual capital and business intelligence to anticipate the future, today.

Barney states that in order for a resource to result in sustained competitive advantage it must meet four criteria, and Wright et al. demonstrate how human resources meet these. First, the resource must be valuable. Wright and his colleagues argue that this is the case where demand for labour is heterogeneous, and where the supply of labour is also heterogeneous – in other words where different firms require different competencies from each other and for different roles in the organization, and where the supply of potential labour comprises individuals with different competencies. On this basis value is created by matching an individual's competencies with the requirements of the firm and/or the job, as individuals will make a variable contribution, and one cannot be substituted easily for another.

The second criterion, rarity, is related to the first. An assumption is made that the most important competence for employees is cognitive ability due to future needs for adaptability and flexibility. On the basis that cognitive ability is normally distributed in the population, those with high levels of this ability will be rare. The talent pool is not unlimited and many employers are currently experiencing difficulties in finding the talent that they require.

Third, resources need to be inimitable. Wright et al. argue that this quality applies to the human resource as competitors will find it difficult to identify the exact source of competitive advantage from within the firm's human resource pool. Also competitors will not be able to duplicate exactly the resource in question, as they will be unable to copy the unique historical conditions of the first firm. This history is important as it will affect the behaviour of the human resource pool via the development of unique norms and cultures. Thus even if a competing firm recruited a group of individuals from a competitor they would still not be able to produce the same outcomes in the new firm as the context would be different. Two factors make this unique history difficult to copy. The first is causal ambiguity – in other words it is impossible to separate out the exact causes of performance, as the sum is always more than the parts; and, second, social complexity – that the complex of relationships and networks developed over time which have an impact on performance is difficult to dissect.

Finally resources need to be non-substitutable. Wright and his co-authors argue that although in the short term it may be possible to substitute human resources with others, for example technological ones, in the long term the human resource is different as it does not become obsolete (like technology) and can be transferred across other products, markets and technologies.

Wright et al. noted that attention has often been devoted to leaders and top management in the context of a resource-based approach, and indeed Boxall contends that this approach provides the theoretical base on which to concentrate in the renewal and development of the critical resource of leaders in the organization. However, Wright and his co-authors view all human resources in the organization as the pool of capital. This sits well with the view of strategy as evolutionary and strategy being influenced from the bottom up as well as from the top down. Also it is likely that top managers are more easily identified for their contribution to the organization and hence are more likely to be mobile, therefore, than other employees who may not be so easily identified. However, different segments of the human resource are viewed differently by organizations in terms of their contribution to competitive advantage, so for some organizations the relevant pool of human capital may not be the total pool of employees.

Whereas fit models focus on the means of competitive advantage (HR practices) the resource-based view focuses on the source (the human capital). Wright et al. argue that while the practices are important they are not the source of competitive advantage as they can be replicated elsewhere, and they will produce different results in different places because of the differential human capital in different places.

Boxall argues that this theoretical perspective provides a conceptual base for asserting that human resources are a source of competitive advantage, and as such valued as generating strategic capability. Thus there is a case for viewing HR strategy as something more than a reactive matching process. Indeed Wright et al. argue that it provides the case for HR to be involved in the formulation of strategy rather than just its implementation. They suggest that it provides a grounding for asserting that not every strategy is universally implementable, and that alternatives may have to be sought or the human capital pool developed further, via human resource practices, where this is possible.

The importance of this perspective is underlined by the current emphasis on a firm's intangible assets. Numerous studies have shown that a firm's market value (the sum of the value of the shares) is not fully explained by its current financial results or its tangible assets and the focus has moved to a firm's intangible assets such as intellectual capital and customer relationships – all of which are derived from human capital. This emphasis has resulted in a great deal of attention being paid to the evaluation of human capital through measuring, reporting and managing it.

But human capital is loaned: 'human capital is not owned by the organization, but secured through the employment relationship' and because this is so, the strategy for the management of people is also critical. Experts believe this will need to include a review about the ways that employees are managed.

The perceived importance of people as an intangible asset is demonstrated in the action of Barclays Group who on their Investor's Day were keen to demonstrate not only their financial results but people strategies and improvements in staff satisfaction which they believe have contributed to the results. This approach has great advantages from an HR point of view. People in the organization become the focus, their contribution is monitored and made more explicit, the way people are managed can be seen to add value and money spent on people can be seen as an investment rather than a cost. Some firms are using the balanced scorecard to demonstrate the contribution that human capital makes to firm performance, such as Norwich Union, and Scarborough argues that this builds a bridge between the role of the HR function and the strategy of the firm. However, there are in-built barriers in the language of the resource-based view. One is the reference to people as 'human capital' which some consider to be unnecessarily instrumental. Another is the focus on 'firms' and 'competitive advantage' which makes it harder to see the relevance of this perspective for organizations in the public sector. There is also the issue of what is being measured and who decides this. The risk is that too much time is spent measuring and that not everything that is measured is of critical value to the organization. So far, such measures appear very varied, although different firms will, of course, need to measure different things. Measures often appear to be taken without a coherent framework, as appears to be the case in the results documented by Scarborough and Elias for their 10 case study organizations. The balanced scorecard and the HR scorecard, however, appear to be a useful mechanism in this respect.

WHY DOES THE THEORY MATTER?

It is tempting to think of these theories of strategic HRM as competing with each other. In other words one is right and the others are wrong. If this were the case HR managers/directors and board members would need only to work out which is the 'right' theory and apply that. This is, of course, a gross oversimplification, as each theory can be interpreted and applied in different ways, and each has advantages and disadvantages. It could be argued that different theories apply in different sectors or competitive contexts. For example Guest suggests that there is the possibility that a 'high performance/high commitment' approach might always be most appropriate in manufacturing, whereas strategic choice (which could be interpreted as choice to fit with business strategy) might be more realistic in the services sector. This could be taken one step further to suggest that different theories apply to different groups in the workforce.

Consequently, these three theories do not necessarily represent simple alternatives. It is also likely that some board directors and even HR managers are not familiar with any of these theories. In spite of that, organizations, through their culture, and individuals within organizations operate on the basis of a set of assumptions, and these assumptions are often implicit. Assumptions about the nature and role of human resource strategy, whether explicit or implicit, will have an influence on what organizations actually do. Assumptions will limit what are seen as legitimate choices.

Understanding these theories enables HR managers, board members, consultants and the like to interpret the current position of HR strategy in the organization, confront current assumptions and challenge current thinking and potentially open up a new range of possibilities.

THE ROLE OF THE HR FUNCTION IN STRATEGY

The extent to which the HR function is involved in both organizational and human resource strategy development is dependent on a range of factors, the most often quoted being whether the most senior HR person is a member of the board of directors. Sparkes identifies a key role for the HR director as promoting the connection between organizational strategy, culture and people strategy. He maintains that being an HR director means that 'we can almost guarantee that a human element is built into everything strategic from the start'.

There is evidence to suggest that over the past 20 years HR board membership has increased and surveys suggest that around three-fifths of larger organizations have an HR, although some surveys indicate lower percentages. However, we found, as did Kelly and Gennard, that board membership, while generally identified as desirable, does not guarantee the involvement of specialists in strategy, and it was not necessarily seen as essential to strategic involvement, and this is perhaps why currently very little attention is given to assessing the percentage of organizations with an HR director:

Thus whilst board membership is often treated as a proxy for strategic involvement, the reality of the situation is far more complex. Even looking at the most favourable evidence from the research, a picture emerges of limited involvement in strategic matters. The good news is that the IPM's survey found that representation on the top management team was predicted to increase, although there is contradictory evidence.

While a seat on the board is undoubtably an advantage and, as Sparkes suggests, improves HR's understanding of the business context in which HR strategies need to be developed and implemented, this is not essential. Other factors influencing the role of the HR function in strategic concerns include the overall philosophy of the organization towards the value of its people, the mindset of the Chief Executive, and the working relationship between the Chief Executive and the most senior HR person.

These influences are not particularly easy to manipulate, but what the HR function can do is look for opportunities in these areas, and use them. Building a good working relationship with the Chief Executive is critical, and doubly so, as Stiles confirms the power of the Chief Executive in selecting who should be appointed to the board. There is evidence that HR managers have to prove themselves before being given a seat on the board so building key competencies is essential. Barney and Wright suggest that one of the real reasons why HR are not involved in strategic planning is that they are not displaying the required competencies.

It is suggested that HR managers need to use business and financial language; describe the rationale for HR activities in terms of added value; act as a business manager first and an HR manager second; appoint line managers into the HR function; concentrate on priorities as defined by the business; understand the business they work in, and offer well-developed change-management skills that can be used immediately. Guest and King argue that, as senior managers and board members appear to have limited knowledge of research linking people management and performance, there is an opportunity for enthusiastic HR managers/ directors to feed new ideas to Chief Executives. Increasingly, HR managers need to become closer to their accounting colleagues. In addition, the function needs to prepare itself by thinking strategically, identifying a functional mission and strategy and involving line management in the development and implementation of human resource strategy.

Note: For a very good study of this chapter see St. Jude Medical, Inc. website. St. Jude Medical is engaged in developing, manufacturing and distributing cardiovascular medical devices for the global cardiac rhythm management, cardiology, cardiac surgery and atrial fibrillation therapy areas. The company also makes implantable neurostimulation medical devices for the management of chronic pain. The company markets its products in about 100 countries across the world. It primarily operates in the US, Europe, Japan and Asia Pacific. It is headquartered in Saint Paul, Minnesota. See www.sjm.com.

4

Planning: Jobs and People

Planning for human resources has experienced a chequered history. In the 1960s and 1970s it was heralded as a critical tool for business success, as planning to get the right people in the right place at the right time was seen to be essential to achieving rapid growth. In the 1980s and 1990s planning was viewed as a suitable tool for managing downsizing and redundancies. On the other hand it has been argued that planning is no longer meaningful in an era of rapid and discontinuous change where it been recognised that strategies emerge rather than being precisely planned in advance. However, good planning still has an important contribution in supporting strategic HRM in this context.

THE CONTRIBUTION AND FEASIBILITY OF HR PLANNING

A useful starting point is to consider the different contributions that strategy and planning make to the organization. A common view has been that they are virtually one and the same – hence the term 'strategic planning'. Henry Mintzberg distinguished between strategic thinking, which is about synthesis, intuition and creativity to produce a not too precisely articulated vision of direction, and strategic planning, which is about collecting the relevant information to stimulate the visioning process and also programming the vision into what needs to be done to get there. In more detail he suggests:

- *Planning as strategic programming* – planning cannot generate strategies, but it can make them operational by clarifying them; working out the consequences of them; and identifying what must be done to achieve each strategy.

- *Planning as tools to communicate and control* – planning can ensure coordination and encourage everyone to pull in the same direction; planners can assist in finding successful experimental strategies which may be operating in just a small part of the organization.
- *Planners as analysts* – planners need to analyse hard data, both external and internal, which managers can then use in the strategy development process.
- *Planners as catalysts* – raising difficult questions and challenging the conventional wisdom which may stimulate managers into thinking in more creative ways.

Organizational and human resource planners make an essential contribution to strategic visioning. Sisson and Storey identify HR planning as 'one of the basic building blocks of a more strategic approach'. Starting with some ideas of Lam and Schaubroeck we identify four specific ways in which HR planning is critical to strategy, as it can identify:

- *Gaps in capabilities* – lack of sufficient skills, people or knowledge in the business which will prevent the strategy being implemented successfully;
- *Surpluses in capabilities* – providing scope for efficiencies and new ventures to capitalise on the skills, people and knowledge that are currently underused in order to influence or shape the strategy;
- *Poor utilisation of people* – suggesting inappropriate human resource practices that need to be altered;
- Developing a talent pool.

If you look again at the resource-based view of the firm you will see how these four aspects are crucial to sustaining competitive advantage through making the most of human resources.

Our environment of rapid and discontinuous change makes any planning difficult, and HR planning is especially difficult as people have free will, unlike other resources, such as finance or technology. The contribution and implementation of HR planning is likely to be enhanced if:

- Plans are viewed as flexible and reviewed regularly, rather than being seen as an end point in the process;
- Stakeholders, including all levels of manager and employee, are

involved in the process. Surveys and focus groups are possible mechanisms, in addition to line manager representatives on the HR planning team;

- Planning is owned and driven by senior managers rather than HR specialists, who need to facilitate the process;
- Plans are linked to business and HR strategy;
- Plans are user-friendly and not overly complex;
- It is recognised that while a comprehensive plan may be ideal, sometimes it may only be feasible to plan on an issue-by-issue basis.

THE SCOPE OF HUMAN RESOURCE PLANNING

Traditionally human resource planning, generally termed manpower planning, was concerned with the numbers of employees and the levels and types of skill in the organization. A typical model of traditional manpower planning is shown in Figure below. In this model the emphasis is on balancing the projected demand for and supply of labour, in order to have the right number of the right employees in the right place at the right time. The demand for manpower is influenced by corporate strategies and objectives, the environment and the way that staff are utilised within the business. The supply of manpower is projected from current employees (via calculations about expected leavers, retirements, promotions, etc.) and from the availability of the required skills in the labour market. Anticipated demand and supply are then reconciled by considering a range of options, and plans to achieve a feasible balance are designed.

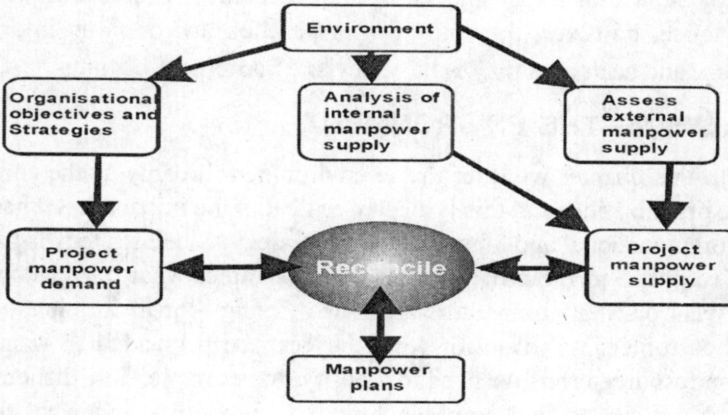

Fig : A Model of Traditional Manpower Planning

As the world has moved on this model has been viewed as too narrow, being heavily reliant on calculations of employee numbers or potential employee numbers. It has also been criticised for giving insufficient attention to skills. In addition there has been an increasing recognition of the need to plan, not just for hard numbers, but for the softer issues of employee behaviour, organization culture and systems; these issues have been identified as having a key impact on business success in the current environment.

Increasingly there is a need for organizations to integrate the process of planning for numbers and skills of employees; employee behaviour and organizational culture; organization design and the make-up of individual jobs; and formal and informal systems. These aspects are all critical in terms of programming and achieving the vision. Each of these aspects interrelates with the others. However, reality has always been recognised as being a long way from identified best practice. Undoubtedly different organizations will place different emphases on each of these factors, and may well plan each separately or plan some and not others.

The framework we shall use in this chapter attempts to bring all aspects of HR planning together, incorporating the more traditional approach to 'manpower planning', but going beyond this to include behaviour, culture, systems and so on. Our framework identifies 'where we want to be', translated from responses to the strategic vision; 'where we are now'; and 'what we need to do to make the transition' – all operating within the organization's environment. An alternative framework to use may be the HR scorecard. We shall now look in more depth at each of these four areas. The steps are presented in a logical sequence. In practice, however, they may run in parallel, and/or in an informal fashion, and each area may well be revisited a number of times.

ANALYSING THE ENVIRONMENT

In this chapter we refer to the environment broadly as the context of the organization, and this is clearly critical in the impact that it has on both organizational and human resource strategy. Much strategy is based on a response to the environment – for example, what our customers now want or what competitors are now offering – or in anticipation of what customers will want or what they can be persuaded to want. In human resource terms we need to identify, for example, how difficult or easy it will be to find employees with scarce skills and what these employees will expect from an employer so that we can attract them. We shall be concerned with legislation which will limit or widen the conditions of employment that we offer, with what competitors are offering and with what training schemes are available locally or nationally.

Data on relevant trends can be collected from current literature, company annual reports, conferences/courses and from contacts and networking. Table below gives examples of the many possible sources for each major area.

Sources of Information on Environment Trends

Trend Area	**Possible Sources**
Social	Census information Journals News media Social Trends General Household Survey Employment Gazette Local papers
Demographics	Labour Market Quarterly Census information Employment Gazette Local Council, Learning and Skills Councils
Political and Legislative	News media Proceedings of European Parliament Proceedings of British Parliament Hansard Industrial Relations Review and Report Industrial Law Journal
Industrial and Technological	Employment Digest

	Journals specifically for the industry Financial Times Employers' association Trade association
Competitors	Annual reports Talk to them!

Once one has acquired and constantly updated data on the environment, a common method of analysis is to produce a map of the environment, represented as a wheel. The map represents a time in the future, say three years away. In the centre of the wheel can be written the core purpose of the organization as it relates to people, or potential future strategies or goals. Each spoke of the wheel can then be filled in to represent a factor of the external environment, for example, potential employees, a specific local competitor, competitors generally, regulatory bodies, customers, government. From all the spokes the six or seven regarded as most important need to be selected.

These can then be worked on further by asking what demands each will make of the organization, and how the organization will need to respond in order to achieve its goals. From these responses can be derived the implications for human resource activities. For example, the demands of potential employees may be predicted as:

- We need a career not just a job.
- We need flexibility to help with childrearing.
- We want to be treated as people and not as machines.
- We need a picture of what the organization has in store for us.
- We want to be better trained.

And so on.

Managers then consider what the organization would need to offer to meet these needs in order to meet a declared organizational goal or strategy. It is a good way of identifying human resource issues which need to be addressed. The analysis can also be fed back into identifying and clarifying the future vision or goals in human resource terms.

FORECASTING FUTURE HUMAN RESOURCE NEEDS

Organization, Behaviour and Culture

There is little specific literature on the methods used to translate the strategic objectives of the organization and environmental influences into qualitative or soft human resource goals. In general terms, they can be summed up as the use of managerial judgement. Brainstorming, combined with the use of structured checklists or matrices, can encourage a more thorough analysis. Organization-change literature and corporate planning literature are helpful as sources of ideas in this area. Three simple techniques are a human resource implications checklist, a strategic brainstorming exercise and a behavioural expectation chart. The HR scorecard may be a useful tool for this aspect of planning, and the use of scenarios may also be helpful. Scenarios can be used to provide a picture of alternative organizational futures and alternative HR responses to these.

EMPLOYEE NUMBERS AND SKILLS (DEMAND FOR ECASTING)

There is far more literature in the more traditional area of forecasting employee number demand based on the organization's strategic objectives. Both objective and subjective approaches can be employed. Objective methods include statistical and work study approaches.

Statistical models generally relate employee number demand to specific organizational circumstances and activities. Models can take account of determining factors, such as production, sales, passenger miles, level of service. A simple model might relate people demand to production, using a constant relationship, without making any assumptions about economies of scale. In this model if output is to be doubled, then employees would also need to be doubled.

More complicated equations can be formulated which describe the way that a combination of independent factors is expected to affect the dependent employee demand. By inserting new values for the independent factors, such as new projected sales figures, we can work out the demand for employees from the equation. The equations can also be represented as graphs, making the relationships clear to see. These models can be adapted to take account of projected changes in utilisation, owing to factors such as the introduction of new technology, or alternative organizational forms, such as high-performance teams.

The work-study method is based on a thorough analysis of the tasks to be done, and the time each takes. From this the person-hours needed per unit of output can be calculated, and standards are developed for the numbers and levels of employees required. These are most useful when one is studying production work. They need to be checked regularly to make sure they are still appropriate. Work study is usually classified as an objective measure; however, it is often accepted that since the development of standards and the grouping of tasks is partly dependent on human judgement, it could be considered as a subjective method.

A Range of Methods to Change Employee Utilisation

- Introducing new materials or equipment, particularly new technology
- Introducing changes in work organization, such as:
  - Quality circles
  - Job rotation
  - Job enlargement
  - Job enrichment
  - Autonomous work groups
  - High-performance teams
  - Participation
- Organization development
- Introducing changes in organization structure, such as:
  - Centralisation/decentralisation
  - New departmental boundaries
  - Relocation of parts of the organization
  - Flexible project structures
- Introducing productivity schemes, bonus schemes or other incentive schemes
- Encouraging greater staff flexibility and work interchangeability
- Altering times and periods of work
- Training and appraisal of staff
- Developing managers and use of performance management

The most common subjective method of demand forecasting is managerial judgement (sometimes referred to as managerial opinion or the inductive method), and this can also include the judgements of other operational and technical staff, as well as all levels of managers. This method relies on managers' estimates of human resource demand based on past experience and on corporate plans. Managerial judgements can be collected from the 'bottom up' with lower-level managers providing estimates to go up the hierarchy for discussion and redrafting. Alternatively, a 'top-down' approach can be used with estimates made by the highest level of management to go down the hierarchy for discussion and redrafting. When this method is used it is difficult to cope with changes that are very different from past experiences. It is also less precise than statistical methods, but it is more comprehensive. Managerial judgement is a simple method, which can be applied fairly quickly and is not restricted by lack of data, particularly historical data, as are statistical techniques. However, managerial judgement is important even when statistical techniques are used.

A specialised procedure for the collection of managerial opinions is based on the idea of the oracle at Delphi. A group of managers anonymously and independently answer questions about anticipated human resource demand. A compilation of the answers is fed back to each individual, and the process is repeated until all the answers converge.

The way that human resources are utilised will change the number of employees required and the necessary skills needed. There are many ways to change how employees are used. Some methods are interrelated or overlap and would therefore be used in combination. Interconnections between most of these areas and soft human resources planning are also apparent.

ANALYSING THE CURRENT SITUATION AND PROJECTING FORWARD

ORGANIZATION, BEHAVIOUR AND CULTURE

It is in this area that more choice of techniques is available, and the possibilities include the use of questionnaires to staff, interviews with staff and managerial judgement. Focus groups are an increasingly popular technique where, preferably, the Chief Executive meets with, say, 20 representative staff from each department to discuss their views of the strengths and weaknesses of the organization, and what can be done to improve. These approaches can be used to provide information on, for example:

- Motivation of employees.
- Job satisfaction.
- Organizational culture.
- The way that people are managed.
- Attitude to minority groups and equality of opportunity.
- Commitment to the organization and reasons for this.
- Clarity of business objectives.
- Goal-focused and other behaviour.
- Organizational issues and problems.
- What can be done to improve.
- Organizational strengths to build on.

Turnover figures, performance data, recruitment and promotion trends and characteristics of employees may also shed some light on these issues.

Data relating to current formal and informal systems, together with data on the structure of the organization, also need to be collected, and the effectiveness, efficiency and other implications of these need to be carefully considered. Most data will be collected from within the organization, but data may also be collected from significant others, such as customers, who may be part of the environment.

CURRENT AND PROJECTED EMPLOYEE NUMBERS AND SKILLS (EMPLOYEE SUPPLY)

Current employee supply can be analysed in both individual and overall statistical terms. To gain an overview of current supply the following factors may be analysed either singly or in combination: number of employees classified by function, department, occupation job title, skills, qualifications, training, age, length of service, performance appraisal results.

Forecasting employee supply is concerned with predicting how the current supply of employees will change, primarily how many will leave, be internally promoted or transferred. These changes are forecast by analysing what has happened in the past, in terms of staff retention and/ or movement, and projecting this into the future to see what would happen if the same trends continued. The impact of changing circumstances would also need to be taken into account when projecting analyses forward. Bell provides an extremely thorough coverage of possible analyses, on which this section is based. Behavioural aspects are also important, such as investigating the reasons why staff leave, the criteria that affect promotions and transfers and changes in working conditions and in HR policy. Analyses fall broadly into two categories: analyses of staff leaving, and analyses of internal movements. The following calculations are the most popular forms of analysing staff leaving the organization.

Annual labour turnover index

The annual labour turnover index is sometimes called the percentage wastage rate, or the conventional turnover index. This is the simplest formula for wastage and looks at the number of staff leaving during the year as a percentage of the total number employed who could have left.

Leavers in year / Average number of staff in post during year × 100 = percentage wastage rate

This measure has been criticised because it gives only a limited amount of information. If, for example, there were 25 leavers over the year, it would not be possible to determine whether 25 different jobs had been left by 25 different people, or whether 25 different people had tried and left the same job. Length of service is not taken into account with this measure, yet length of service has been shown to have a considerable influence on leaving patterns, such as the high number of leavers at the time of induction.

Stability index

The stability index is based on the number of staff who could have stayed throughout the period. Usually, staff with a full year's service are expressed as a percentage of staff in post one year ago.

Number of staff with one year's service at date/ Number of staff employed exactly one year before × 100 = percent stability

This index, however, ignores joiners throughout the year and takes little account of length of service.

Cohort analysis

A cohort is defined as a homogeneous group of people. Cohort analysis tracks what happens as some people leave a group of people with very similar characteristics who all joined the organization at the same time. Graduates are an appropriate group for this type of analysis. A graph showing what happens to the group can be in the form of a survival curve or a log-normal wastage curve, which can be plotted as a straight line and can be used to make predictions. The disadvantage of this method of analysis is that it cannot be used for groups other than the specific group for which it was originally prepared. The information has also to be collected over a long time-period, which produces problems of availability and reliability of data.

Half-life

The half-life is a figure expressing the time taken for half the cohort to leave the organization. The figure does not give as much information as a survival curve, but it is useful as a summary and as a method of comparing different groups. The census method is an analysis of leavers over a reasonably short period of time – often over a year.

Retention profile

Staff retained, that is those who remain with the organization, are allocated to groups depending on the year they joined. The number in each year group is translated into a percentage of the total number of individuals who joined during that year.

We move now to methods of analysing internal movements. These focus on either overall analyses of movement patterns in the organization or succession planning, which has a more individual emphasis.

Analyses of internal movements

And now we turn to employee movements. Age and length of service distributions can be helpful to indicate an overall pattern of problems that may arise in the future, such as promotion blocks. They need to be used in conjunction with an analysis of previous promotion patterns in the organization. An alternative is a stocks and flows analysis of the whole organization or a part of it, such as a department. The model is constructed to show the hierarchy of positions and the numbers employed in each. Numbers moving between positions, and in and out of the organization over any time-period, can be displayed. The model displays visually promotion and lateral move channels in operation, and shows what happens in reality to enable comparison to be made with the espoused approach, but users need to recognise, and work within, the limitation that the structure of jobs will change more rapidly than in the past.

Succession planning

Succession planning has a very high profile at present. This has developed from the original process of replacement planning which tended to be an informal approach to promotion with a short-term focus on who would be able to replace senior people if they left suddenly, so that disruption and dislocation were minimised. In the 1980s more formal approaches were used which included careful analysis of the jobs to be filled, a longer-term focus, developmental plans for individuals who were identified as successors, and the possibility of cross-

functional moves. This approach was typically applied to those identified as having high potential, and was generally centred on the most senior positions. Larger organizations would produce tables of key jobs on which were named immediate successors, probable longer-term successors and potential longer-term successors, all with attached development plans. Alternatively, high-potential individuals were identified with likely immediate moves, probable longer-term moves and possible longer-term moves. However, as Hirsh points out, this model is appropriate to a stable environment and career structure, and the emphasis in current succession planning has changed yet again.

The focus now is on the need to build and develop a pool of talent, without such a clear view of how the talent will be used in the future. This is a more dynamic approach and fits well with the resource-based view of the firm. While the link to business strategy is emphasised, there is more recognition of individual aspirations and a greater opportunity for people to put themselves forward to be considered for the talent pool. Developing talent at different leadership levels in the organization is considered important. Much greater openness in succession planning is encouraged, and more consideration is given to the required balance between internal talent development and external talent.

RECONCILIATION, DECISIONS AND PLANS

We have already said that, in reality, there is a process of continuous feedback between the different stages of human resource planning activities, as they are all interdependent. On the soft side (organization, behaviour and culture) there is a dynamic relationship between the future vision, environmental trends and the current position. Key factors to take into account during reconciliation and deciding on action plans are the acceptability of the plans to both senior managers and other employees, the priority of each plan, key players who will need to be influenced and the factors that will encourage or be a barrier to successful implementation.

On the hard side, feasibility may centre on the situation where the supply forecast is less than the demand forecast. Here, the possibilities are to:

- Alter the demand forecast by considering changes in the utilisation of employees (such as training and productivity deals, or high-performance teams): by using different employees with higher skills; employing staff with insufficient skills and training them immediately; or outsourcing the work.
- Alter the supply forecast by, say, reducing staff turnover or delaying retirement.
- Change the company objectives, as lack of human resource will prevent them from being achieved in any case. Realistic objectives need to be based on the resource that is, and is forecast to be, available either internally or externally.

When the demand forecast is less than the internal supply forecast in some areas, the possibilities are to:

- Consider and calculate the costs of overemployment over various timespans.
- Consider the methods and cost of losing staff.
- Consider changes in utilisation: work out the feasibility and costs of retraining, redeployment and so on.
- Consider whether it is possible for the company objectives to be changed. Could the company diversify, move into new markets, etc.?

We have also noted the interrelationship between the soft and the hard aspects of planning. For example, the creation of high-performance teams may have implications for different staffing numbers, a different distribution of skills, alternative approaches to reward and a different management style. The relocation of supplier's staff on to premises of the company that they supply, in order to get really close to this customer, could have implications for relocation, recruitment, skills required and culture encouraged. The development of a learning organization may have implications for turnover and absence levels, training and development provision, culture encouraged and approach to reward.

Once all alternatives have been considered and feasible solutions decided, specific action plans can be designed covering all appropriate areas of HRM activity. For example:

1. *Human resource supply plans*. Plans may need to be made concerning the timing and approach to recruitment or downsizing. For example, it may have been decided that in order to recruit sufficient staff, a public relations campaign is needed to promote a particular company image. Promotion, succession, transfer and redeployment and redundancy and retirement plans would also be relevant here. Increasingly there is the need to focus on plans for the development and retention of the talent pool.
2. *Organization and structure plans*. These plans may concern departmental existence, remit and structure and the relationships between departments. They may also be concerned with the layers of hierarchy within departments and the level at which tasks are done, and the organizational groups within which they are done. Changes to organization and structure will usually result in changes in employee utilisation.
3. *Employee utilisation plans*. Any changes in utilisation that affect human resource demand will need to be planned. Some changes will result in a sudden difference in the tasks that employees do and the numbers needed; others will result in a gradual movement over time. Other plans may involve the distribution of hours worked, for example the use of annual hours contracts; or the use of functional flexibility where employees develop and use a wider range of skills. There are implications for communications plans as the employees involved will need to be consulted about the changes and be prepared and trained for what will happen. There will be interconnections with supply plans here: for example, if fewer employees will be needed, what criteria will be used to determine who should be made redundant and who should be redeployed and retrained, and in which areas?
4. *Learning and development plans*. There will be development implications from both the human resource supply and utilisation plans. The timing of development can be a critical aspect. For

example, training for specific new technology skills loses most of its impact if it is done six months before the equipment arrives. If the organization wishes to increase recruitment by promoting the excellent development that it provides for employees, then clear programmes of what will be offered need to be finalised and resourced so that these can then be used to entice candidates into the organization. If the organization is stressing customer service or total quality, then appropriate development will need to be developed to enable employees to achieve this.

5. *Performance management and motivation plans*. These plans may include the development or renewal of a performance management system; ensuring that employees are assessed on objectives or criteria that are key to organizational success, and which may then be linked to reward. They may also include setting performance and quality standards; culture change programmes aimed at encouraging specified behaviour and performance; or empowerment or career support to improve motivation.

6. *Reward plans*. It is often said that what gets rewarded gets done, and it is key that rewards reflect what the organization sees as important. For example, if quantity of output is most important for production workers, bonuses may relate to number of items produced. If quality is most important, then bonuses may reflect reject rate, or customer complaint rate. If managers are only rewarded for meeting their individual objectives there may be problems if the organization is heavily dependent on teamwork.

7. *Employee relations plans*. These plans may involve unions, employee representatives or all employees. They would include any matters which need to be negotiated or areas where there is the opportunity for employee involvement and participation.

8. *Communications plans*. The way that planned changes are communicated to employees is critical. Plans need to include not only methods for informing employees about what managers expect of them, but also methods to enable employees to express their concerns and needs for successful implementation. Communications plans will also be important if, for example, managers wish to generate greater employee commitment by keeping employees better informed about the progress of the organization.

Once the plans have been made and put into action, the planning process still continues. It is important that the plans be monitored to see if they are being achieved and if they are producing the expected results. Plans will also need to be reconsidered on a continuing basis in order to cope with changing circumstances.

MANAGERIAL FACE-TO-FACE SKILLS

Managers of all types spend most of their time talking with people; information is the stock in which they trade. HR specialists have skilfulness in interaction as their core expertise. We have already seen how interactive skill is essential to enable HR people to have an impact on strategy formulation. Throughout this book we shall see how effective handling of face-to-face situations is essential throughout human resource management. As well as being articulate and receptive in any face-to-face situation, HR specialists need to develop their skills in various different types of encounter.

The recruiter has to be effective in the highly specialised interaction of the selection interview, where the task is to find out a great deal of relevant information about an applicant on which to base a judgement as to whether or not that person would match the skills, experience and attitudes required in the job to be filled. The skilled recruiter knows that such information will only come from an applicant who has confidence in the interviewer's integrity and who volunteers the information, responding willingly and helpfully to the questions that are posed.

FOCUS ON SKILLS

The industrial relations manager, in contrast, needs to be an effective negotiator, explaining a position that those on the other side of the table may not appreciate and who have themselves a position which the industrial relations manager may not appreciate. Common ground has to be established, differences clarified and possibilities for reconciling those differences explored.

Both interactions have things in common, but they require different skills. Each Part of this book is rounded up by focusing on an interaction central to the theme of the Part. Understanding that interaction helps with understanding the other activities that have been reviewed.

Our objectives in this introductory Focus on skills are to:

1. Explain what makes for effectiveness in interaction

2. Explain the different types of interaction
3. Review the fundamental skills of (a) setting the tone, (b) listening, (c) questioning and (d) feedback

EFFECTIVENESS IN INTERACTION

In the remainder of this focus on skills we concentrate on methods, but we also must remember the need to understand non-verbal behaviour. We all reveal our feelings by what we do as well as in what we say. Someone blushing is obviously embarrassed and someone crying is clearly distressed, but there are a host of other signs or tells that indicate what a person is feeling. The person who is able to read these signals has a great advantage in interactions. The term 'tell' comes from the study of poker players, who are as anxious to conceal their own hand as they are to guess what is in someone else's.

Effective face-to-face people are likely to have some basic qualities. Poise enables a person to be at ease in a wide variety of social situations, often enjoying them, and able to talk with different types of people in a relaxed and self-confident way. This self-confidence derives partly from the feedback of willing responses constantly provided by other people.

Another element of poise is knowing what you are talking about, so we demonstrate our poise much more in situations with which we are familiar than we do in strange circumstances. There is less fear of what the other may say and less apprehension about appearing naive. Questions, and even criticism, are easier to deal with and are often wanted, so stimulating the interchange.

Poise is often associated with maturity, due to a person having succeeded in developing a rounded view of themselves without feeling too much anxiety about the possible adverse opinions of others. The process of acquiring poise can be accelerated by experience which involves meeting a variety of people from differing backgrounds.

A necessary adjunct to poise is the quality of being responsive to the needs, feelings and level of understanding in other people. This prevents poise from becoming too egocentric. The teacher, for instance, will be looking for signs of misunderstanding in the student so that the message can be restated or clarified, and the market research interviewer will be looking for signals that the question has been accurately construed, or that it needs elabouration. Responsiveness can also include offering rewards, like friendliness, warmth, sympathy and helpfulness as features of general style or as part of a relationship with other participants. These not only sustain and strengthen the relationship, but may also be held back as a means of trying to get one's own way.

There are certain general problems that impair effectiveness. They mostly concern ways in which people tend to hear what they expect to hear rather than what they are being told.

The frame of reference is the standpoint from which a person views an issue, and understanding of the issue will be shaped by that perspective rather than any abstract 'reality'. It is a set of basic assumptions or standards that frame our behaviour. These are developed through childhood conditioning, through social background, education and affiliations. Differences in the frames of reference held by participants in interactions present inescapable problems. Can Israelis and Arabs ever really understand each other? How can those who manage and direct ever appreciate the point of view of those who are managed and directed?

The frame of reference on any particular matter is largely determined by opinions developed within a group with which we identify, as few of us alter our opinions alone. We both follow and participate in the formulation of opinion in our group, and most of us are in a number of such reference groups. Because this is so, complexities arise: some people can be vociferously anti-union as citizens and voters in general elections, yet support a union of which they are members at their workplace.

The stereotype is the standardised expectation we have of those who have certain dominant characteristics: typical stereotypes are that all Scots are mean, all shop stewards are disruptive, women are more caring than men and that men are more aggressive than women. The behaviour of some people in a category makes us expect all in that category to behave in the same way. This is obviously invalid, but is a tendency to which we are prone. We must always listen to what people are actually saying to us rather than hearing what we think a person of that type would say.

At first making use of stereotypes is necessary in working relationships; it is not feasible to deal with every individual we meet as being a void until we have collected enough information to know how to treat them, so we always try to find a pigeon-hole in which to put someone. We begin conversations with a working stereotype, so that, for example, we stop someone in the street to ask directions only after we have selected a person who looks intelligent and sympathetic. If we are giving directions to a stranger we begin our explanation having made an assessment of their ability to understand quickly, or their need for a more detailed, painstaking explanation. The stereotype becomes a handicap only when we remain insensitive to new information enabling us to develop a fuller and more rational appraisal of the individual with whom we are interacting.

Being aware of the dangers of stereotyping others, and trying to exercise self-discipline, can reduce the degree to which you misunderstand other people, but you still have the problem that your respondents will put you into a stereotype and hear what you say in accordance with whatever their predetermined notion may be.

Cognitive dissonance is the difficulty we all have in coping with behaviour that is not consistent with our beliefs. Such behaviour will make us uncomfortable and we will try to cope with the dissonance in various ways in order to reduce the discomfort. Either we persuade ourselves that we believe in what we are doing, or we avoid the necessary behaviour. When we are given new information that is not consistent with what we already believe, we are likely to massage it to fit our existing pattern of behaviour rather than discard the beliefs of a lifetime.

DIFFERENT TYPES OF INTERACTION

Meetings are needed to make decisions, to overcome misunderstanding and to develop ideas. Interviews are used for selection, discipline, appraisal, counselling, problem solving and grievance handling. Managers 'put things across' in selling, persuasion, presentation and negotiation.

It is helpful to group interactions into four broad types: enquiry, exposition, joint problem solving and conflict resolution, as indicated in Figure below.

Four Categories of Interaction

Enquiry	*Exposition*	*Joint Problem solving*	*Conflict Resolution*
Selection	Presentation	Appraisal	Negotiation
Attitude survey	Lecture	Counselling	Arbitration
Health	screening	Briefing	Discipline

Enquiry is that group of situations where the HR specialist needs to find things out from someone else, with the selection interview being the classic example. What needs to be found out may be factual information, attitudes, feelings, levels of understanding or misunderstanding. The main skill is in types of questioning.

Exposition is almost the direct opposite. Instead of finding things out, the HR person is trying to convey information, to develop in the other person a level of knowledge and understanding, acceptance of an argument or agreement with a proposition. Although some questioning is often an integral part of exposition, the main skill is in clear articulation, fluency, good organization of material and effective illustration.

Joint problem solving is a different type of activity as it involves developing an exchange in which both parties work together to unravel a problem or understand a situation which neither fully understands beforehand. It is not one person transferring an 'answer' to another, but both trying to understand together something which they can only partly understand alone. The skills involve some questioning and explanation, but also careful listening and feedback.

Joint problem solving assumes that both parties trust each other and see a common interest in helping the other. Conflict resolution begins without that mutual confidence, as the parties have interests that inevitably conflict and they are not likely fully to trust each other. The skills here are first those of presentation and then listening, questioning and feedback.

FUNDAMENTAL SKILLS IN SETTING THE TONE

Any interaction begins by someone setting the tone of what is to follow. A shop assistant who says, 'Can I help you', or the peculiarly common, 'Are you all right there?' is trying to set a tone of knowledgeable helpfulness to a customer that might eventually result in a sale. It is the inclusion of the apparently superfluous 'there' that is puzzling. Of course you are there; where else would you be? Presumably the reason is to make the question less blunt, avoiding the implication that you are not all right. The HR specialist will set the tone of a selection interview, for instance, by explaining what is to happen and providing other contextual information that will enable the candidate to engage in the process constructively. There will also be a process of conveying more subtle messages to say, 'I'm in charge; I know what I'm doing; you can trust me.' In other interactions the way of setting the tone is different, but some features are common:

– Speak first.

- Smile, looking confident and relaxed (much easier said than done).
- Have brief, harmless exchanges that enable the parties to speak to each other without the answers mattering (weather, travel problems, etc.), but always react appropriately to answers.
- Explain your understanding of what is to happen.
- Check that that is understood and accepted.

FUNDAMENTAL SKILLS IN LISTENING

Tone of voice

Different feelings express themselves in different voice characteristics. Possible meanings for various characteristics are tabulated below:

Characteristic	*Probable Meaning*
Monotone voice	Boredom
Slow speed, low pitch	Depression
High voice, emphasis	Enthusiasm
Ascending tone	Astonishment
Abrupt speech	Defensiveness
Terse speed, loud tone	Anger
High pitch, drawn out speech	Disbelief

Giving attention

Inclining the body towards the other person is a signal of attentiveness, so our posture should be inclined forward and facing the other squarely with an open posture: folded arms can be inhibiting.

Eye contact is crucial to good listening, but is a subtle art:

Effective eye contact expresses interest and a desire to listen. It involves focusing one's eyes softly on the speaker and occasionally shifting the gaze from his face to other parts of the body, to a gesturing hand, for example, and then back to the face and then to eye contact once again. Poor eye contact occurs when a listener repeatedly looks away from the speaker, stares at him constantly or blankly, or looks away as soon as the speaker looks at the listener.

The distinction between 'focusing one's eyes softly' and staring is vital, though difficult to describe, and competence in eye contact is never easy to establish. It is one of the most intimate ways of relating to a person and many managers fear that the relationship may become too close.

We also show physical responses in our attentiveness. First we have to avoid distracting the other person by physical behaviour that is unrelated to what is being said; fiddling with a pen, playing with car keys, scrutinising our fingernails, wringing our hands, brushing specks of dust off our sleeves are a few typical behaviours that indicate inattention. Skilled listeners not only suppress these, they also develop minor gestures and posture variants that are directly responsive to what the other is saying.

Being silent helps you to listen by providing space for incoming messages, but it also provides opportunities to observe the other person and to think about what is being said. Most people are uncomfortable with silence and try to fill it with inconsequential chat, but this interferes with listening. Silence still has to be attentive and the longer the silence, the harder it is to be attentive: think of the last lecture you attended and how hard it was to maintain attentiveness.

FUNDAMENTAL SKILLS IN QUESTIONING

Closed questions seek precise, terse information and are useful when you want clear, straightforward data. Most encounters feature closed questioning at some point.

Open-ended questions avoid terse replies by inviting respondents to develop their opinions without the interviewer prescribing what the answer should be. The question does little more than introduce a topic to talk about. Their main purpose is to obtain the type of deeper information that the closed question misses, as the shape of the answer is not predetermined by the questioner. You are informed not simply by the content of the answers, but by what is selected and emphasised.

Indirect questions take an oblique approach on a difficult matter. A blunt 'Did you like that job?' almost suggests you didn't, or at least raises the suspicion that the interviewer thinks you didn't; it is a bit like the shop assistant avoiding being too blunt. Put indirectly as 'What gave you the most satisfaction in that job?' it has the merit of concentrating on the work rather than the person.

The probe is a form of questioning to obtain information that the respondent is trying to conceal. When the questioner becomes aware that the respondent is doing so he or she has to make an important, and perhaps difficult, decision: whether to respect the candidate's unwillingness and let the matter rest, or to persist with the enquiry. Reluctance is quite common in selection interviews where a candidate may wish to gloss over an aspect of the recent employment history. The most common sequence for the probe takes the following form: (a) direct questions, replacing the more comfortable open-ended approach ('What were you doing in the first six months of 2001?'). Careful phrasing may avoid a defensive reply, but those skilled at avoiding unwelcome enquiries may still deflect the question, leading to (b) supplementaries, which reiterate the first question with different phrasing ('Yes, I understand about that period. It's the first part of 2001 that I'm trying to get clear: after you came back from Belgium and before you started with Amalgamated Widgets'). Eventually this should produce the information the questioner needs. (c) Closing. If the information has been wrenched out like a bad tooth and the interviewer looks horrified or sits in stunned silence, then the candidate will feel put down beyond redemption. The interviewer needs to make the divulged secret less awful than the candidate had feared, so that the interview can proceed with reasonable confidence ('Yes, well you must be glad to have that behind you'). It may be that the interviewer will feel able to develop the probe by developing the answer by a further question such as 'And how did that make you feel?' or 'And how did you react to that? It must have been a terrible blow.' It is only reasonable to do this if the resultant exchange adds something useful to the questioner's understanding of the client: simple nosiness is not appropriate.

Some common lines of questioning should be avoided because they can produce an effect that is different from what is intended.

Leading questions ('Would you agree with me that ... ?') will not necessarily produce an answer that is informative, but an answer in line with the lead that has been given.

Multiple questions give the candidate too many inputs at one time ('Could you tell me something of what you did at university, not just the degree, but the social and sporting side as well, and why you chose to backpack your way round the world? You didn't travel on your own, did you?'). This sort of questioning is sometimes adopted by interviewers who are trying very hard to efface themselves and let the respondent get on with the talking. However helpful the interviewer intends to be, the effect is that the candidate will usually forget the later parts of the question, feel disconcerted and ask, 'What was the last part of the question?' By this time the interviewer has also forgotten, so they are both embarrassed.

Taboo questions are those that infringe the reasonable personal privacy of the candidate. There is a proper place for the probe, but some questions have to be avoided, especially in selection interviews, as they could be interpreted as discriminatory. It is at least potentially discriminatory, for instance, to ask women how many children they have and what their husbands do for a living. Questions about religion or place of birth are also to be avoided. Some questions may do no more than satisfy the idle curiosity of the questioner. If there is no point in asking them, they should not be put.

FUNDAMENTAL SKILLS IN FEEDBACK

As well as listening, it is necessary to provide feedback to demonstrate that you have received and understood what you are being told.

In reflection, the listener picks up and re-states the content of what has just been said. In a difficult situation the listener picks out the emotional overtones of a statement and 'reflects' them back to the respondent without any attempt to evaluate them. The interviewer expresses neither approval nor disapproval, neither sympathy nor condemnation.

At a more prosaic level, there is summary and re-run to show you are listening and providing the opportunity for any misunderstanding to be pointed out. In appraisal, for instance, the respondent will produce lots of information in an interview and you will be selecting that which is to be retained and understood. From time to time you interject a summary sentence or two with an interrogative inflection. This shows that you are listening, gives the respondent the chance to correct any false impressions and reinforces the key points that are being retained. It is also a useful way of making progress, as the interjection is easily followed by another open-ended question – 'Now perhaps we can turn to ...?'

The standard method in both reflection and summary is paraphrasing, by which the listener states the essence of what has been said. This is done concisely, giving the speaker a chance to review what has been said and, perhaps, to correct it.

We all respond positively when a listener shows interest in what is being said. If it is possible also to agree with what is being said, the reinforcement of the respondent will be greater.

The most common form of affirmation in feedback is the head nod, and many public speakers look for head nods (not to be confused with nodding off) as a way of judging the supportive mood of the audience. Other ways of affirming involve the use of the eyes. These are too subtle and individual to describe, but we each have a repertoire of signals to indicate such reactions as encouragement, surprise and understanding. When the eyes are part of a smile, there will be stronger reward to the talker. There are also words and phrases: 'Really?' 'Go on . . .', 'Yes . . .', 'Of course .. .', 'My word . . .', 'You were saying . . .'

Interaction contains a variety of noises that are ways of feeding back to the other party. They are impossible to reproduce in words but are usually variations of a theme of 'Mmm . . .' and they form a part of the exchanges that is inarticulate yet meaningful, keeping things going without interrupting.

Note: For detailed information & understanding more on this chapter reader may visit this site www.saksincorporated.com *of* Saks Incorporated. Saks Incorporated (Saks) and its subsidiaries operate free-standing stores and mall based specialty stores. The company operates in the US. It is headquartered in East 49th street, New York and employs about 16,700 people.

5

Strategic Aspects of Resourcing

The first major activity of the human resource specialist is to find and bring in the people that the business needs for its success. The people may not be employees; they may be consultants or subcontractors. They may be temporary, full time, part time or occasional, and the working relationship between the business and its people is the contract, which sums up the features of that relationship so that both parties know where they stand. Nearly always there is a face-to-face meeting between the parties to agree terms before the relationship begins. The process of 'coming to terms' is one of mutual assessment. Many prospective employees reject a prospective employer by deciding not to apply for a post, or by discontinuing their application. Employers usually choose between many, and often feel there are too few applicants. Once recruited, people have to be retained within the business by a series of strategies that sustain their interest and motivation as well as keeping the focus of their activities within a changing organizational and business context. Contracts end as well as begin, and we have to be sure that the arrangements to end the contract are as sound as those for it to start.

The whole resourcing process is symbolised by the mutual assessment of the selection interview: 'Is this person right for us?' and 'Is this job and situation right for me?' The answers to both those questions have major implications for both parties. The uncertainty about whether or not the right answers are found at the interview is why we have to examine resourcing so closely.

All too often employee resourcing is a reactive activity, without any link to organizational strategy and without internal coherence. To bridge this gap we suggest a range of aspects which together can form the framework for a resourcing strategy to facilitate the future direction of the business. Each of these aspects offers choices for managers.

RESPONDING TO LABOUR MARKET TRENDS

The starting point for all strategic activity in HRM is to understand the environment in which an organization operates. It is only possible to formulate the most appropriate policies and practices once its key features have been identified and their importance grasped. In the field of employee resourcing the environment with which we are concerned is the labour market, the pool of available talent in which employers compete to recruit and subsequently retain staff. Later we look at different types of labour market and their implications for employers. Here we focus on three major trends in the India labour market as a whole and look at how they are affecting decision making in organizations.

DEMOGRAPHIC DEVELOPMENTS

In 2003 the India's population numbered 1 billion, of whom just under half were in work. Both figures are projected to rise marginally during the coming decade. The overall population is increasing, despite falling birth rates, because of lengthening life expectancy. The number of people who are economically active is increasing largely because of women spending a greater proportion of their lives in paid work than has been the case historically. Over the longer term, however, the proportion of the population that is of working age will shrink in comparison with the total population as more and more people live longer after reaching retirement age. This process has already begun in countries such as Japan and Germany with significant implications for the provision of care and pensions for the growing number of elderly people. The coming years will therefore see a substantial change in the age profile of the workforce, as the population as a whole gets older and a greater proportion of young people remain in full-time education for longer. There are two major implications for employers. First, because their numbers will fall, it will be progressively harder to recruit and retain the more talented younger workers. Organizations that have sought to resource their organizations by recruiting and training new graduates or school leavers will either have to work a good deal harder at competing for them or have to bring in older people in their place. Second, there are implications for the capacity of the state to provide a reasonable level of pension for so many retired people. Increasingly, therefore, people are likely to look at the nature of occupational pension being provided by employers when deciding on their career options. Organizations offering good, well-communicated pension benefits will be better placed than others to attract and retain the employees they need.

DIVERSITY

According to the most recent government figures 84 per cent of men and 73 per cent of women are either in work or actively seeking work. Increased female participation in the workforce has been one of the most significant social trends over recent decades. In 1980 the employment rate for women of working age was 59 per cent, since when the figure has risen steadily, while that for men has declined somewhat. This has happened as more women with young children have opted to work while more men have taken early retirement. As a result there has been some decline in the number of workplaces where women are heavily outnumbered by men and an increase in the number where men are outnumbered by women. Although the vast majority of management posts are still held by men, we have also seen a substantial increase in the number of women occupying such positions – another trend that is going to continue in the years ahead. Despite these developments there remain many areas of work which are dominated by either men or women and a continued substantial gender gap in overall pay levels (women's average salary is 82 per cent of that for men). A trend which has been identified in many surveys is the growth in the number of part-time workers. They now account for over a quarter of the total workforce and over 80 per cent of them are women. Representation of ethnic minorities has also increased over recent years. In the early 1980s around 4.5 per cent of employees came from ethnic minorities. Twenty years on the figure is 6.5 per cent. Whereas in 1980 two-thirds of workplaces employed no one from an ethnic minority, over half now do. Increases in representation have occurred across the industrial sectors. Taken together, these various trends mean that the workforce is steadily becoming more diverse in its make-up. While there remains a strong degree of segregation in terms of the types of work performed, the trend is towards heterogeneity at all organizational levels. There are a number of important implications for human resource managers:

- In order to attract and retain the best employees it is necessary to take account of the needs of dual-career families. The law now requires employers to offer a measure of support with recent measures on parental leave, the right to time off for family emergencies, and the right to request flexible working, but there is a great deal more that can be done. Career-break entitlements, crèches and job-share schemes are the most common initiatives.

– There is a heightened need for awareness of the possibility of discrimination against any group which is underrepresented in the workplace. The perception of inequity, however justifiable in practice, is all that is needed for staff turnover rates to increase and for an employer to gain a poor reputation in its labour markets.

– Employers are required to pay more serious attention to the issue of sexual and racial harassment in a workplace characterised by diversity than in one which is less heterogeneous. It is advisable to have written policies covering such matters and to ensure that line managers are fully aware of the developing law on harassment.

SKILLS AND QUALIFICATIONS

The third major development in the labour market is the changing occupational structure, leading to a greater demand for skilled staff. In recent decades the chief job growth areas have been in the managerial and professional occupations, and in service industries such as retailing, security and catering. By contrast there has been an ongoing decline in demand for people to work in the manufacturing and agricultural sectors. While technical skills are not required for all the new jobs, social skills are necessary, as is the ability to work effectively without close supervision.

The past two decades have also seen a strong increase in demand for graduates. Over 400,000 now graduate from universities in the India every year, including 260,000 with first degrees. Unemployment among this group is considerably lower than for the rest of the population whatever the economic conditions, indicating a capacity on the part of employers to absorb the growing numbers into their labour forces. However, despite the increasing numbers of people gaining formal qualifications at all levels, there remain skills shortages. When the economy is performing well these can be significant. There are still too few people with high-level IT and scientific qualifications entering the labour market and far too many people lacking basic numeracy and literacy skills. It is estimated that 20 per cent of adults in the India are innumerate and unable to read beyond the most basic level.

Policy initiatives are in place to improve skills levels at both ends of the scale, but it will take a number of years before the effects are apparent in the labour market. Until then employers have to devise strategies to deal with skills shortages in key areas. One approach is simply to work harder at recruiting and retaining employees. Another is to find ways of reducing reliance on the hard-to-recruit groups by reorganizing work and dividing tasks up differently so that people with particular skills spend 100 per cent of their time undertaking the duties for which only they are qualified. A third response is to look overseas for recruits interested in working in the India. Where skills shortages are particularly acute there is also the possibility of relocating one or more organizational functions abroad. Finally, of course, it is possible to recruit people without the required skills and to provide the necessary training and development opportunities.

ANALYSING LABOUR MARKETS

While the general trends outlined above have significant implications for employers, more important for individual organizations are developments in the particular labour markets which have relevance to them. An understanding of what is going on in these can then form the basis of decision making across the employee resourcing field. There are several different ways in which labour markets vary.

GEOGRAPHICAL DIFFERENCES

For most jobs in most organizations the relevant labour market is local. Pay rates and career opportunities are not so great as to attract people from outside the district in which the job is based. The market consists of people living in the 'travel to work area', meaning those who are able to commute within a reasonable period of time. In determining rates of pay and designing recruitment campaigns there is a need to compare activities with those of competitors in the local labour market and to respond accordingly. Skills shortages may be relieved by increases in the local population or as a result of rival firms contracting. New roads and improved public transport can increase the population in the travel to work area, with implications for recruitment budgets and the extent to which retention initiatives are necessary. For other jobs, usually but not always those which are better paid, the relevant labour market is national or even international. Here different approaches to recruitment are necessary and there is a need to keep a close eye on what a far larger number of rival employers are doing to compete for staff.

TIGHT V. LOOSE

A tight labour market is one in which it is hard to recruit and retain staff. Where the labour market is loose, there are few problems finding people of the required calibre. Labour market conditions of this type clearly vary over time. The higher the rate of unemployment in an area, the looser the labour market will be. However, some labour markets always remain tight whatever the economic conditions simply because there are insufficient numbers of people willing or able to apply for the jobs concerned. In recent years, even at the depths of the recessions of the 1980s and 1990s, it has been difficult to find good IT staff and effective sales people.

A number of researchers have looked at the responses of employers faced with either loose or tight labour markets. Windolf identified four types of approach used in the UK and Germany which varied depending not only on the tightness of the market, but also on the capacity of the organization to respond intelligently to the situation. He found that many organizations with high market power (that is, faced with a relatively loose labour market) made little effort at all in the employee resourcing field. They simply took the opportunity to spend as little as possible on recruitment and selection and waited for people to come to them. When there was a vacancy it tended to be filled by a similar person to the one who had left, thus maintaining the status quo. According to Windolf, the more intelligent organizations took the opportunity afforded by favourable labour market conditions to seek out people with the capacity to innovate and who would develop their roles proactively. All available recruitment channels were used, leading to the development of a richly diverse and creative workforce. A similar dichotomy was identified in the case of tight labour markets. Here many organizations simply 'muddled through', finding people where they could, giving them training and hoping that they would stay long enough to give a decent return on the investment. By contrast, the more intelligent organizations were looking at restructuring their operations, introducing flexible working patterns and devising ways of reducing their reliance on people who were difficult to recruit.

OCCUPATIONAL STRUCTURE

Labour markets also differ according to established behavioural norms among different occupational groups. The attitudes of people to their organizations and to their work vary considerably from profession to profession, with important implications for their employers. A useful model developed by Mahoney (1989) illustrates these differences. He identifies three distinct types of occupational structure: craft, organization career and unstructured. In craft-oriented labour markets, people are more committed over the long term to their profession or occupation than they are to the organization for which they work. In order to develop a career they perceive that it is necessary for them to move from employer to employer, building up a portfolio of experience on which to draw. Remaining in one organization for too long is believed to damage or at least to slow down career prospects. Examples include teaching, where there is often a stronger loyalty to the profession as a whole than towards the employing institution. By contrast, an organization-career occupation is one in which progress is primarily made by climbing a promotion ladder within an organization. People still move from employer to employer, but less frequently, and will tend to stay in one organization for as long as their careers are advancing. Mahoney's third category, the unstructured market, consists of lower-skilled jobs for which little training is necessary. Opportunities for professional advancement are few, leading to a situation where people move in and out of jobs for reasons which are not primarily career related.

To an extent employers can seek to influence the culture prevailing among members of each type of occupational group. There is much to be gained in terms of employee retention, for example, by developing career structures which encourage craft-oriented workers to remain for longer than they otherwise would. However, a single employer can have limited influence of this kind. It is therefore necessary to acknowledge the constraints associated with each labour market and to manage within them. Different areas of HR activity have to be prioritised in each case. It is necessary to work harder at retaining people in craft-oriented labour markets than in those which are organization oriented, because people will be more inclined to stay with one employer in the latter than in the former. Recruitment and selection will be different too. Where career advancement is generally achieved within organizations, as in banking or the civil service, there is a good case for giving a great deal of attention to graduate recruitment. It is worth spending large sums to ensure that a good cohort is employed and subsequently developed because there is likely to be a long period in which to recoup the investment. The case is a good deal weaker in craft-oriented labour markets where there is less likelihood of a long association with individual employees.

GENERATIONAL DIFFERENCES

Employee resourcing practices should also be adapted to take account of variations in the age profile of those whom the organization is seeking to employ. While it is clearly wrong to assert that everyone of a certain age shares the same attitudes and characteristics, broad differences between the generations can be identified. Sparrow and Cooper , in their review of recent research in this area, argue that there are good reasons for believing that the workforce of the future (i.e. made up of young people currently in full-time education) will have decidedly different 'work values' from those of the current workforce. This is because the shared experiences which shape the attitudes and expectations of each generation are different. Evidence suggests that future employees will be less trusting of organizations, more inclined to switch jobs, and more prepared to relocate, and indeed emigrate, than is the case today.

Research on generational differences from a management perspective remains underdeveloped, but a number of writers have put forward interesting ideas. Zemke et al. , for example, identify four groups defined by their dates of birth. They go on to argue that each must be treated rather differently if they are to be successfully managed. The four categories are Veterans (born before and during the Second World War), Baby Boomers (late 1940s and 1950s), Generation X (1960s and 1970s) and a group labelled 'Nexters' (born after 1980). Some of the points made about each are as follows:

- Veterans are attracted to workplaces which offer stability and which value experience.
- Boomers place a high value on effective employee participation.
- Xers enjoy ambiguity and are at ease with insecurity.
- Nexters are wholly intolerant of all unfair discrimination.
- Boomers do not object to working long hours.
- Xers require a proper 'work-life balance'.
- Veterans are loyal to their employers and are less likely to look elsewhere for employment opportunities than younger colleagues.
- Xers are strongly resistant to tight control systems and set procedures.

- Nexters, being serious minded and principled, prefer to work for ethical employers.
- Xers and Nexters work more easily with new technology than veterans and boomers.

Where a workforce is dominated by a particular age group, it makes sense to manage the workers in a way with which they feel comfortable. Organizational performance as well as turnover rates improve as a result. Similarly, where a recruitment drive is aimed at a particular age group, it is important to give out appropriate messages about what the organization is able to offer.

FLEXIBLE RESOURCING CHOICES

Understanding the dynamics of the organizational environment is only one part of taking a strategic approach to employee resourcing. Having gained an understanding one must decide how the organization can best interact with its environment to maximise its performance. One set of key choices concerns the extent to which the organization can aspire to flexibility and in what ways this can be achieved. Three types of flexibility are often identified in the literature: numerical flexibility, temporal flexibility and functional flexibility.

NUMERICAL FLEXIBILITY

Numerical flexibility allows the organization to respond quickly to the environment in terms of the numbers of people employed. This is achieved by using alternatives to traditional full-time, permanent employees. The use, for example, of short-term contract staff, staff with rolling contracts, staff on short-term, government-supported training schemes, outworkers, and so on, enable the organization to reduce or expand the workforce quickly and cheaply.

Atkinson is one of a number of commentators who has described the way in which firms may develop flexibility in their approach to employment, as shown in figure below. The flexible firm in this analysis has a variety of ways of meeting the need for human resources. First are core employees, who form the primary labour market. They are highly regarded by the employer, well paid and involved in those activities that are unique to the firm or give it a distinctive character. These employees have improved career prospects and offer the type of flexibility to the employer that is so prized in the skilled craftworker who does not adhere rigidly to customary protective working practices.

THE FLEXIBLE FIRM

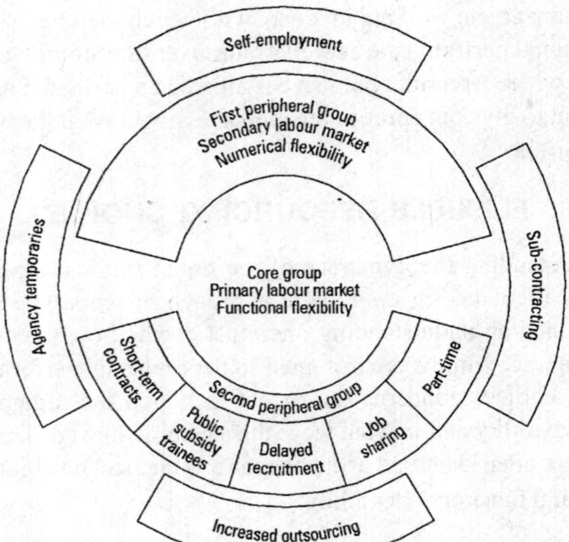

Fig : Atkinson's Model of the Flexible Firm

There are then two peripheral groups: first, those who have skills that are needed but not specific to the particular firm, like typing and word processing. The strategy for these posts is to rely on the external labour market to a much greater extent, to specify a narrow range of tasks without career prospects, so that the employee has a job but not a career. Some employees may be able to transfer to core posts, but generally limited scope is likely to maintain a fairly high turnover, so that adjustments to the vagaries of the product market are eased.

The second peripheral group is made up of those enjoying even less security, as they have contracts of employment that are limited, either to a short-term or to a part-time attachment. There may also be a few job sharers and many participants on government training schemes find themselves in this category. An alternative or additional means towards this flexibility is to contract out the work that has to be done, either by employing temporary personnel from agencies or by subcontracting the entire operation. A slightly different version of the peripheral workforce is the way in which the organization boundary may be adjusted by redefining what is to be done in-house and what is to be contracted out to various suppliers.

TEMPORAL FLEXIBILITY

Temporal flexibility concerns varying the pattern of hours worked in order to respond to business demands and employee needs. Moves away from the 9–5, 38-hour week include the use of annual hours contracts, increased use of part-time work, job sharing and flexible working hours. For example, an organization subject to peaks and troughs of demand (such as an ice cream manufacturer) could use annual hours contracts so that more employee hours are available at peak periods and less are used when business is slow. Flexitime systems can benefit the employer by providing employee cover outside the 9–5 day and over lunchtimes, and can also provide employee benefits by allowing personal demands to be fitted more easily around work demands.

The research evidence suggests increased usage of all forms of temporal flexibility in recent years. Longer opening hours in retailing and the growth of the leisure sector means that many more people now work in the evening (17 per cent) and at night (6 per cent) than used to be the case. The proportion of jobs that are part time also continues to rise, albeit at a slower rate than in the 1970s and 1980s, while the length of the working week for full-time workers has increased by three hours on average during the past decade. There has also been some growth in the use of annual hours, but these arrangements have not become as widespread as was predicted in the early 1990s. The vast majority of employers have not chosen to adopt this approach.

FUNCTIONAL FLEXIBILITY

The term 'functional flexibility' refers to a process in which employees gain the capacity to undertake a variety of tasks rather than specialising in just one area. Advocates of such approaches have been influenced by studies of Japanese employment practices as well as by criticisms of monotonous assembly-line work. Horizontal flexibility involves each individual employee becoming multiskilled so that they can be deployed as and where required at any time. It is often associated with shop-floor manufacturing work, but can be applied equally in other workplace settings.

Vertical flexibility entails gaining the capacity to undertake work previously carried out by colleagues higher up or lower down the organizational hierarchy.

The primary purpose of functional flexibility initiatives is to deploy human resources more efficiently. It should mean that employees are kept busy throughout their working day and that absence is more easily covered than in a workplace with rigidly defined demarcation between jobs. Another source of efficiency gains arises because employees are more stretched, fulfiled and thus productive than is the case in a workplace with narrowly defined jobs. According to Blyton, this is primarily because of a reluctance to invest in the training necessary to support these new forms of working. By contrast, Reilly points to employee resistance and the increased likelihood of errors occurring when functional flexibility programmes are introduced.

DEBATES ABOUT FLEXIBILITY

The growth in flexible working arrangements combined with their promotion by governments since the 1990s has led to the development of robust debates about their desirability and usage in practice. As much controversy has centred on the Atkinson model of the flexible firm as on the rather different elements that go to make it up. There has been a continuing debate, for example, about whether the model of core and periphery is a description of trends or a prescription for the future. Two streams of research have flowed from these interpretations. The first concerns the extent to which the model has been adopted in practice, the second focuses on the advantages and disadvantages of the model as a blueprint for the future organization of work.

Evidence on the first of these questions is patchy. There is no question that rhetoric about flexibility and the language of flexibility is increasingly used. The flexible firm model appears to be something that managers aspire to adopt, but the extent to which they have actually adopted it is questionable. In many organizations the drive for economies of scale means that far from becoming more flexible, organizations are just as likely to introduce bureaucratic systems and standardised practices in response to competitive pressures. And yet we also have seen for a long period now increased use of part-time workers, consultants, subcontractors, agency workers and of moves towards multiskilling. Karen Legge's conclusion that flexibility is used in a pragmatic and opportunistic way rather than as a strategic HRM initiative thus seems to hold true today.

On the question of the desirability of flexibility a number of views have been expressed. The theoretical advantages for organizations arise from productivity gains. In different ways each type of flexibility aims to deploy employee time and effort more efficiently so that staff are only at work when they need to be and are wholly focused on achieving organizational objectives throughout that time. However, the extent to which this is achieved in practice is not clear. Many writers equate the term 'flexibility' with 'insecurity' and argue that the consequences for organizations in terms of staff commitment and willingness to work beyond contract are damaging. Staff turnover is likely to increase in response to the introduction of flexible working practices, while recruitment of talented people will be harder too. In short it is plausibly argued that the flexible firm model, at least as far as the 'peripheral' workforce is concerned, is incompatible with best practice approaches to HRM which seek to increase employees' commitment. Sisson and Storey make the further observation that too much 'hollowing out' can impair organizational learning and lead to the loss of expertise, a loss from which it is difficult to recover. These unintended consequences, it is argued, can worsen rather than improve an organization's competitive position. Others see too much flexibility as having damaging longer- term economic consequences. For example, it can lead to a reduced willingness on the part of employers to invest in training, the absence of which creates skills shortages that hold back economic development. It can also lead to a situation in which managers exploit the vulnerability of peripheral workers by intensifying their work to an unacceptable degree. Finally, it can be argued that in dividing people into 'core' and 'peripheral' groups, flexible firms perpetuate inequality in society more generally and that this leads to poverty, crime, family breakdown and political alienation.

READY MADE OR HOME GROWN

Organizations have a choice whether to depend extensively on the talent available in the external labour market or to invest heavily in training and development and career systems to exploit the potential in the internal labour market. Some organizations thrive despite having high levels of staff turnover, while others thrive on the development of employees who remain with the organization in the long term. The emphasis on either approach, or a balance between the two, can be chosen to support organizational strategy.

Sonnenfield et al. propose a model which relates entry and exit of staff with promotion and development of staff in the organization. One axis of the model is supply flow. They argue that, strategically, organizations that focus on internal supply tend to see people as assets with a long-term development value rather than costs in terms of annual expenditure. The other axis is labelled the assignment flow, which describes the basis on which individuals are assigned new tasks in the organization. The criteria for allocation may be in terms of individual contribution to organizational performance, or on group contribution – which Sonnenfield et al. identify as factors such as loyalty, length of service and support of others. They argue that, strategically, organizations that emphasise individual contribution expect individuals to provide value on a continuous basis, whereas those that emphasise group contribution see employees as having intrinsic value. In this chapter we are concerned with the characteristics of the career systems, which are discussed below.

Academies

In academies there is a heavy emphasis on individual contribution, in terms of reward and promotion. They are characterised by stability and low turnover of staff, with many employees remaining until retirement. There is an emphasis on development and often competitions for promotion and barriers to leaving the organization. Examples of typical industries where academies operate are pharmaceuticals and automobiles.

Clubs

Again there is a heavy emphasis on the internal labour market, but promotion in clubs is more likely to be based on loyalty, length of service, seniority and equality rather than individual contribution. There is an emphasis on staff retention. Sectors where this type of system is likely to operate include public bodies, although the introduction of competitive forces will mean that a different career system may be appropriate.

Baseball Teams

Organizations characterised as baseball teams use external labour sources at all levels to seek the highest contributors. There is an emphasis on recruitment to maintain staffing levels. Employees will tend to identify with their profession rather than the organization, and examples given are advertising, accountancy and legal firms.

Fortresses

Fortress organizations are concerned with survival and cannot afford to be concerned with individuals, in terms of either reward or promotion. They are more likely to depend on external recruitment, often for generalists who meet the needs of a retrenchment or turnaround situation. Examples given are publishing, retailing and the hotel sector.

Note : For a case study visit Goodrich Corporation's site. Goodrich is a supplier of aerospace components, systems and services to the commercial and general aviation airplane markets. The company primarily operates in the US. It is headquartered in Charlotte, North Carolina and employs about 25,000 people. www.goodrich.com

6

Contracts, Contractors and Consultants

Although a great deal is written about 'psychological contracts' and 'contracts for performance', the association between employer and employee remains at base a legal relationship governed by 'a contract of employment'. Whatever expectations employers and employees have of one another when the employment begins, the basic terms and conditions will be agreed and understood at the start and may, if necessary, be enforced in a court. In law the existence of such a contract confers on both parties important obligations as well as giving the employee access to significant legal rights which are not available to people who work under different contractual arrangements.

Employment contracts are very varied, and in recent years all industrialised countries have seen a trend away from what are usually described as being 'traditional' arrangements in which employees are employed on an open-ended basis for 38 hours or so over a 5-day standard 'working week' towards a variety of different alternative types of contract. In some industrial sectors we have seen a move away from employment altogether as people have chosen, or been required, to switch to self-employment. These developments have given employers more options in terms of how they resource their organizations and there is evidence that some are making use of the outermost ring of Atkinson's flexible firm model to a greater extent than they were previously. The more consultants, specialist employment agencies and outsourcing specialists that exist and the more effective the services they provide, the more they are considered to provide a viable alternative to the more traditional forms of employment.

CONTRACTS OF EMPLOYMENT

As far as the law is concerned around 80 per cent of people who work in the India are employees. This means that they have a contract of employment with their employer, with the duties and privileges that that implies. The employer may be an individual, as with most small businesses, or the contract may be with a large corporation. Throughout this book we use terms like 'organization' and 'business' more or less interchangeably and 'employer' is the legal term to describe the dominant partner in the employment relationship. This derives from the old notion of a master and servant relationship and indicates that the employee (or servant) has obligations to the employer or master and vice versa. In contrast, those who are self-employed or subcontractors have greater autonomy, but no one standing between them and legal accountability for their actions.

The law makes an important distinction between the two groups, employees having access to a wider range of legal rights than non-employees. While some areas of employment law apply to all workers, others only apply to employees. Non-employees are deemed to be working under 'a contract for services' rather than 'a contract of service' as is the case for employees. In 2004 the main statutory rights that applied to each were those shown in table below.

In addition to the statutory rights conferred by Acts of Parliament, a range of common law duties are owed by employers to employees and vice versa which do not apply in the case of other forms of relationship. The major obligations are as follows:

Access to Statutory Employment Rights

Employment rights which apply to all workers:	Employment rights which apply only to employees:
Equal pay for equal work	Right to a statement of terms and
Non-discrimination on grounds of sex, race, religious belief, sexual orientation and disability	Right to an itemised pay statement
Right not to have unauthorised deductions from pay	Statutory Sick Pay conditions of employment
Basic health and safety	RightsTime off for public duties
Minimum wage	Twenty-six weeks' maternity leave
Working time regulations	Trade union rights
Data protection rights	Minimum notice periods
Time off to care for dependants	Fixed-term workers regulations
Part-time workers regulations	Statutory Maternity Pay

	(after six months' service)
	Additional maternity leave (after one year's service)
	Unfair dismissal rights (after one year's service)
	Parental leave (after one year's service)

1. Owed by employers to employees:
   - A general duty of care
   - A duty to pay agreed wages
   - A duty to provide work
   - A duty not to treat employees in an arbitrary or vindictive manner
   - A duty to provide support to employees
   - A duty to provide safe systems of work
2. Owed by employees to employers:
   - A duty to cooperate
   - A duty to obey reasonable/lawful instructions
   - A duty to exercise reasonable care and skill
   - A duty to act in good faith
3. Owed by employers to employees and vice versa:
   - To maintain a relationship of mutual trust and confidence
4. Owed by employees and ex-employees:
   - Duty of fidelity

A contract of employment, contrary to common perception, need not exist in written form. It is much more satisfactory for both parties if there is documentary evidence of what terms and conditions have been offered and accepted, but a contract of employment exists whether agreed verbally on the telephone or sealed with no more than a handshake. Where there is any doubt about whether someone is an employee or not, the courts look at the evidence presented to them concerning the reality of the existing relationship between the two parties. If they consider, on balance, that it is governed by a 'contract of service' rather than a 'contract for services', they will consider the worker to be an employee and entitled to the full range of rights outlined above.

An employment contract comes into existence when an unambiguous offer of employment is made and is unconditionally accepted. Once agreed neither side can alter the terms and conditions which govern their relationship without the agreement of the other. An employer cannot therefore unilaterally cut employees' pay, lengthen their hours of work, reduce their holiday entitlement, change their place of work or move them to another kind of work. To do so the employer either has to secure the employees' agreement (by offering some kind of sweetener payment) or has to ensure that the right to make adjustments to terms and conditions is written into the contract by means of flexibility clauses. Where an employer forces changes through without securing the agreement of employees directly, or in many cases through negotiation with union representatives, legal action may follow. An employee may simply bring a claim for breach of contract and ask that the original contract be honoured. In such circumstances compensation may or may not be appropriate. Alternatively, where the employer's breach is serious or where it is one of the implied duties listed above that has not been honoured, employees are entitled to resign and claim constructive dismissal in an Employment Tribunal, in which case their situation is treated as if they had actually been dismissed.

WORKING PATTERNS

Aside from payment arrangements, for full-time workers the pattern of hours which they are expected to work is the most important contractual issue. The total number of hours worked by the average full-time worker in the India fell substantially for much of the past 150 years, but started to rise again in the 1990s. In 1850 the normal working week was established as 60 hours spread over six days of 10 hours each. The average number of hours weekly worked in 2003, including paid and unpaid overtime, was 44 hours for men and 39 hours for women. Interestingly, in the last two or three years there is evidence that people have started working rather fewer hours again, the number working in excess of 45 hours a week falling by nearly 10 per cent.

Checklist for Preparing a Contract of Employment

1. Name of employer; name of employee.
2. Date on which employment began.

3. Job title.
4. Rate of pay, period and method of payment.
5. Normal hours of work and related conditions, such as meal-breaks.
6. Arrangements for holidays and holiday pay, including means whereby both can be calculated precisely
7. Terms and conditions relating to sickness, injury and sick pay.
8. Terms and conditions of pension arrangements.
9. Length of notice due to and from employee.
10. Disciplinary rules and procedure.
11. Arrangements for handling employee grievances.
12. (Where applicable) Conditions of employment relating to trade union membership.

While some people remain attached to the 'normal' working week and would avoid working 'unsocial hours' wherever possible, others like the flexibility it gives them, especially where they are rewarded with shift premia for doing so. Shift- working particularly appeals to people with family responsibilities as it permits at least one parent to be present at home throughout the day. Several types of distinct shift pattern can be identified, each of which brings with it a slightly different set of problems and opportunities.

Part-timer shifts require employees to come to work for a few hours each day. The most common groups are catering and retail workers employed to help cover the busiest periods of the day (such as a restaurant at lunchtime) and office cleaners employed to work early in the morning or after hours in the evening. This form of working is convenient for many and clearly meets a need for employers seeking people to come in for short spells of work.

Permanent night shifts create a special category of employee set apart from everyone else. They work full time, but often have little contact with other staff who leave before they arrive and return after they have left. Apart from those working in 24hour operations, the major categories are security staff and maintenance specialists employed to carry out work when machinery is idle or when roads are quiet. There are particular problems from an HR perspective as they are out of touch with company activities and may be harder to motivate and keep committed as a result. Some people enjoy night work and maintain this rhythm throughout their working lives, but for most such work will be undertaken either reluctantly or for relatively short periods.

Double day shifts involve half the workforce coming in from early in the morning until early afternoon (an early shift), while the other half work from early afternoon until 10.00 or 11.00 at night (a late shift). A handover period occurs between the two shifts when everyone is present, enabling the organization to operate smoothly for 16–18 hours a day. Such approaches are common in organizations such as hospitals and hotels which are busy throughout the day and evening but which require relatively few people to work overnight. Rotation between early and late shifts permits employees to take a 24-hour break every other day.

Three-shift working is a well-established approach in manufacturing industry and in service-sector organizations which operate around the clock. Common patterns are 6–2, 2–10 and 10–6 or 8–4, 4–12 and 12–8. A further distinction can be made between discontinuous three-shift working, where the plant stops operating for the weekend, and continuous three-shift working, where work never stops. Typically the workforce rotates between the three shifts on a weekly basis, but in doing so workers suffer the consequences of a 'dead fortnight' when normal evening social activities are not possible. This is avoided by accelerating the rotation with a 'continental' shift pattern, whereby a team spends no more than three consecutive days on the same shift.

Split shifts involve employees coming into work for two short periods twice in a day. They thus work on a full-time basis, but are employed on part-timer shifts to cover busy periods. They are most commonly used in the catering industry so that chefs and waiting staff are present during meal times and not during the mornings and afternoons when there is little for them to do. Drawbacks include the need to commute back and forth from home to work twice and relatively short rest-periods in between shifts in which staff can wind down. For these reasons split shifts are unpopular and are best used in workplaces which provide live-in accommodation for staff.

Compressed hours shifts are a method of reducing the working week by extending the working day, so that people work the same number of hours but on fewer days. An alternative method is to make the working day more concentrated by reducing the length of the midday meal-break. The now commonplace four-night week on the night shift in engineering was introduced in Coventry as a result of absenteeism on the fifth night being so high that it was uneconomic to operate.

FLEXIBLE WORKING HOURS

Another way of dealing with longer operating hours and unpredictable workloads is to abandon regular, fixed hours of working altogether. This allows an organization to move towards the 'temporal flexibility'. The aim is to ensure that employees are present only when they are needed and are not paid for being there during slack periods. However, there are also advantages for employees.

FLEXITIME

A flexitime system allows employees to start and finish the working day at different times. Most systems identify core hours when everyone has to be present (for example 10–12 and 2–4) but permit flexibility outside those times. Staff can then decide for themselves when they start and finish each day and for how long they are absent at lunchtime. Some systems require a set number of hours to be worked every day, while others allow people to work varying lengths of time on different days provided they complete the quota appropriate for the week or month or whatever other settlement period is agreed. This means that someone can take a half-day or full day off from time to time when they have built up a sufficient bank of hours.

There are great advantages for employees working under flexitime. Aside from the need formally to record time worked or to clock in, the system allows them considerable control over their own hours of work. They can avoid peak travel times, maximise the amount of time they spend with their families and take days off from time to time without using up holiday entitlement. From an employer's perspective flexitime should reduce the amount of time wasted at work. In particular, it tends to eliminate the frozen 20-minute periods at the beginning and end of the day when nothing much happens. If the process of individual start-up and slowdown is spread over a longer period, the organization is operational for longer. Moreover, provided choice is limited to a degree, the system encourages staff to work longer hours at busy times in exchange for free time during slack periods.

ANNUAL HOURS

Annual hours schemes involve an extension of the flexitime principle to cover a whole year. They offer organizations the opportunity to reduce costs and improve performance by providing a better match between working hours and a business's operating profile. Unlike flexitime, however, annual hours systems tend to afford less choice for employees.

Central to each annual hours agreement is that the period of time within which full-time employees must work their contractual hours is defined over a whole year. All normal working hours contracts can be converted to annual hours; for example, an average 38-hour week becomes 1,732 annual hours, assuming five weeks' holiday entitlement. The principal advantage of annual hours in manufacturing sectors, which need to maximise the utilisation of expensive assets, comes from the ability to separate employee working time from the operating hours of the plant and equipment. Thus we have seen the growth of five-crew systems, in particular in the continuous process industries. Such systems are capable of delivering 168 hours of production a week by rotating five crews. In 365 days there are 8,760 hours to be covered, requiring 1,752 annual hours from each shift crew, averaging just over 38 hours for 46 weeks. All holidays can be rostered into 'off' weeks, and 50 or more weeks of production can be planned in any one year without resorting to overtime. Further variations can be incorporated to deal with fluctuating levels of seasonal demand.

The move to annual hours is an important step for a company to take and should not be undertaken without careful consideration and planning. Managers need to be aware of all the consequences. The tangible savings include all those things that are not only measurable but capable of being measured before the scheme is put in. Some savings, such as reduced absenteeism, are quantifiable only after the scheme has been running and therefore cannot be counted as part of the cost justification. A less tangible issue for both parties is the distance that is introduced between employer and employee, who becomes less a part of the business and more like a subcontractor. Another problem can be the carrying forward of assumptions from the previous working regime to the new. One agreement is being superseded by another and, as every industrial relations practitioner knows, anything that happened before, which is not specifically excluded from a new agreement, then becomes a precedent.

ZERO HOURS

A zero-hours contract is one in which individuals are effectively employed on a casual basis and are not guaranteed any hours of work at all. Instead they are called in as and when there is a need. This has long been the practice in some areas of employment, such as nursing agencies and the acting profession, but it has recently been used to some extent in other areas, such as retailing, to deal with emergencies or unforeseen circumstances. Such contracts allow employers to cope with unpredictable patterns of business, but they make life rather more unpredictable for the individuals involved. The lack of security associated with such arrangements makes them an unattractive prospect for many.

ATYPICAL CONTRACTUAL ARRANGEMENTS

Recent decades have seen the growth of contractual arrangements that differ from the permanent, open-ended, full-time, workplace-based form of employment that has always been regarded as representing the norm. There is considerable disagreement about the significance of these trends. For some they mark the 'beginning of the end' for jobs as we have come to experience them over the past 100 years, while for others they represent a modest adjustment of traditional practices in response to evolving labour market developments and to industrial restructuring. Either way they have important implications for the effective management of people.

CONTRACTS OF LIMITED DURATION

Contracts of employment vary in all manner of ways. One of the most important distinctions relates to their length. Here it is possible to identify three basic forms:

- ***Permanent***: This is open-ended and without a date of expiry.
- ***Fixed term***: This has a fixed start and finish date, although it may have provision for notice before the agreed finish date.
- ***Temporary***: Temporary contracts are for people employed explicitly for a limited period, but with the expiry date not precisely specified. A common situation is where a job ends when a defined source of funding comes to an end. Another is where someone is employed to carry out a specified task, so that the expiry date is when the task is complete. The employer is obliged to give temporary workers an indication in writing at the start of their employment of the expected duration of the job.

Around half of all employers in the India, including a good majority of public sector bodies, employ some people on a fixed-term basis or make use of agency temps. In 2003 a total of 1.5 million people worked under some form of non-permanent contract, which is 6.4 per cent of all employees. This is appreciably more than the 5 per cent who were employed on such a basis in the 1980s, but represents a substantial fall over the past few years; in 1998 the figure was close to 1.8 million. As unemployment has fallen and the economy has grown employers have found that they have to offer permanent positions if they are to attract effective employees. Although only around a quarter of temporary staff now claim that they would prefer a permanent job, in the mid-1990s this figure was close to half.

Some of the reasons for employing people on a temporary or fixed-term basis are obvious. Retail stores need more staff immediately before Christmas than in February and ice cream manufacturers need more people in July than November, so both types of business have seasonal fluctuations. Nowadays, however, there is the additional factor of flexibility in the face of uncertainty. Will the new line sell? Will there be sustained business after we have completed this particular contract? In the public sector fixed-term employment has grown with the provision of funds to carry out one-off projects, while the signing of time-limited service provision agreements with external private-sector companies has also become a great deal more common.

Often temporary staff are needed to cover duties normally carried out by a permanent employee. This can be due to sickness absence or maternity leave, or it may occur when there is a gap between one person resigning and another taking up the post. Another common approach is to employ new starters on a probationary basis, confirming their appointments as permanent when the employer is satisfied that they will perform their jobs successfully.

Some argue (e.g. Geary 1992) that managers have a preference for temporary staff because the use of such people gives them a greater degree of control over labour. This control derives from the fact that many temporary staff would dearly love to secure greater job security in order to gain access to mortgages and to allow them to plan their future lives with greater certainty. As a result temporary workers are often keenest to impress and will work beyond their contract in a bid to gain permanent jobs. Their absence levels also tend to be low. Because they work under the constant, unspoken threat of dismissal, they feel the need to behave with total compliance to avoid this. Managers sometimes take advantage of such a situation and push people into working harder than is good for them.

The law on the employment of fixed-term workers has changed in recent years and this may well in part account for the reduction in their numbers. Until October 1999 it was possible to employ staff on fixed-term contracts which contained clauses waiving the right to claim unfair dismissal. This meant that the employer could terminate the relationship by failing to renew the contract whether or not there was a good reason for doing so. It was thus possible substantially to avoid liability for claims of unfair dismissal by employing people on a succession of short contracts. For fixed- term contracts entered into after October 1999 waiver clauses no longer apply. Henceforth employers who do not renew a fixed-term contract have had to be able justify their decision just as they do with any other dismissal, if they want to avoid court action. Temporary and fixed-term workers also gained a number of further rights via the Employment Act 2002 which implemented the EU's Fixed-term Work Directive. This seeks to ensure that temporary employees enjoy the same terms and conditions as permanent employees undertaking equivalent roles, that employers inform them of permanent vacancies and allow them access to training opportunities. The new law also seeks to limit the number of times that an employer can renew a fixed-term contract without making it permanent without good reason. After October 2006 people who have been employed on a temporary basis for four years or more will be entitled to permanent contracts unless the employer can objectively justify less favourable treatment. People entering temporary contracts after October 2002 are also now entitled to redundancy payments if they are laid off.

A special type of contract is that for apprenticeship. Although this is not to be seen as a contract of employment for the purpose of accumulating employment rights, it is a form of legally binding working relationship that pre-dates all current legislative rights in employment, and the apprentice therefore has additional rights at common law relating to training. An employer cannot lawfully terminate an apprentice's contract before the agreed period of training is complete, unless there is closure or a fundamental change of activity in the business to justify redundancy.

PART-TIME CONTRACTS

At one time part-time working was relatively unusual and was scarcely economic for the employer as the national insurance costs of the part-time employee were disproportionate to those of the full-timer. The part-time contract was regarded as an indulgence for the employee and only a second-best alternative to the employment of someone full time. This view was endorsed by lower rates of pay, little or no security of employment and exclusion from such benefits as sick pay, holiday pay and pension entitlement. The situation has now wholly changed.

Since the 1960s the proportion of the employed workforce on part-time contracts has increased dramatically. Over a quarter of us (seven million) now work on a part- time basis, compared to just 9 per cent in 1961.

Women account for four-fifths of all part-time workers in the India, 44 per cent of all female workers being employed on a part-time basis and only 10 per cent of men. Male part-timers are overwhelmingly in the 16–19 and over 65 age groups, suggesting that full-time work is the preference for most men between leaving school and retiring. In the case of women the age pattern is markedly different. Around a quarter of women work on a part-time basis in their twenties, but this figure rises to 40 per cent for women aged 30–34 and to 50 per cent for those aged 35–39. After that the proportion declines somewhat until close to retirement. Among women, therefore, part-time work appears very frequently to be undertaken during the time that their children are at school and that it is the preference for many. Among women with dependent children who work part time, government statistics report that 94 per cent do not want a full-time job.

Many part-timers work short shifts and sometimes two will share a full working day. Others will be in positions for which only a few hours within the normal day are required or a few hours at particular times of the week. Retailing is an occupation that has considerable scope for the part-timer, as there is obviously a greater need for counter personnel on Saturday mornings than on Monday mornings. Also many shops are now open for longer periods than would be normal hours for a full- time employee, so that the part-timer helps to fill the gaps and provide the extra staffing at peak periods. Catering is another example, as is market research interviewing, office cleaning, clerical work and some posts in education.

All benefits must also be provided to part-timers on a pro-rata basis. Moreover, the regulations state that employers cannot subject workers to a detriment of any kind simply because they work part time. This means, for example, that both part-time and full-time workers must be given equal access to training. It also means that the fact that an employee works part time should not be taken into account when deciding who is to be made redundant. Unlike other forms of direct discrimination, however, in the case of part-timers employers can seek to justify their actions on objective grounds.

DISTANCE WORKING

In the quest for greater flexibility many employers are beginning to explore new ways of getting work done which do not involve individuals working full time on their premises. Working overseas, selling in the field and home-working are the most obvious types of distance working, but advances in information technology have led to increased interest in the concepts of teleworking and tele-cottaging. The term tele is the Greek for distant, which is familiar to us in words such as telegram and television.

The main advantage, for both the employer and the employee, is the flexibility that teleworking can provide, but the employer also benefits from reduced office accommodation costs and potential increases in productivity. Employees avoid the increasingly time-consuming activity of commuting to work and can manage their own workload around their home responsibilities and leisure interests. But there is a downside too. Many find working from home all the time to be a rather isolating experience and miss the social life and sense of belonging to a community of colleagues that comes with traditional employment.

The main problem for employers, aside from fostering staff morale, commitment and a sense of corporate identity, is the need to maintain a reasonable degree of management control when the workforce is so geographically diffused. Drawing up an appropriate job specification is thus particularly important in the case of teleworking jobs. It is important to set out clearly defined parameters of action, criteria for decisions and issues which need reference back. Person specifications are also crucial since in much distance working there is less scope for employees to be trained or socialised on the job. In addition, 'small business' skills are likely to be needed by teleworkers, networkers, consultants and subcontractors.

Attention also needs to be given to the initial stages of settling in distance workers. Those off-site need to know the pattern of regular links and contacts to be followed. Those newly recruited to the company need the same induction information as regular employees. In fact, those working independently with less supervision may need additional material, particularly on health and safety. Heightened team- building skills will also be needed to encompass staff who are working on a variety of different contracts and at different locations.

The final key aspect of employing distance workers is the need for a close link between pay and performance. Managers must be able to specify job targets and requirements accurately and to clarify and agree these with the employees concerned. Where a fee rather than a salary is paid, the onus is on the manager to ensure the work has been completed satisfactorily.

SELF-EMPLOYMENT

In the India just over three million people are self-employed, which is around 11 per cent of the total workforce. The proportion is somewhat higher in London and the south-east than elsewhere in the country because that is where the industries which employ most self-employed people are most common. Weir shows that demand for the services of self-employed people is lowest in manufacturing and in the public services. By contrast there are many more opportunities for self- employment in the construction, retailing, property, business services and personal services industries. Three-quarters of self-employed people work for themselves or in partnership with one other person and they are heavily concentrated in skilled trades and professional services occupations. They also tend to be a good deal older than average workers, as many as 31 per cent of older workers employing themselves.

The 1980s saw a substantial growth in the number of self-employed people, but the growth slowed down in the 1990s and has now apparently come to an end. Why this should be is not clear, but it may simply reflect a preference among most people for employment if they are able to secure a job which they enjoy. The growth in self- employment in previous decades, like the growth in temporary working, may therefore simply be a reaction to conditions of relatively high unemployment and low job security. What is clear is that most employed people earn considerably more than most self-employed people. While around 17 per cent of self-employed people earn well in excess of the national average, the big majority earn substantially less. Some running fledgling businesses struggle to earn anything at all. Some of these earnings figures may be subject to some under-reporting for tax avoidance reasons, but they firmly dispel the myth that self-employment is a route to affluence and an easy life. Many more self-employed people work longer hours for less reward than those employed by organizations.

Increasing the proportion of the workforce that is hired on a self-employed basis has both attractions and drawbacks for employers. While self-employed people typically cost more per hour to employ, they only need to be paid for the time they actually spend completing a job or can simply be paid a set fee for the completion of a project irrespective of how long it takes. The fact that they can be asked to tender for work in competition with others tends to further reduce costs, as does the fact that a self-employed person manages their own taxation and pension arrangements. So overall there are often major savings to be made in replacing certain jobs in an organization with self-employed people. Moreover, as was shown at the start of this chapter, huge swathes of employment rights such as unfair dismissal and paid maternity leave apply only to employees and not to those employed on a subcontracted basis. The negative implications derive from the inevitable fact that a self-employed person is not obliged to work exclusively for one employer or even to work uniquely in the interests of any one organization. The relationship is thus more distant and conditional on external influences for its continuance. This can mean that only the minimum acceptable levels of quality are achieved in practice and that the contribution made by the worker to longer-term business development is severely limited. An employer can buy a self-employed person's expertise, but cannot draw on the full range of their energies and commitment as is possible in the case of well- managed employees to whom a longer-term commitment has been made and with whom a closer personal relationship has been forged.

CONSULTANTS

Some management consultants are self-employed people who have gained considerable experience over some years and are in a position to sell their expertise to organizations for a fee. Many more are employed by larger firms which also provide a range of other business services. These tend to be younger people who have substantial, specialist, technical knowledge of particular areas of business activity. Consultants offer advice about issues faced by organizations, but they are also in a position to carry out research, to design new policies and procedures, and to brief or train staff in their effective use. Nowadays a lot of their work involves selling already developed IT products to clients and assisting them to put these into operation. In the HR field this is true of consultancies that specialise in job evaluation and in the provision of personnel information systems.

In many ways consultants thus provide a service analogous to that of an accountant, a lawyer or a financial adviser. However the service is packaged, organizations are being invited to buy their professional expertise and to apply it (or not) as they see fit. The following quotation from the leading industrialist Lord Weinstock is born of disappointing experiences:

Consultants are invariably a waste of money. There has been the occasional instance where a useful idea has come up, but the input we have received has usually been banal and unoriginal, wrapped up in impressive sounding but irrelevant rhetoric. The use of consultants is thus a matter about which managers are very divided. In some companies, and increasingly in public-sector organizations, they are employed regularly and found to offer a useful if expensive service. Elsewhere it appears almost to be a matter of policy to resist their blandishments and to tap into alternative sources of advice. The best approach, as with all major purchasing decisions, is to employ them only in situations where there is a good business case for doing so and where they are likely to add value. The most likely scenario is where the organization needs specialist advice and cannot gain access to it through its internal resources. In the HR field an example would be the need to develop a competitive employment package for an individual who is being sent on long-term expatriate assignment to a country with which people within the organization are largely unfamiliar. It makes sense in such a situation to take advice from someone who has technical knowledge of the tax systems, pay rates and living standards in that country. Another common situation in which consultants are employed in the HR field is to administer psychometric selection tests to candidates applying for jobs and then to interpret and provide feedback on the results. However, there can also be other reasons for their employment, as Duncan Wood (1985) found in his interviews with well-established HR consultants:

- To provide specialist expertise and wider knowledge not available within the client organization.
- To provide an independent view.
- To act as a catalyst.
- To provide extra resources to meet temporary requirements.
- To help develop a consensus when there are divided views about proposed changes.
- To demonstrate to employees the impartiality/objectivity of personnel changes or decisions.
- To justify potentially unpleasant decisions.

The likelihood of securing a positive outcome when employing consultants depends on two conditions being present. First, it is essential that the consultant is given very clear instructions both about the nature of the issue or problem that they are being asked to advise about, and about what the client expects of them. Second, they should only be employed once it has first been established that they are likely to be able to provide knowledge and ideas that cannot be sourced in-house, and that the costs associated with their employment are justified.

Typical views about using outside consultants

Favourable views

1. The HR manager knows what to do, but proposals are more likely to be implemented if endorsed by outside experts.

2. The outsider can often clarify the HR manager's understanding of an issue.

3. Specialist expertise is sometimes needed.

4. The HR manager has insufficient time to deal with a particular matter on which a consultant could work full time.

5. The consultant is independent.

6. Using consultants can be cheaper than employing your own full-time, permanent specialists.

Less favourable views

1. The HR function should contain all the necessary expertise.
2. In-house HR specialists know what is best for the company.
3. Other members of the organization are prejudiced against the use of outside advisers.
4. Using consultants can jeopardise the position of the HR specialists and reduce their influence.

OUTSOURCING

Consultants are mainly employed to give advice or to carry out a defined project. In employing them an organization is effectively subcontracting part of its management process. But organizations can and do subcontract out to specialist service providers a great deal more. The outsourcing of functions which either could be or were previously carried out in-house has become more common in recent years. It is a trend that creates its own momentum because the more outsourcing that occurs, the bigger and better the providers become, making it an increasingly viable proposition for more organizations. Of particular interest to readers of this book is the strong trend that can now be discerned towards the outsourcing (either in whole or in part) of activities that have traditionally been carried out by the HR function in organizations.

According to Colling the organizational functions which are most commonly outsourced by Indian organizations are ancillary services such as cleaning, catering, security, transportation and buildings maintenance. There is nothing new about organizations subcontracting such functions to external providers, but there is clearly an increased trend in that direction. Twenty years ago most larger corporations and the entire public sector managed these ancillary services themselves, employing their own people to carry them out. This is less and less true. Increasingly managers are keen to focus all their energies on their 'core business activities', by which they mean those activities which are the source of competitive advantage and which determine the success or failure of their organizations. There is thus a desire to minimise the amount of management time and effort which is spent carrying out more marginal activities. The decision to outsource is made easier by the fact that specialist security, cleaning and catering companies are often in a position to provide a higher-quality standard of service at a lower cost than can be achieved by in-house operations. This is because for them the provision of ancillary services is the core business and they have the expertise, up-to-date equipment, and staff to run highly efficient operations. Moreover, their size means that they can benefit from economies of scale that are not available to the far smaller locally run operations.

The nature and standard of services that the external company provides are determined by the service level agreement that is signed. This will usually follow on from a competitive tendering exercise in which providers of outsourced services compete with one another to secure a three- or five-year contract. If the standards of service fall short of those set out in the agreement, the purchasing organization is then able to look elsewhere, and can in any case sign a new agreement with a different provider at the end of the contract. This should ensure that high standards are maintained, but the evidence suggests that outsourcing frequently disappoints in practice. Reilly (2001, p. 135) lists all manner of problems that occur due to poor communication, differences of opinion about the service levels being achieved and different interpretations of terms in the

contract. These occur because it will always be in the interests of the providing company to keep its costs low and in the interests of the purchasing company to demand higher standards of service and value for money.

In practice the theoretical advantages of outsourcing thus often fail to materialise. Serious cost savings are often difficult to achieve, largely because the Transfer of Undertakings laws require existing staff to be retained by the new service provider on their existing terms and conditions, yet standards of service may actually decline. Loss of day-to-day control means that problems take longer to rectify because complaints have to be funnelled through to managers of the providing company and cannot simply be addressed on the spot. It is also hard in practice to replace one contractor with another, as well as being costly, because there are a limited number of companies that are both viable over the long term and interested in putting in a bid. So great care has to be taken when adopting this course of action. Expectations need to be managed and deals should only be signed with providers who can demonstrate a record of satisfactory service achieved in comparable organizations.

These potential obstacles have not stopped a number of large corporations from outsourcing large portions of their HR functions in recent years. The service level agreements that are signed typically involve a specialist provider taking over responsibility for the more routine administrative tasks that are traditionally carried out by in-house HR teams. These include payroll administration, the maintenance of personnel databases, the provision of intranet services which set out HR policies, recruitment administration and routine training activities. Such arrangements enable the organization to dispense with the services of junior HR staff and to retain small teams of more senior people to deal with policy issues, sensitive or confidential matters and union negotiations.

Note: For further knowledge regarding this chapter, reader can visit Ryland Group Inc website. The Ryland Group (Ryland) is engaged in home building and mortgage financing activities. The company primarily operates in the US. It is headquartered in Calabasas, California and employs 1,303 people. Its website is www.ryland.com

7

Recruitment

There is always a need for replacement employees and those with unfamiliar skills that business growth makes necessary. Recruitment is also an area in which there are important social and legal implications, but perhaps most important is the significant part played in the lives of individual men and women by their personal experience of recruitment and the failure to be recruited. Virtually everyone reading these pages will know how significant those experiences have been in their own lives.

Over three million people are recruited by employers in the India each year. It can be a costly and difficult process when skills are in short supply and labour markets are tight. In such circumstances the employer needs to 'sell' its jobs to potential employees so as to ensure that it can generate an adequate pool of applicants. According to Barber it is important that employers do not consider the recruitment process to be finished at this point. It continues during the shortlisting and interviewing stages and is only complete when an offer is made and accepted. Until that time there is an ongoing need to ensure that a favourable impression of the organization as an employer is maintained in the minds of those whose services it wishes to secure.

DETERMINING THE VACANCY

Is there a vacancy? Is it to be filled by a newly recruited employee? These are the first questions to be answered in recruitment. Potential vacancies occur either through someone leaving or as a result of expansion. When a person leaves, there is no more than a prima facie case for filling the vacancy thus caused. There may be other ways of filling the gap. Vacancies caused by expansion may be real or imagined. The desperately pressing need of an executive for an assistant may be a plea more for recognition than for assistance. The creation of a new post to deal with a specialist activity may be more appropriately handled by contracting that activity out to a supplier. Recruiting a new employee may be the most obvious tactic when a vacancy occurs, but it is not necessarily the most appropriate. Listed below are some of the options:

- Reorganize the work
- Use overtime
- Mechanise the work
- Stagger the hours
- Make the job part time
- Subcontract the work
- Use an agency

The conventional HR approach to these questions is to produce job descriptions and personnel specifications. Methods of doing this are well established. Good accounts are provided by Pearn and Kandola, Brannick and Levine. The approach involves breaking the job down into its component parts, working out what its chief objectives will be and then recording this on paper. A person specification listing the key attributes required to undertake the role can then be derived from the job description and used in recruiting the new person.

An alternative approach which allows for more flexibility is to dispense with the job description and to draw up a person specification using other criteria. One way of achieving this is to focus on the characteristics or competences of current job holders who are judged to be excellent performers. Instead of asking 'What attributes are necessary to undertake this role?' this second method involves asking 'What attributes are shared by the people who have performed best in the role?' According to some the disadvantage of the latter approach is that it tends to produce employees who are very similar to one another and who address problems with the same basic mindset (corporate clones). Where innovation and creativity are wanted it helps to recruit people with more diverse characteristics.

INTERNAL RECRUITMENT

Vacancies, of course, are often filled internally. Sometimes organizations advertise all vacancies publicly as a matter of course and consider internal candidates along with anyone from outside the organization who applies. This approach is generally considered to constitute good practice and is widely used in the India's public sector. However, many organizations prefer to invite applications from internal candidates before they look to their external labour markets for new staff. There are considerable advantages from the employer's perspective. First it is a great deal less expensive to recruit internally, there being no need to spend money on job advertisements or recruitment agencies. Instead a message can simply be placed in a company newsletter or posted on its intranet or staff noticeboards. Further cost savings and efficiency gains can be made because internal recruits are typically able to take up new posts much more quickly than people being brought in from outside. Even if they have to work some notice in their current positions, they are often able to take on some of their new responsibilities or undergo relevant training at the same time. The other advantage stems from the fact that internal candidates, as a rule, are more knowledgeable than new starters coming in from other organizations about what exactly the job involves. They are also more familiar with the organization's culture, rules and geography, and so take less time to settle into their new jobs and to begin working at full capacity.

Giving preference to internal recruits, particularly as far as promotions are concerned, has the great advantage of providing existing employees with an incentive to work hard, demonstrate their commitment and stay with the organization when they might otherwise consider looking for alternative employment. The practice provides a powerful signal from management to show that existing employees are valued and that attractive career development opportunities are available to them. Failing to recruit internally may thus serve to put off good candidates with potential from applying for the more junior positions in an organization.

The main disadvantage of only advertising posts internally stems from the limited field of candidates that it permits an organization to consider. While it may mean that someone who 'fits in well' is recruited, it may also very well mean that the best available candidate is not even considered. Over the long term the organization can thus end up being less well served than it would have been had internal candidates been required to compete with outside people for their posts. For this reason internal recruitment sits uneasily with a commitment to equal opportunities and to the creation of a diverse workforce. Talented candidates from under-represented groups are not appointed because they never get to know about the vacancies that the organization has.

It is also important to note that the management of internal recruitment practices is difficult to carry out effectively in practice. Research carried out in this field shows that serious problems often occur when internal candidates fail to be selected. This is because they tend to enter the selection process with higher expectations of being offered the position than is the case with external candidates. Bitterness, antipathy and low morale are thus likely to follow. Moreover, failed internal candidates are considerably more likely to pursue claims of unfair discrimination following a selection process than external candidates. For these reasons it is essential that great care is taken when managing internal recruitment to ensure that the approach taken is both fair and seen to be fair. Giving honest, full, accurate and constructive feedback to failed candidates is an essential part of the process.

METHODS OF RECRUITMENT

Once an employer has decided that external recruitment is necessary, a cost-effective and appropriate method of recruitment must be selected. There are a number of distinct approaches to choose from, each of which is more or less appropriate in different circumstances. As a result most employers use a wide variety of different recruitment methods at different times. In many situations there is also a good case for using different methods in combination when looking to fill the same vacancy.

It is interesting to compare the figures in table below with those reported in surveys of how people actually find their jobs in practice. These repeatedly show that informal methods (such as word of mouth and making unsolicited applications) are as common as, if not more common than, formal methods such as recruitment advertising. In 2002, the Labour Force Survey asked over a million people how they had obtained their current job.

Usage of various methods of recruitment by 557 organizations in 2003

Advertisements in local press	84%	Recruiting temporary employees	43%
Specialist journals and trade press	73%	Executive recruitment consultants	41%
Corporate website	72%	Promotional events/careers fairs	37%
Recruitment agencies	71%	Apprentices/work placements	34%
National newspaper advertisements	64%	Speculative applications	34%
Internal intranet	61%	Secondments	32%
Word of mouth	58%	Commercial job-board internet sites	15%
Job Centres/Employment Service	46%	Radio/TV	14%
Education liaison	45%	Posters/billboards	13%

Methods of Obtaining a Job		
	Men	***Women***
Hearing from someone who worked there	30%	25%
Reply to an advertisement	25%	31%
Direct application	14%	17%
Private employment agency	10%	10%
Job centre	9%	8%
Other	12%	9%

THE RECRUITMENT METHODS COMPARED

All the various methods of recruitment have benefits and drawbacks, and the choice of a method has to be made in relation to the particular vacancy and the type of labour market in which the job falls. A general review of advantages and drawbacks is given in table below.

Advantages and Drawbacks of Different Methods of Recruitment

Job centres

Advantages:

(a) Applicants can be selected from nationwide sources with convenient, local availability of computer-based data.

(b) Socially responsible and secure.

(c) Can produce applicants very quickly.

(d) Free service for employers.

Drawbacks:

(a) Registers are mainly of the unemployed rather than of the employed seeking a change.

(b) Produces people for interview who are not genuinely interested in undertaking the job.

Commercial employment agencies and recruitment consultancies

Advantages:

(a) Established as the normal method for filling certain vacancies, e.g. secretaries in London.

(b) Little administrative chore for the employer.

Drawbacks:

(a) Can produce staff who are likely to stay only a short time.

(b) Widely distrusted by employers.

(c) Can be very expensive.

Management selection consultants

Advantages:

(a) Opportunity to elicit applicants anonymously.

(b) Opportunity to use expertise of consultant in an area where employer will not be regularly in the market.

Drawbacks:

(a) Internal applicants may feel, or be, excluded.

(b) Cost.

Executive search consultants ('headhunters')

Advantages:

(a) Known individuals can be approached directly.

(b) Useful if employer has no previous experience in specialist field.

(c) Recruiting from, or for, an overseas location.

Drawbacks:

(a) Cost.

(b) Potential candidates outside the headhunter's network are excluded.

(c) Recruits remain on the consultant's list and can be hunted again.

Visiting universities

Advantages:

(a) The main source of new graduates from universities.

(b) Rated by students as the most popular method.

Drawbacks:

(a) Need to differentiate presentations from those of other employers.

(b) Time taken to visit a number of universities (i.e. labour intensive).

Schools and the Careers Service

Advantages:

(a) Can produce a regular annual flow of interested enquirers.

(b) Very appropriate for the recruitment of school-leavers, who seldom look further than the immediate locality for their first employment.

Drawbacks:

(a) Schools and the advisers are more interested in occupations than organizations.

(b) Taps into a limited potential applicant pool.

RECRUITMENT ADVERTISING

In order to assist them in drafting advertisements and placing them in suitable media, many employers deal with a recruitment advertising agency. Such agencies provide expert advice on where to place advertisements and how they should be worded and will design them attractively to achieve maximum impact. Large organizations often subcontract all their advertising work to an agency with whom a mutually acceptable service-level agreement has been signed.

Recruitment advertising companies (as opposed to headhunters and recruitment consultants) are often inexpensive because the agency derives much of its income from the commission paid by the journals on the value of the advertising space sold, the bigger agencies being able to negotiate substantial discounts because of the amount of business they place with the newspapers and trade journals. A portion of this saving is then passed on to the employer so that it can easily be cheaper and a great deal more effective to work with an agent providing this kind of service. The HR manager placing, say, Rs.50,000 of business annually with an agency will appreciate that the agency's income from that will be between Rs.5,000 and Rs.7,500, and will expect a good standard of service. The important questions relate to the experience of the agency in dealing with recruitment, as compared with other types of advertising, the quality of the advice they can offer about media choice and the quality of response that their advertisements produce.

In choosing where to place a recruitment advertisement the aim is to attract as many people as possible with the required skills and qualifications. You also want to reach people who are either actively looking for a new job or thinking about doing so. The need is therefore to place the advertisement where job seekers who are qualified to take on the role are most likely to look. Except in very tight labour markets, where large numbers of staff are required at the same time, there is no point in placing a recruitment advertisement outside a newspaper or journal's recruitment pages. In some situations newspaper readership figures are helpful when deciding where to advertise. An example would be where there are two or more established trade journals or local newspapers competing with one another, both of which carry extensive numbers of recruitment advertisements. Otherwise readership figures are unimportant because people tend to buy different newspapers when job searching than they do the rest of the time. It is often more helpful to look at the share of different recruitment advertising markets achieved by the various publications, as this gives an indication of where particular types of job are mostly advertised. In the India in recent years the Guardian newspaper has gained and sustained a 40 per cent market share of national recruitment advertising. For many jobs in the media, education and the public sector it is now established as the first port of call for job seekers. This has been achieved by cutting rates to less than half those charged by other national newspapers. For the more senior private sector jobs, however, the established market leaders are the Times of India, the Indian Express and the Hindustan Times. While recruitment advertising agents are well placed to advise on these issues, it is straightforward to get hold of information about rates charged by different publications and their respective market shares.

DRAFTING THE ADVERTISEMENT

The decision on what to include in a recruitment advertisement is important because of the high cost of space and the need to attract attention; both factors will encourage the use of the fewest number of words. Where agencies are used they will be able to advise on this, as they will on the way the advertisement should be worded, but the following is a short checklist of items that must be included.

- Name and brief details of employing organization
- Job role and duties
- Training to be provided
- Key points of the personnel specification or competency profile
- Salary
- Instructions about how to apply

Many employers are coy about declaring the salary that will accompany the advertised post. Sometimes this is reasonable as the salary scales are well known and inflexible, as in much public sector employment. Elsewhere the coyness is due either to the fact that the employer has a general secrecy policy about salaries and does not want to publicise the salary of a position to be filled for fear of dissatisfying holders of other posts, or does not know what to offer and is waiting to see 'what the mail brings'. All research evidence, however, suggests that a good indication of the salary is essential if the employer is to attract a useful number of appropriate replies.

E-RECRUITMENT

The use of the internet for recruitment purposes is undoubtedly the most striking recent development in the field, but its practical significance remains a question of debate. When the internet first became widely used a decade ago it was often predicted that it would revolutionise the recruitment industry. In the future, it was argued, most of us would find out about jobs through web searches. It now appears that these predictions greatly overstated the influence that the internet would have.

While advertising on the Internet is fairly common – many organizations now place vacancies on their own websites and make use of third party job boards – among the employers featured in this study this is clearly seen as complementary to, rather than replacing traditional advertising media. Placing advertisements in local and national newspapers and in the trade press continues to be the most important way for many companies to reach potential applicants.

Internet recruitment takes two basic forms. The first is centred on the employer's own website, jobs being advertised alongside information about the products and services offered by the organization. The second approach makes use of the growing number of cyber-agencies which combine the roles traditionally played by both newspapers and employment agents. They advertise the job and undertake shortlisting before sending on a selection of suitable CVs to the employer.

For employers the principal attraction is the way that the internet allows jobs to be advertised inexpensively to a potential audience of millions. According to Frankland the cost of setting up a good website is roughly equivalent to that associated with advertising a single high-profile job in a national newspaper. Huge savings can also be made by dispensing with the need to print glossy recruitment brochures and other documents to send to potential candidates. The other big advantage is speed. People can respond within seconds of reading about an opportunity by emailing their CV to the employer. Shortlisting can also be undertaken quickly with the use of CV-matching software or online application forms.

In principle e-recruitment thus has a great deal to offer. In practice, however, there are major problems which may take many years to iron out. A key drawback is the way that employers advertising jobs tend to get bombarded with hundreds of applications. This occurs because of the large number of people who read the advertisement and because it takes so little effort to email a copy of a pre-prepared CV to the employer concerned. In order to prevent 'spamming' of this kind it is necessary to make use of online shortlisting software which is able to screen out unsuitable applications. Such technologies, however, are not wholly satisfactory. Those which work by looking for key words in CVs inevitably have a 'hit and miss' character and can be criticised for being inherently unfair. The possibility that good candidates may not be considered simply because they have not chosen a particular word or phrase is strong. The alternative is to require candidates to apply online by completing an application form or pschyometric test. This approach has the advantage of deterring candidates who are not prepared to invest the time and effort required to complete the forms, but is unreliable in important respects – there is no guarantee that the test is in fact being completed by the candidate, nor is it completed within a standard, pre-determined time limit. Other problems concern fears about security and confidentiality which serve to deter people from submitting personal details over the web:

Everybody should be familiar with the fear of using a credit card on-line even though good e-commerce sites have secure servers that enable these transactions to take place safely. The job-seeker's equivalent of this is 'how safe is it to put my CV on-line?' Although the figures prove that plenty of people have overcome this fear (there are an estimated 4.5 million CVs on-line), horror stories of candidates' CVs ending up on their employer's desktop aren't entirely without foundation.

Criticisms have also been made about poor standards of ethicality on the part of cyber-agencies. As with conventional employment agents there are a number who employ sharp practices such as posting fictional vacancies and falsely inflating advertised pay rates in order to build up a bank of CVs which can be circulated to employers on an unsolicited basis. Some cyber-agencies also copy CVs from competitors' sites and send them on to employers without authorisation. Over time, as the industry grows, professional standards will be established and a regulatory regime established, but for the time being such problems remain.

The fact that there are so many drawbacks alongside the advantages explains why so many employers appear to use the internet for recruitment while rating it relatively poorly. When asked to rank recruitment methods in terms of their effectiveness very few employers place the internet at the top of the list. Established approaches such as newspaper advertising and education liaison are much more highly rated and are thus unlikely to be replaced by e-recruitment in the near future. However, over the longer term, technological developments and increased web usage may improve the effectiveness of e-recruitment considerably. This will occur when one or two very well-funded job sites emerge from the current mass and are able command substantial shares of the market. We will then have a situation in which anyone seeking a new job in a particular field will make a familiar website rather than the newspaper or journal their first port of call.

EMPLOYER BRANDING

In recent years considerable interest has developed in the idea that employers have much to gain when competing for staff by borrowing techniques long used in marketing goods and services to potential customers. In particular, many organizations have sought to position themselves as 'employers of choice' in their labour markets with a view to attracting stronger applications from potential employees. Those who have succeeded have often found that their recruitment costs fall as a result because they get so many more unsolicited applications.

Central to these approaches is the development over time of a positive 'brand image' of the organization as an employer, so that potential employees come to regard working there as highly desirable. Developing a good brand image is an easier task for larger companies with household names than for those which are smaller or highly specialised, but the possibility of developing and sustaining a reputation as a good employer is something from which all organizations stand to benefit.

The key, as when branding consumer products, is to build on any aspect of the working experience that is distinct from that offered by other organizations competing in the same broad applicant pool. It may be relatively high pay or a generous benefits package, it may be flexible working, or a friendly and informal atmosphere, strong career development potential or job security. This is then developed as a 'unique selling proposition' and forms the basis of the employer branding exercise.

The best way of finding out what is distinct and positive about working in your organization is to carry out some form of staff attitude survey. Employer branding exercises simply amount to a waste of time and money when they are not rooted in the actual lived experience of employees because people are attracted to the organization on false premises. As with claims made for products that do not live up to their billing, the employees gained are not subsequently retained, and resources are wasted recruiting people who resign quickly after starting.

Once the unique selling propositions have been identified they can be used to inform all forms of communication that the organization engages in with potential and actual applicants. The aim must be to repeat the message again and again in advertisements, in recruitment literature, on internet sites and at careers fairs. It is also important that existing employees are made aware of their employer's brand proposition too as so much recruitment is carried out informally through word of mouth. Provided the message is accurate and provided it is communicated effectively over time, the result will be a 'leveraging of the brand' as more and more people in the labour market begin to associate the message with the employer.

CONTROL AND EVALUATION

The HR manager needs to monitor the effectiveness of advertising and all other methods of recruitment, first, to ensure value for money and, second, to ensure that the pool of applicants produced by the various methods is suitable.

Wright and Storey suggest that information on the following should be collected:

1. Number of initial enquiries received which resulted in completed application forms.
2. Number of candidates at various stages in the recruitment and selection process, especially those shortlisted.
3. Number of candidates recruited.
4. Number of candidates retained in organization after six months.

There is also a good case for monitoring the numbers of men and women who are successful at each stage of the process and the numbers of people from different ethnic minorities. Where an imbalance becomes apparent the organization can then take remedial action.

There needs, however, to be more information than this in order to get to the more intangible questions, such as 'Did the best candidate not even apply?' The most important source of information about the quality of the recruitment process is the people involved in it. Do telephonists and receptionists know how to handle the tentative employment enquiry? What did they hear from applicants in the original enquiries that showed the nature of their reaction to the advertisement? Is it made simple for enquirers to check key points by telephone or personal visit? Is there an unnecessary emphasis on written applications before anything at all can be done? Useful information can also be obtained from both successful and unsuccessful applicants. Those who have been successful will obviously believe that recruitment was well done, while the unsuccessful may have good reason to believe that it was flawed. However, those who are unsuccessful sometimes ask for feedback on the reasons. If a recruiter is able to give this, it is also a simple development to ask the applicant for comment on the recruitment process.

CORRESPONDENCE

If an organization is to maximise its chances of recruiting the best people to the jobs it advertises it must ensure that all subsequent communication with those who express an interest is carried out professionally. The same is true of casual enquirers and those who find out about possible vacancies informally through word of mouth. Failing to make a positive impression may well result in good candidates losing interest or developing a preference for a rival organization which takes greater care to project itself effectively in its labour markets. Providing information to would-be candidates who express an interest is the first step. This is often seen as unnecessary and costly, but it should be seen as the organization's opportunity to sell itself as an employer to its potential applicant pool. The following are commonly provided:

- A copy of the relevant job description and personnel specification;
- A copy of the advertisement for reference purposes;
- A copy of any general recruitment brochure produced by the organization;
- The staff handbook or details of a collective agreement;
- Details of any occupational pension arrangements;
- General information about the organization (e.g. a mission statement, annual report or publicity brochures).

It is also essential to have some method of tracking recruitment, either manually or by computer, so that an immediate and helpful response can be given to applicants enquiring about the stage their application has reached. Moreover, it is necessary to ensure that all applicants are informed about the outcome of their application. This will reduce the number of enquiries that have to be handled, but it is also an important aspect of public relations, as the organization dealing with job applicants may also be dealing with prospective customers. Many people have the experience of applying for a post and then not hearing anything at all. Particularly when the application is unsolicited, HR managers may feel that there is no obligation to reply, but this could be bad business as well as disconcerting for the applicant. Standard letters ('I regret to inform you that there were many applications and yours was not successful . . .') are better than nothing, but letters containing actual information ('out of the seventy-two applications, we included yours in our first shortlist of fifteen, but not in our final shortlist of eight') are better. Best of all are the letters that make practical suggestions, such as applying again in six months' time, asking if the applicant would like to be considered for another post elsewhere in the organization, or pointing out the difficulty of applying for a post that calls for greater experience or qualifications than the applicant at that stage is able to present.

SHORTLISTING

Shortlisting of candidates can be difficult in some instances because of small numbers of applicants and in other instances because of extremely large numbers of applicants. Such difficulties can arise unintentionally when there is inadequate specification of the criteria required or intentionally in large-scale recruitment exercises such as those associated with an annual intake of graduates.

In such circumstances it is tempting for the HR department to use some form of arbitrary method to reduce the numbers to a more manageable level. Examples include screening people out because of their age, because of their handwriting style or because their work history is perceived as being unconventional in some way. No doubt there are other whimsical criteria adopted by managers appalled at making sense of 100 or so application forms and assorted curricula vitae. Apart from those that are unlawful, these criteria are grossly unfair to applicants if not mentioned in the advertisement, and are a thoroughly unsatisfactory way of recruiting the most appropriate person.

It is far more satisfactory to have in place a fair and objective system for short- listing candidates which produces the best group of alternative candidates to move forward to the interview stage. This can be achieved in one of three basic ways – which can be used separately or in combination. The first involves using a panel of managers to undertake shortlisting, reducing the likelihood that individual prejudices will influence the process. A number of distinct stages can be identified:

- *Stage 1*: Panel members agree essential criteria for those to be placed on the shortlist.
- *Stage 2*: Using those criteria, selectors individually produce personal lists of, say, ten candidates. An operating principle throughout is to concentrate on who can be included rather than

who can be excluded, so that the process is positive, looking for strengths rather than shortcomings.

- *Stage 3*: Selectors reveal their lists and find their consensus. If stages 1 and 2 have been done properly the degree of consensus should be quite high and probably sufficient to constitute a shortlist for interview. If it is still not clear, they continue to:
- *Stage 4*: Discuss those candidates preferred by some but not all in order to clarify and reduce the areas of disagreement. A possible tactic is to classify candidates as 'strong', 'possible' or 'maverick'.
- *Stage 5*: Selectors produce a final shortlist by discussion, guarding against including compromise candidates: not strong, but offensive to no one.

The second approach involves employing a scoring system as advocated by Roberts and Wood and Payne. As with the panel method, the key shortlisting criteria are defined at the start of the process (e.g. three years' management experience, a degree in a certain discipline, current salary in the range of Rs.20,000–Rs.30,000, evidence of an ability to drive change, etc.). The shortlister then scores each CV or application form received against these criteria awarding an A grade (or high mark) where clear evidence is provided that the candidate matches the criteria, a B grade where there is some evidence or where the candidate partially meets the criteria and a C grade where no convincing evidence is provided. Where a structured application form has been completed by the candidates, this process can be undertaken quickly (two or three minutes per application) because a candidate can be screened out whenever, for example, more than one C grade has been awarded.

The third approach involves making use of the software systems on the market which shortlist candidates electronically. The different types of system and some of the drawbacks were described above in the section on e-recruitment. Despite the problems, such systems can be useful where the criteria are very clearly and tightly defined, and where an online application form is completed which makes use of multiple-choice answers. Such forms can be scored speedily and objectively, the candidate being given feedback on whether or not they have been successful. Only those who make the 'right' choices when completing the online questionnaire are then invited to participate in the next stage of the recruitment process.

Note: For a very good case study regarding this topic, reader can visit company's website of C.H. Robinson Worldwide Inc. C.H. Robinson Worldwide (CHRW) is a global provider of multimodal transportation services and logistics solutions. It also provides fresh produce sourcing and information services. The company primarily operates in the US. It is headquartered in Eden Prairie, Minnesota and employs about 7,961 people. www.chrobinson.com.

8

Selection Methods and Decisions

While the search for the perfect method of selection continues, in its absence HR and line managers continue to use a variety of imperfect methods to aid the task of predicting which applicant will be most successful in meeting the demands of the job, and/or be the best fit with the work group and culture of the organization. Selection is increasingly important as more attention is paid to the costs of poor selection, in a very competitive market for talent. This context has promoted greater attention to the applicant's perspective and increasing use of technology in selection. In addition equal opportunities legislation has underlined the importance of using well- validated selection procedures, so that the selection process discriminates fairly, and not unfairly, between applicants.

SELECTION AS A TWO-WAY PROCESS

The various stages of the selection process provide information for decisions by both the employer and the potential employee. While employment decisions have long been regarded as a management prerogative there is considerable evidence that the two-way nature of the process is now being widely acknowledged, and Lievens et al. suggest that labour market shortages have promoted a concern for the organization's image and the treatment of applicants during the recruitment and selection process. We must also be concerned not only with the job to be done, but also with the work and the organizational context that is offered.

Throughout the selection process applicants choose between organizations by evaluating the developing relationship between themselves and the prospect. This takes place in the correspondence from potential employers; in their experience of the selection methods used by the employer; and in the information they gain on interview. Applicants will decide not to pursue some applications. Either they will have accepted another offer, or they will find something in their dealings with the organization that discourages them and they withdraw. When large numbers of candidates withdraw it may be because the information provided by the organization was sufficiently detailed, accurate and realistic that they were able to make a wise decision that they were not suited to the organization and that time would be wasted by continuing. On the other hand, it might be that potentially admirable recruits were lost because of the way in which information was presented, lack of information, or the interpretation that was put on the 'flavour' of the correspondence.

The frame of reference for the applicant is so different from that of the manager in the organization that the difference is frequently forgotten. It would not be unrealistic to suggest that the majority of applicants have a mental picture of their application being received by the company and immediately being closely scrutinised and discussed by powerful figures. The fact that the application is one element in a varied routine for the recipient is incomprehensible to some and unacceptable to many. The thought that one person's dream is another's routine is something the applicant cannot cope with.

If they have posted or emailed an application with high enthusiasm about the fresh prospects that the new job would bring, they are in no mood for delay and they may quickly start convincing themselves that they are not interested, because their initial euphoria has not been sustained. If candidates get as far as interview they will also be influenced by recruiter behaviour in deciding whether to accept a job offer, if one is made. Papadopoulou et al., for example, demonstrated that candidates were influenced by the recruiter's ability to supply adequate and accurate information, as this is what they had expected from the interview. In addition they were influenced by the way the recruiter managed the interaction, as well as the content, so the recruiter's control of the interaction, their listening ability and in particular their ability/willingness to allow the candidate to present themselves effectively are all important.

Some of the points that seem to be useful about interacting with the candidate are:

- Reply, meaningfully, fast. The printed postcard of acknowledgement is not a reply, neither is the personal letter or email which says nothing more than that the application has been received. Web-based selection can speed things up considerably.
- Conduct correspondence in terms of what the applicants want

to know. How long will they have to wait for an answer? If you ask them in for interview, how long will it take, what will it involve, do you defray expenses, can they park their car, how do they find you, etc.?

- Interviewers should be trained to ensure that they have not only full knowledge of the relevant information, but also the skills to manage the interaction effectively.

SELECTION CRITERIA AND THE PERSON SPECIFICATION

Unless the criteria against which applicants will be measured are made explicit, it is impossible to make credible selection decisions. It will be difficult to select the most appropriate selection procedure and approach, and it will be difficult to validate the selection process. Selection criteria are typically presented in the form of a person specification representing the ideal candidate, and cover such areas as skills, experience, qualifications, education, personal attributes, special attributes, interests and motivation. Although it is also have been found that person specifications were used by three-quarters of the organizations in their study, Lievens et al. challenge the use of traditional person specifications as jobs become less defined and constantly change. Three perspectives can be used to determine selection criteria – organizational fit, team/functional fit and job fit.

FIT WITH THE ORGANIZATION

The organizational criteria are those attributes that an organization considers valuable in its employees and that affect judgements about a candidate's potential to be successful within an organization. For example, the organization may be expanding and innovating and require employees who are particularly flexible and adaptable. Previously, these organizational criteria were rarely made explicit and they were often used at an intuitive level. However, Townley argues that organizations are increasingly likely to focus on more general attitudes and values than narrow task-based criteria. Barclay explains how fit with the organization is often expressed in terms of personality, attitudes, flexibility, commitment and goals, rather than the ability to do the specific job for which the person is being recruited. Such organizational criteria are important where jobs are ill defined and constantly changing. There are also some groups who are recruited into the organization rather than into specific jobs or even a specific function

– new/recent graduates, for example, and, here again, organization criteria are important.

FUNCTIONAL AND TEAM FIT

Between the generality of the organizational criteria and the preciseness of job criteria there are functional criteria, such as the definition of appropriate interpersonal skills for all members of the HR department. Criteria may also be important when the new appointee will have to fit into a pre-existing work team.

INDIVIDUAL JOB CRITERIA

Individual job criteria contained in job descriptions and person specifications are derived from the process of job analysis. Although it is reasonably easy to specify the factors that should influence the personnel specification, the process by which the specification is formed is more difficult to describe. Van Zwanenberg and Wilkinson offer a dual perspective. They describe 'job first – person later' and 'person first – job later' approaches. The first starts with analysing the task to be done, presenting this in the form of a job description and from this deriving the personal qualities and attributes or competencies that are necessary to do the task. The difficulty here is in the translation process and the constant change of job demands and tasks. The alternative approach suggested by van Zwanenberg and Wilkinson starts with identifying which individuals are successful in a certain job and then describing their characteristics. There is also a trend towards making the person specification appropriate for a broad band of jobs rather than one particular job.

In addition to, or sometimes instead of, a person specification, many organizations are developing a competency profile as a means of setting the criteria against which to select. Competencies have been defined as underlying characteristics of a person which result in effective or superior performance; they include personal skills, knowledge, motives, traits, self-image and social role. The advantage of competencies is that they can be used in an integrated way for selection, development, appraisal and reward activities; and also that from them behavioural indicators can be derived against which assessment can take place. Woodruffe and Whiddett and Hollyforde are useful practical sources of information on how to use competencies in the selection process. It should be noted, however, that using competencies as the only selection criteria is considered to be limiting and unhelpful.

Choosing Selection Methods

It is unusual for one selection method to be used alone. A combination of two or more methods is generally used, and the choice of these is dependent upon a number of factors:

- *Selection criteria for the post to be filled.* For example, group selection methods and assessment centre activities would be most useful for certain types of job, such as managerial, professional, supervisory and those who will be part of self-managing teams.
- *Acceptability and appropriateness of the methods.* For the candidates involved, or likely to be involved, in the selection. The use, for example, of intelligence tests may be seen as insulting to applicants already occupying senior posts.
- *Abilities of the staff involved in the selection process.* This applies particularly in the use of tests and assessment centres. Only those staff who are appropriately qualified by academic qualification and/or attendance on a recognised course may administer psychological tests.
- *Administrative ease.* For administrative purposes it may be much simpler, say, to arrange one or two individual interviews for a prospective candidate than to organize a panel consisting of four members, all needing to make themselves available at the same time. Web-based testing may save much administrative time, particularly when there are large numbers of candidates.
- *Time factors.* Sometimes a position needs to be filled very quickly, and time may be saved by using telephone or video-based interviews, or organizing individual interviews rather than group selection methods, which would mean waiting for a day when all candidates are available.
- *Accuracy.* Accuracy in selection generally increases in relation to the number of appropriate selection methods used.
- *Cost.* Tests may cost a lot to set up but once the initial outlay has been made they are reasonably cheap to administer. Assessment centres would involve an even greater outlay and continue to be fairly expensive to administer. Interviews, on the other hand, cost only a moderate amount to set up in terms of interviewer training and are fairly cheap to administer. For the costlier methods great care needs to be taken in deciding whether the improvement

in selection decision making would justify such costs.

SELECTION METHODS

APPLICATION FORMS

Growing use is being made of the application form as a basis for employment decisions, and it has been found that they were used in 80 per cent of the organizations they surveyed. For a long time the application form was not suitable for use in that way; it was a personal details form, which was intended to form the nucleus of the personnel record for the individual when they began work. As reservations grew about the validity of interviews for employment purposes, the more productive use of the application form was one of the avenues explored for improving the quality of decisions.

Forms were considered to act as a useful preliminary to employment interviews and decisions, either to present more information that was relevant to such deliberations, or to arrange such information in a standard way. This made sorting of applications and shortlisting easier and enabled interviewers to use the form as the basis for the interview itself, with each piece of information on the form being taken and developed in the interview. While there is heavy use of CVs for managerial and professional posts, many organizations, especially in the public sector, require both – off-putting to the applicant but helpful to the organization in eliciting comparable data from all applicants.

The application form has been extended by some organizations to take a more significant part in the employment process. One form of extension is to ask for very much more, and more detailed, information from the candidate.

Another extension of application form usage has been in weighting, or biodata. Biodata have been defined by Anderson and Shackleton as 'historical and verifiable pieces of information about an individual in a selection context usually reported on application forms'. Biodata are perhaps of most use for large organizations filling fairly large numbers of posts for which they receive extremely high numbers of applications. This method is an attempt to relate the characteristics of applicants to characteristics of a large sample of successful job holders. The obvious drawbacks of this procedure are, first, the time that is involved and the size of sample needed, so that it is only feasible where there are many job holders in a particular type of position. Second, it smacks of witchcraft to the applicants who might find it difficult to believe that success in a position correlates with being, inter alia, the first born in one's family. Such methods are not currently well used and Taylor notes the controversial nature and high development costs.

Generally, application forms are used as a straightforward way of giving a standardised synopsis of the applicant's history. This helps applicants present their case by providing them with a predetermined structure, it speeds the sorting and shortlisting of applications and it guides the interviewers as well as providing the starting point for personnel records. Application forms are increasingly available electronically; this not only speeds up the process but also enables 'key word' searches of the data on the forms (for alternative ways in which this may be carried out, but there are questions about the legality of this method when used alone.

SELF-ASSESSMENT AND PEER ASSESSMENT

There is increasing interest in providing more information to applicants concerning the job. This may involve a video, an informal discussion with job holders or further information sent with the application form. This is often termed giving the prospective candidate a 'realistic job preview', enabling them to assess their own suitability to a much greater extent. However, the survey found that only 2 per cent of organizations have taken the opportunity to provide a self-selection questionnaire on the company website. Another way of achieving this is by asking the candidates to do some form of pre-work. This may also involve asking them questions regarding their previous work experiences which would relate to the job for which they are applying.

TELEPHONE INTERVIEWING

Telephone interviews can be used if speed is particularly important, and if geographical distance is an issue, as interviews with appropriate candidates can be arranged immediately. According to a report 28 per cent of organizations use this method of selection. There is evidence that telephone interviews are best used as a part of a structured selection procedure, rather than alone – generally in terms of pre-selection for a face-to-face interview. However, they may also have in important role when selecting for jobs in which telephone manner is critical such as call centre and contact centre staff. This survey also report problems such as lack of non-verbal information and difficulties getting hold of the applicant. However, positive aspects have been reported, such as concentration on content rather than the person.

TESTING

The use of tests in employment procedures is surrounded by strong feelings for and against. Those in favour of testing in general point to the unreliability of the interview as a predictor of performance and the greater potential accuracy and objectivity of test data. Tests can be seen as giving credibility to selection decisions. Those against them either dislike the objectivity that testing implies or have difficulty in incorporating test evidence into the rest of the evidence that is collected. Questions have been raised as to the relevance of the tests to the job applied for and the possibility of unfair discrimination and bias. Also, some candidates feel that they can improve their prospects by a good interview performance and that the degree to which they are in control of their own destiny is being reduced by a dispassionate routine.

Tests remain heavily used, and the key issue debated currently is the extent to which tests should be administered over the web. It has been reported that 80 per cent of organizations studied used ability tests and 85 per cent used personality tests. This survey found that testing is more likely to be used for management, professional and graduate jobs – although as testing on the web becomes more common it is likely to be used for a wider range of jobs.

Tests are chosen on the basis that test scores relate to, or correlate with, subsequent job performance, so that a high test score would predict high job performance and a low test score would predict low job performance.

CRITICAL FEATURES OF TEST USE

Validity

Different types of validity can be applied to psychological tests. Personnel managers are most concerned with predictive validity, which is the extent to which the test can predict subsequent job performance. Predictive validity is measured by relating the test scores to measures of future performance, such as error rate, production rate, appraisal scores, absence rate or whatever criteria are important to the organization. Sometimes performance is defined as the level of the organization to which the individual has been promoted – so the criteria here are organizational rather than job specific. If test scores relate highly to future performance, however defined, then the test is a good predictor.

Reliability

The reliability of a test is the degree to which the test measures consistently whatever it does measure. If a test is highly reliable, then it is possible to put greater weight on the scores that individuals receive on the test. However, a highly reliable test is of no value in the employment situation unless it also has high validity.

Problems with using tests

A number of problems can be incurred when using tests.

- Validation procedures are very time consuming, but are essential to the effective use of tests. There are concerns that with the growth of web testing, new types of tests, such as emotional intelligence tests, are being developed without sufficient validation.
- The criteria that are used to define good job performance in developing the test are often inadequate. They are subjective and may account to some extent for the mediocre correlations between test results and job performance.
- Tests are often job specific. If the job for which the test is used changes, then the test can no longer be assumed to relate to job performance in the same way. Also, personality tests only measure how individuals see themselves at a certain time and cannot therefore be reliably reused at a later time.
- Tests may not be fair as there may be a social, sexual or racial bias in the questions and scoring system. People from some cultures may, for example, be unused to 'working against the clock'.
- Increasingly organizations are using competencies as a tool to identify and develop the characteristics of high performance. However, as Fletcher has pointed out, it is difficult to relate these readily to psychological tests. Rogers reports research which suggests the two approaches are compatible – but there is little evidence to support this so far.

TYPES OF TEST FOR OCCUPATIONAL USE

Aptitude tests

People differ in their performance of tasks, and tests of aptitude (or ability) measure an individual's potential to develop in either specific or general terms. This is in contrast to attainment tests, which measure the skills an individual has already acquired. When considering the results from aptitude tests it is important to remember that a simple relationship does not exist between a high level of aptitude and a high level of job performance, as other factors, such as motivation, also contribute to job performance.

Aptitude tests can be grouped into two categories: those measuring general mental ability or general intelligence, and those measuring specific abilities or aptitudes.

General intelligence tests

Intelligence tests, sometimes called mental ability tests, are designed to give an indication of overall mental capacity. A variety of questions are included in such tests, including vocabulary, analogies, similarities, opposites, arithmetic, number extension and general information. Ability to score highly on such tests correlates with the capacity to retain new knowledge, to pass examinations and to succeed at work. However, the intelligence test used would still need to be carefully validated in terms of the job for which the candidate was applying. And Ceci and Williams note that intelligence is to some extent determined by the context – so an individual's test score may not reflect capacity to act intelligently. Indeed practical intelligence, associated with success in organizations, may be different from the nature of intelligence as measured by tests.

Special aptitude tests

There are special tests that measure specific abilities or aptitudes, such as spatial abilities, perceptual abilities, verbal ability, numerical ability, motor ability (manual dexterity) and so on. An example of a special abilities test is the Critical Reasoning Test developed by Smith and Whetton.

Trainability tests

Trainability tests are used to measure a potential employee's ability to be trained, usually for craft-type work. The test consists of the applicants doing a practical task that they have not done before, after having been shown or 'trained' how to do it. The test measures how well they respond to the 'training' and how their performance on the task improves. Because it is performance at a task that is being measured, these tests are sometimes confused with attainment tests; however, they are more concerned with potential ability to do the task and response to training.

Attainment tests

Whereas aptitude tests measure an individual's potential, attainment or achievement tests measure skills that have already been acquired. There is much less resistance to such tests of skills. Few candidates for a secretarial/administrative post would refuse to take a typing speed test, or a test on 'Word', 'PowerPoint' or 'Excel' software before interview. The candidates are sufficiently confident of their skills to welcome the opportunity to display them and be approved. Furthermore, they know what they are doing and will know whether they have done well or badly. They are in control, while they feel that the tester is in control of intelligence and personality tests as the candidates do not understand the evaluation rationale. Attainment tests are often devised by the employer.

Personality tests

The debate still rages as to the importance of personality for success in some jobs and organizations. The need for personality assessment may be high but there is even more resistance to tests of personality than to tests of aptitude, partly because of the reluctance to see personality as in any way measurable. There is much evidence to suggest that personality is also context dependent, and Iles and Salaman also argue that personality changes over time. Both of these factors further complicate the issue. Personality tests are mainly used for management, professional and graduate jobs, although there is evidence of their use when high-performance teams are developed.

Theories of human personality vary as much as theories of human intelligence. Jung, Eysenck and Cattell, among others, have all proposed different sets of factors/ traits which can be assessed to describe personality. Based on research to date Robertson argues that it is now possible to state that there are five basic building blocks of personality: extroversion/introversion; emotional stability; agreeableness; conscientiousness and openness to new experiences.

It is dangerous to assume that there is a standard profile of 'the ideal employee' (although this may fit nicely with theories of culture change) or the ideal personality for a particular job, as the same objectives may be satisfactorily achieved in different ways by different people. Another problem with the use of personality tests is that they rely on an individual's willingness to be honest, as the socially acceptable answer or the one best in terms of the job are seemingly easy to pick out, although 'lie detector' questions are usually built in. There is a further problem that some traits measured by the test will not be relevant in terms of performance on the job. Myers–Briggs is a well used personality test. There is at the time of writing an interest in emotional intelligence – tests measure self-awareness, self-motivation, emotional control, empathy and the ability to understand and inspire others.

Online Testing: The Case for and Against

While online tests are not widely used at present, there is much interest in developing this area. Tests can be used in one of three different ways:

- *Uncontrolled* – anyone can register to use them on the open internet;
- *Controlled* – the candidate needs first to be registered by the organization using the test, and their identity must be checked;
- *Supervised* – as above, and a qualified tester from the organization also logs on and ensures that time limits and other requirements are met.

For:

- Cheaper in the long run
- Immediate analysis
- Immediate feedback to candidate
- Can be used for wider range of (lower-paid) jobs
- Speeds processes and helps to retain potential candidates
- Good for company image
- Can use a wider range of different tests – e.g. video scenarios, followed by 'what would you do next?'
- Can be convenient for applicants

Against:

- Worries over confidentiality and security of personal data
- Appears cold and impersonal
- Open to misuse – who is actually completing the test?
- Can encourage the rapid development of new tests which are not properly validated.

Group Selection Methods and Assessment Centres

Group methods

The use of group tasks to select candidates is not new – the method dates back to the Second World War – but such measures have gained greater attention through their use in assessment centres. Plumbley describes the purpose of group selection methods as being to provide evidence about the candidate's ability to:

- Get on with others;
- Influence others and the way they do this;
- Express themselves verbally;
- Think clearly and logically;
- Argue from past experience and apply themselves to a new problem;
- Identify the type of role they play in group situations.

These features are difficult on the whole to identify using other selection methods and one of the particular advantages of group selection methods is that they provide the selector with examples of behaviour on which to select. When future job performance is being considered it is behaviour in the job that is critical, and so selection using group methods can provide direct information on which to select rather than indirect verbal information or test results. The increasing use of competencies and behavioural indicators, as a way to specifiy selection criteria, ties in well with the use of group methods.

Plumbley identifies three main types of group task that can be used, each of which would be observed by the selectors:

1. *Leaderless groups*: A group of about 6–8 individuals are given a topic of general interest to discuss.
2. *Command or executive exercises*: The members of the group are allocated roles in an extensive brief based on a real-life situation. Each member outlines his or her solution on the basis of their role and defends it to the rest of the group.
3. *Group problem solving*: The group is leaderless and has to organize itself in order to solve, within time limits, a problem that is relevant to the job to be filled. Such tasks may be developed into business

games and case studies.

Group selection methods are most suitable for management, graduate and sometimes supervisory posts. One of the difficulties with group selection methods is that it can be difficult to assess an individual's contribution, and some people may be unwilling to take part.

ASSESSMENT CENTRES

Assessment centres incorporate multiple selection techniques, and group selection methods outlined above form a major element, together with other work simulation exercises such as in-basket tasks, psychological tests, a variety of interviews and presentations. Assessment centres are used to assess, in depth, a group of broadly similar applicants, using a set of competencies required for the post on offer and a series of behavioural statements which indicate how these competencies are played out in practice. Even assuming that the competencies for the job in question have already been identified, assessment centres require a lengthy design process to select the appropriate activities so that every competency will be measured via more than one task.

A matrix is usually developed to show how the required competencies and the activities link up together. In terms of running the centre sufficient well-trained assessors will be needed, usually based on the ratio of one assessor for two candidates to ensure that the assessor can observe each candidate sufficiently carefully. Lists of competencies and associated behaviours will need to be drawn up as checklists and a careful plan will need to be made of how each candidate will move around the different activities. Clearly candidates will need to be very well briefed both before and at the start of the centre.

At the end of the procedure the assessors have to come to agreement on a cumulative rating for each individual, related to job requirements, taking into account all the selection activities. The procedure as a whole can then be validated against job performance rather than each separate activity. The predictive validities from such procedures are not very consistent, but there is a high 'face validity' – a feeling that this is a fairer way of selecting people. Reliability can also be improved by the quality of assessor training, careful briefing of assessors and a predetermined structured approach to marking. The chief disadvantages of these selection methods are that they are a costly and time-consuming procedure, for both the organization and the candidates. The time commitment is extended by the need to give some feedback to candidates who have been through such a long procedure which involves psychological assessment – although feedback is still not always available for candidates. There is evidence of increasing use of assessment centres reports that 47.5 per cent of organiztaions in its survey used such centres for selection. Some organizations have been improving their centres by making the activities more connected or by using longer simulations or scenarios which are a reflection of real-life experience on the job, and are carrying out testing separately from the centre. Some are assessing candidates against the values of the company rather than a specific job, in view of the rapid change in the nature of jobs, and others, such as Britvic, are running a series of assessment centres which candidates must attend, rather than only one.

WORK SAMPLING/PORTFOLIOS

Work sampling of potential candidates for permanent jobs can take place by assessing candidates' work in temporary posts or on government training schemes in the same organization. For some jobs, such as photographers and artists, a sample of work in the form of a portfolio is expected to be presented at the time of interview. Kanter suggests that managers and professionals should also be developing portfolios of their work experiences and achievements as one way of enhancing their employability.

REFERENCES

One way of informing the judgement of managers who have to make employment offers to selected individuals is the use of references. Candidates provide the names of previous employers or others with appropriate credentials and then prospective employers request them to provide information. Reference checking is increasing as organizations react to scandals in the media and aim to protect themselves from rogue applicants. There are two types: the factual check and the character reference.

THE FACTUAL CHECK

The factual check is fairly straightforward as it is no more than a confirmation of facts that the candidate has presented. It will normally follow the employment interview and decision to offer a post. It simply confirms that the facts are accurate. The knowledge that such a check will be made – or may be made – will help focus the mind of candidates so that they resist the temptation to embroider their story.

THE CHARACTER REFERENCE

The character reference is a very different matter. Here the prospective employer asks for an opinion about the candidate before the interview so that the information gained can be used in the decision-making phases. The logic of this strategy is impeccable: who knows the working performance of the candidate better than the previous employer? The wisdom of the strategy is less sound, as it depends on the writers of references being excellent judges of working performance, faultless communicators and – most difficult of all – disinterested. The potential inaccuracies of decisions influenced by character references begin when the candidate decides who to cite. They will have some freedom of choice and will clearly choose someone from whom they expect favourable comment, perhaps massaging the critical faculties with such comments as: 'I think references are going to be very important for this job' or 'You will do your best for me, won't you?'

OTHER METHODS

A number of other less conventional methods such as physiognomy, phrenology, body language, palmistry, graphology and astrology have been suggested as possible selection methods. While these are fascinating to read about there is little evidence to suggest that they could be used effectively. Thatcher suggests that the use of graphology is around 10 per cent in Holland and Germany and that it is regularly used in France; in the UK he found nine per cent of small firms (with fewer than 100 employees), one per cent of medium-sized firms (100–499 employees) and five per cent of larger firms used graphology as a selection method. There are also concerns about the quality of graphologists – who can indeed set themselves up with no training whatsoever.

FINAL SELECTION DECISION MAKING

The selection decision involves measuring each candidate against the selection criteria defined in the person specification, and not against each other. This is a good method of ensuring that every candidate is assessed against each selection criterion and in each box in the matrix the key details can be completed. The box can be used whether a single selection method was used or multiple methods. If multiple methods were used and contradictory information is found against any criterion, this can be noted in the decision-making process.

When more than one selector is involved there is some debate about how to gather and use the information and judgement of each selector. One way is for each selector to assess the information collected separately, and then for all selectors to meet to discuss assessments. When this approach is used, there may be some very different assessments, especially if the interview was the only selection method used. Much heated and time-consuming debate can be generated, but the most useful aspect of this process is sharing the information in everyone's matrix to understand how judgements have been formed. This approach is also helpful in training interviewers.

An alternative approach is to fill in only one matrix, with all selectors contributing. This may be quicker, but the drawback is that the quietest member may be the one who has all the critical pieces of information. There is a risk that all the information may not be contributed to the debate in progress. Iles, referring to assessment centre decisions, suggests that the debate itself may not add to the quality of the decision, and that taking the results from each selector and combining them is just as effective.

VALIDATION OF SELECTION PROCEDURES

We have already mentioned how test scores may be validated against eventual job performance for each individual in order to discover whether the test score is a good predictor of success in the job. In this way we can decide whether the test should be used as part of the selection procedure. The same idea can be applied to the use of other individual or combined selection methods.

The critical information that is important for determining validity is the selection criteria used, the selection processes used, an evaluation of the individual at the time of selection and current performance of the individual.

Unfortunately we are never in a position to witness the performance of rejected candidates and compare this with those we have employed. However, if a group of individuals are selected at the same time, for example, graduate trainees, it will be unlikely that they were all rated equally highly in spite of the fact that they were all considered employable. It is useful for validation purposes if a record is made of the scores that each achieved in each part of the selection process. Test results are easy to quantify, and for interview results a simple grading system can be devised.

Current performance includes measures derived from the job description, together with additional performance measures:

1. Measures from the job description: quantitative measures such as volume of sales, accuracy, number of complaints and so on may be used, or qualitative measures such as relations with customers and quality of reports produced.

2. Other measures: these may include appraisal results, problems identified, absence data and, of course, termination.

Current performance is often assessed in an intuitive, subjective way, and while this may sometimes be useful it is no substitute for objective assessment.

Selection ratings for each individual can be compared with eventual performance over a variety of time periods. Large discrepancies between selection and performance ratings point to further investigation of the selection criteria and methods used. The comparison of selection rating and performance rating can also be used to compare the appropriateness of different selection criteria, and the usefulness of different selection methods.

Note: For further knowledge regarding this chapter, reader can visit site of Cooper Tire & Rubber Company. Cooper Tire & Rubber (Cooper Tire) is engaged in the designing, manufacturing and selling of tires for passenger cars, light trucks, medium trucks, and motorcycles and racing vehicles. The company primarily operates in the US. It is headquartered in Findlay, Ohio and employs 13,311 people. www.coopertire.com

9

Staff Retention

It is estimated that the costs associated with recruiting and training a new employee average between half and one and a half times the annual salary for the post in question, depending on the approaches used. In this chapter we consider the most important way in which human resource managers seek to reduce the time and money spent on these activities, namely by trying to ensure that people choose not to leave an organization voluntarily in the first place.

The extent of interest in employee retention issues varies over time as labour markets become successively tighter and looser depending on economic conditions. In recent years, as unemployment has fallen, making it harder to recruit staff with the necessary skills and attitudes, the subject has again moved up the HRM agenda. This has led to the publication of several new books and articles exploring how organizations can ensure that they have the best chance of retaining the people they employ. The authors tend to take one of two distinct perspectives on the subject. The first focuses on the organization as a whole, tracking staff turnover rates over time, benchmarking the figures against industry or regional averages and developing organizational policy aimed at improving retention generally. The second, illustrated in recent work by Hiltrop, Woodruffe, Williams and Cappelli , concentrates primarily on retaining high-performing key players. Each of these authors uses the expression 'the war for talent' to illustrate the significance and difficulty faced by those competing for the services of individuals who have the capacity to make a real difference to an organization's competitive position. While the methods put forward to reduce turnover are similar in each case, the second group advocate more sophisticated retention practices aimed specifically at those whose talents are the most scarce.

TURNOVER RATES AND TRENDS

In recent years there has been a mismatch between the rhetoric about job tenure and the reality. Much mileage continues to be made by some consultants, academics and management gurus out of the claim that 'there are no longer any jobs for life', suggesting that the length of time we spend working for organizations has fallen substantially in recent years. In fact this is a misleading claim. Detailed analyses of data from the New Earnings Survey, the General Household Survey and the British Labour Force Survey show that relatively little actually changed in terms of employee retention during recent decades. Turnover always rises when the economy is strong and jobs are plentiful because there are more opportunities available for people to change employers. Conversely, during recessions staff turnover falls because relatively few attractive permanent positions are advertised. Gregg and Wadsworth show that the biggest increase has been among women with children. In 1975, on average, they remained in a job for 20 months; the figure in 1998 was 46 months. This reflects the greater propensity of women during this period to return to work following maternity leave and the improved career opportunities available to them. These trends continue today. Table below shows that long periods of job tenure remain the norm for a substantial portion of the working population. People tend to move from employer to employer early on in their careers, often staying in one employment for just a few months. But once they find a job (or an employer) that they like, the tendency is to remain for several years. 'Jobs for life' have, in truth, always been a relative rarity, but the evidence suggests that they remain a reality for many employees, despite the predictions of the management gurus. Nearly a third of workers have been in their current jobs for over ten years.

Job tenure in the India since 1975

Year	*Male job tenure*	*Female job tenure*	*Average tenure*
1975	6 years, 6 months	3 years, 7 months	4 years, 9 months
1985	7 years, 2 months	3 years, 10 months	5 years, 6 months
1990	6 years	3 years, 9 months	4 years, 4 months
1995	6 years, 10 months	4 years, 6 months	5 years, 7 months
1998	5 years, 9 months	4 years, 4 months	4 years, 10 months

Length of service	*% of the workforce*
0–3 months	6%
3–6 months	6%
6–12 months	10%
1–2 years	12%
2–5 years	21%
5–10 years	15%
10–20 years	19%
Over 20 years	10%

The overall figures mask substantial differences between tenure and turnover rates in different industries. Studies undertaken annually by the Chartered Institute of Personnel and Development persistently show retailing and catering to be the sectors with the highest turnover levels, with rates averaging over 40 per cent in recent years. By contrast the most stable workforces are to be found in the public services, where reported annual turnover rates are only 10 or 11 per cent. Rates also vary from region to region and over time, being highest when and where average pay levels are highest and unemployment is low, and between different professions. As a rule, the more highly paid a person is, the less likely they are to switch jobs, but there remain some highly paid professions such as sales where turnover is always high. It is also interesting to observe how much more inclined younger workers are to switch jobs than their older colleagues. Macaulay recently calculated what proportion of employees had completed more than a year's service with their employer. For the over-fifties the figure was 86 per cent, for the 18–24 age group it was only 51 per cent.

THE IMPACT OF STAFF TURNOVER

There is some debate about the level which staff turnover rates have to reach in order to inflict measurable damage on an employer. The answer varies from organization to organization. In some industries it is possible to sustain highly successful businesses with turnover rates that would make it impossible to function in other sectors. Some chains of fast food restaurants, for example, are widely reported as managing with turnover rates in excess of 300 per cent. This means that the average tenure for each employee is only four months, yet the companies concerned are some of the most successful in the world. By contrast, in a professional services organization, where the personal relationships established between employees and clients are central to ongoing success, a turnover rate in excess of 10 per cent is likely to cause damage to the business.

There are sound arguments that can be made in favour of a certain amount of staff turnover. First, it is fair to say that organizations need to be rejuvenated with 'fresh blood' from time to time if they are to avoid becoming stale and stunted. This is particularly true at senior levels, where new leadership is often required periodically to drive change forward. More generally, however, new faces bring new ideas and experiences which help make organizations more dynamic. Second, it is possible to argue that a degree of turnover helps managers to keep firmer control over labour costs than would otherwise be the case. This is particularly true of organizations which are subject to regular and unpredictable changes in business levels. When income falls it is possible to hold back from replacing leavers until such time as it begins to pick up again. In this way organizations are able to minimise staffing budgets while maintaining profit levels during leaner periods. Redundancy bills are also lower in organizations with relatively high staff turnover because they are able to use natural wastage as the main means of reducing their workforce before compulsory lay-offs are needed. Third, it can be plausibly argued that some employee turnover is 'functional' rather than 'dysfunctional' because it results in the loss of poor performers and their replacement with more effective employees.

The arguments against staff turnover are equally persuasive. First are the sheer costs associated with replacing people who have left, ranging from the cost of placing a recruitment advertisement, through the time spent administering and conducting the selection process, to expenses required in inducting and training new employees. On top of these there are less easily measurable losses sustained as a result of poorer performance on the part of less experienced employees. For larger organizations employing specialist recruiters these costs can add up to millions of pounds a year, with substantial dividends to be claimed from a reduction in staff turnover levels by a few percentage points. The second major argument in favour of improving staff retention results from a straightforward recognition that people who leave represent a lost resource in whom the organization has invested time and money. The damage is all the greater when good people, trained and developed at the organization's expense, subsequently choose to work for competitors. Finally, it is argued that high turnover rates are symptomatic of a poorly managed organization. They suggest that people are dissatisfied with their jobs or with their employer and would prefer to work elsewhere. It thus sends a negative message to customers and helps create a poor image in the labour market, making it progressively harder to recruit good performers in the future.

We may thus conclude that the case for seeking to reduce staff turnover varies from organization to organization. Where replacement employees are in plentiful supply, where new starters can be trained quickly and where business levels are subject to regular fluctuation it is possible to manage effectively with a relatively high level of turnover. Indeed, it may make good business sense to do so if the expenditure required to increase employee retention is greater than the savings that would be gained as a result. In other situations the case for taking action on turnover rates is persuasive, particularly where substantial investment in training is required before new starters are able to operate at maximum effectiveness. Companies which achieve turnover rates below their industry average are thus likely to enjoy greater competitive advantage than those whose rates are relatively high.

TURNOVER ANALYSIS AND COSTING

There is little that an organization can do to manage turnover unless there is an understanding of the reasons for it. Information about these reasons is notoriously difficult to collect. Most commentators recommend exit interviews (that is, interviews with leavers about their reasons for resigning), but the problem here is whether the individual will feel able to tell the truth, and this will depend on the culture of the organization, the specific reasons for leaving and support that the individual will need from the organization in the future in the form of references. Despite their disadvantages, exit interviews may be helpful if handled sensitively and confidentially – perhaps by the HR department rather than the line manager. In addition, analyses of turnover rates between different departments and different job groups may well shed some light on causes of turnover. Attitude surveys can also provide relevant information. People leave jobs for a variety of different reasons, many of which are wholly outside the power of the organization to influence. One very common reason for leaving, for example, is retirement. It can be brought forward or pushed back for a few years, but ultimately it affects everyone. In many cases people leave for a mixture of reasons, certain factors weighing more highly in their minds than others. The following is one approach to categorising the main reasons people have for voluntarily leaving a job, each requiring a different kind of response from the organization.

OUTSIDE FACTORS

Outside factors relate to situations in which someone leaves for reasons that are largely unrelated to their work. The most common instances involve people moving away when a spouse or partner is relocated. Others include the wish to fulfil a long-term ambition to travel, pressures associated with juggling the needs of work and family and illness. To an extent such turnover is unavoidable, although it is possible to reduce it somewhat through the provision of career breaks, forms of flexible working and/or childcare facilities.

FUNCTIONAL TURNOVER

The functional turnover category includes all resignations which are welcomed by both employer and employee alike. The major examples are those which stem from an individual's poor work performance or failure to fit in comfortably with an organizational or departmental culture. While such resignations are less damaging than others from an organization's point of view they should still be regarded as lost opportunities and as an unnecessary cost. The main solution to the reduction of functional turnover lies in improving recruitment and selection procedures so that fewer people in the category are appointed in the first place. However, some poorly engineered change management schemes are also sometimes to blame, especially where they result in new work pressures or workplace ethics.

PUSH FACTORS

With push factors the problem is dissatisfaction with work or the organization, leading to unwanted turnover. A wide range of issues can be cited to explain such resignations. Insufficient development opportunities, boredom, ineffective supervision, poor levels of employee involvement and straightforward personality clashes are the most common precipitating factors. Organizations can readily address all of these issues. The main reason that so many fail to do so is the absence of mechanisms for picking up signs of dissatisfaction. If there is no opportunity to voice concerns, employees who are unhappy will inevitably start looking elsewhere.

PULL FACTORS

The opposite side of the coin is the attraction of rival employers. Salary levels are often a factor here, employees leaving in order to improve their living standards. In addition there are broader notions of career development, the wish to move into new areas of work for which there are better opportunities elsewhere, the chance to work with particular people, and more practical questions such as commuting time. For the employer losing people as a result of such factors there are two main lines of attack. First, there is a need to be aware of what other employers are offering and to ensure that as far as possible this is matched – or at least that a broadly comparable package of pay and opportunities is offered. The second requirement involves trying to ensure that employees appreciate what they are currently being given. The emphasis here is on effective communication of any 'unique selling points' and of the extent to which opportunities comparable to those offered elsewhere are given.

Most Common Reasons

Taylor and his colleagues interviewed 200 people who had recently changed employers about why they left their last jobs. They found a mix of factors at work in most cases but concluded that push factors were a great deal more prevalent than pull factors as causes of voluntary resignations. Very few people appear to leave jobs in which they are broadly happy in search of something even better. Instead the picture is overwhelmingly one in which dissatisfied employees seek alternatives because they no longer enjoy working for their current employer.

Interestingly this study found relatively few examples of people leaving for financial reasons. Indeed more of the interviewees took pay cuts in order to move from one job to another than said that a pay rise was their principal reason for switching employers. Other factors played a much bigger role:

1. Dissatisfaction with the conditions of work, especially hours.
2. A perception that they were not being given sufficient career development opportunities
3. A bad relationship with their immediate supervisor.

This third factor was by far the most commonly mentioned in the interviews, lending support to the often stated point that people leave their managers and not their organizations.

COSTING

When deciding what kind of measures to put in place in order to improve staff retention generally or the retention of particular individuals, organizations need to balance the costs involved against those that are incurred as a direct result of voluntary resignations. Although it is difficult to cost turnover accurately, it is possible to reach a fair estimate by taking into account the range of expenses involved in replacing one individual with another. Once a figure has been calculated for a job, it is relatively straightforward to compute the savings to be gained from a given percentage reduction in annual turnover rates.

STAFF RETENTION STRATEGIES

The straightforward answer to the question of how best to retain staff is to provide them with a better deal, in the broadest sense, than they perceive they could get by working for alternative employers. Terms and conditions play a significant role, but other factors are often more important. For example, there is a need to provide jobs which are satisfying, along with career development opportunities, as much autonomy as is practicable and, above all, competent line management. Indeed, at one level, most of the practices of effective human resource management described in this book can play a part in reducing turnover. Organizations which make use of them will enjoy lower rates than competitors who do not.

PAY

There is some debate in the retention literature about the extent to which raising pay levels reduces staff turnover. On the one hand there is evidence to show that, on average, employers who offer the most attractive reward packages have lower attrition rates than those who pay poorl, an assumption which leads many organizations to use pay rates as their prime weapon in retaining staff. On the other, there is questionnaire-based evidence which suggests that pay is a good deal less important than other factors in a decision to quit one's job. The consensus among researchers specialising in retention issues is that pay has a role to play as a satisfier, but that it will not usually have an effect when other factors are pushing an individual towards quitting. Raising pay levels may thus result in greater job satisfaction where people are already happy with their work, but it will not deter unhappy employees from leaving. Sturges and Guest, in their study of leaving decisions in the field of graduate employment, summed up their findings as follows:

As far as they are concerned, while challenging work will compensate for pay, pay will never compensate for having to do boring, unstimulating work. Recent research findings thus appear to confirm the views expressed by Herzberg that pay is a 'hygiene factor' rather than a motivator. This means that it can be a cause of dissatisfaction at work, but not of positive job satisfaction. People may be motivated to leave an employer who is perceived as paying badly, but once they are satisfied with their pay additional increases have little effect.

The other problem with the use of pay increases to retain staff is that it is an approach that is very easily matched by competitors. This is particularly true of 'golden handcuff' arrangements which seek to tie senior staff to an organization fora number of years by paying substantial bonuses at a defined future date. As Cappelli argues, in a buoyant job market, recruiters simply 'unlock the handcuffs' by offering equivalent signing-on bonuses to people they wish to employ.

It is important that employees do not perceive their employers to be treating them inequitably. Provided pay levels are not considerably lower than those paid by an organization's labour market competitors, other factors will usually be more important contributors towards high turnover levels. Where the salaries that are paid are already broadly competitive, little purpose is served by increasing them further. The organization may well make itself more attractive in recruitment terms, but the effect on staff retention will be limited. Moreover, of course, wage costs will increase.

There is potentially more to be gained from enhancing benefits packages, because these are less easily imitated or matched by competitors. Where particular benefits, such as staff discounts, holiday entitlements or private healthcare schemes, are appreciated by staff, they are more likely to have a positive effect on staff turnover than simply paying higher base wages. Potentially the same is true of pension schemes, which are associated with relatively high levels of staff retention. However, the research evidence suggests that except for older employees who have completed many years of service, most pension schemes are not sufficiently valued by staff to cause them to stay in a job with which they are dissatisfied. Arguably, the best way of using benefits to keep a lid on staff turnover is to move towards flexible schemes. An employer which allows individual employees to choose how they make up their own remuneration package will generally be more attractive than one which only offers a 'one size fits all' set of benefits.

MANAGING EXPECTATIONS

For some years research evidence has strongly suggested that employers benefit from ensuring that potential employees gain a 'realistic job preview' before they take up a job offer. The purpose is to make sure that new staff enter an organization with their eyes wide open and do not find that the job fails to meet their expectations. A major cause of job dissatisfaction, and hence of high staff turnover, is the experience of having one's high hopes of new employment dashed by the realisation that it is not going to be as enjoyable or stimulating as anticipated.

Several researchers have drawn attention to the importance of these processes in reducing high turnover during the early months of employment. The need is to strike a balance at the recruitment stage between sending out messages which are entirely positive and sending out those which are realistic. In other words, it is important not to mislead candidates about the nature of the work that they will be doing.

Realistic job previews are most important when candidates, for whatever reason, cannot know a great deal about the job for which they are applying. This may be because of limited past experience or it may because the job is relatively unusual and not based in a type of workplace with which job applicants are familiar. An example quoted by Carroll et al. concerns work in nursing homes, which seems to attract people looking to undertake a caring role but who are unfamiliar with the less attractive hours, working conditions and job duties associated with the care assistant's role. The realistic job preview is highly appropriate in such a situation as a means of avoiding recruiting people who subsequently leave within a few weeks.

The importance of unmet expectations as an explanation for staff turnover is also stressed by Sturges and Guest in their work on the retention of newly recruited graduates. Here the problem is one of employers overselling graduate careers when competing with others to secure the services of the brightest young people:

False impressions are given and a positive spin put on answers to questions so as to deter able applicants from taking up alternative offers. As a result, graduates start work confident in the belief that their days will be filled with interesting work, that they will be treated fairly and objectively in terms of performance assessment, that their career development will be fostered judiciously, and that their working lives will in some way be 'fun' and 'exciting'. That is fine if it really can be guaranteed. Unfortunately such is often not the case, and unsurprisingly it leads to early dissatisfaction and higher turnover rates than are desirable.

A solution, aside from the introduction of more honest recruitment literature, is to provide periods of work experience for students before they graduate. A summer spent working somewhere is the best possible way of finding out exactly what a particular job or workplace is really like. The same argument can be deployed in support of work experience for young people who are about to leave school in order to enter the job market.

INDUCTION

Another process often credited with the reduction of turnover early in the employment relationship is the presence of effective and timely induction. It is very easy to overlook in the rush to get people into key posts quickly and it is often carried out badly, but it is essential if avoidable early turnover is to be kept to a minimum. Gregg and Wadsworth show in their analysis of 870,000 workers starting new jobs in 1992 that as many as 17 per cent had left within three months and 42 per cent within 12 months. No doubt a good number of these departures were due either to poorly managed expectations or to ineffective inductions.

Induction has a number of distinct purposes, all of which are concerned with preparing new employees to work as effectively as possible and as soon as is possible in their new jobs. First, it plays an important part in helping new starters to adjust emotionally to the new workplace. It gives an opportunity to ensure that they understand where things are, who to ask when unsure about what to do and how their role fits into the organization generally. Second, induction provides a forum in which basic information about the organization can be transmitted. This may include material about the organization's purpose, its mission statement and the key issues it faces. More generally a corporate induction provides a suitable occasion to talk about health and safety regulations, fire evacuation procedures and organizational policies concerning matters like the use of telephones for private purposes. Third, induction processes can be used to convey to new starters important cultural messages about what the organization expects and what employees can expect in return. It thus potentially forms an important stage in the establishment of the psychological contract, leaving new employees clear about what they need to do to advance their own prospects in the organization. All these matters will be picked up by new starters anyway in their first months of employment, but incorporating them into a formal induction programme ensures that they are brought up to speed a good deal quicker, and that they are less likely to leave at an early date.

There is no 'right' length for an induction programme. In some jobs it can be accomplished effectively in a few days, for others there is a need for some form of input over a number of weeks. What is important is that individuals are properly introduced both to the organization and to their particular role within it. These introductons are usually best handled by different people. Organizational induction, because it is given to all new starters, is normally handled centrally by the HR department and takes place in a single place over one or two days. Job-based induction takes longer, will be overseen by the individual's own line manager and will usually involve shadowing colleagues. The former largely takes the form of a presentation, while the latter involves the use of a wider variety of training methods.

FAMILY-FRIENDLY HR PRACTICES

Labour Force Survey statistics show that between 5 per cent and 10 per cent of employees leave their jobs for 'family or personal reasons', while Hom and Griffeth quote American research indicating that 33 per cent of women quit jobs to devote more time to their families – a response given by only one per cent of men. To these figures can be added those quoted by Gregg and Wadsworth which show average job tenure among women with children in the India to be over a year shorter than that of women without children and almost two years shorter than that of men. These statistics suggest that one of the more significant reasons for voluntary resignations from jobs is the inability to juggle the demands of a job with those of the family. They indicate that there is a good business case, particularly where staff retention is high on the agenda, for considering ways in which employment can be made more family friendly.

Many employers, however, have decided to go a good deal further down this road than is required by law. The most common example is the provision of more paid maternity leave and the right, where possible, for mothers to return to work on a part-time or job-share basis if they so wish. Crèche provision is common in larger workplaces, while others offer childcare vouchers instead. Career breaks are offered by many public sector employers, allowing people to take a few months off without pay and subsequently to return to a similar job with the same organization. Flexitime systems are also useful to people with families and may thus serve as a retention tool in some cases.

TRAINING AND DEVELOPMENT

There are two widely expressed, but wholly opposed, perspectives on the link between training interventions and employee turnover. On the one hand is the argument that training opportunities enhance commitment to an employer on the part of individual employees, making them less likely to leave voluntarily than they would if no training were offered. The alternative view holds that training makes people more employable and hence more likely to leave in order to develop their careers elsewhere. The view is thus put that money spent on training is money wasted because it ultimately benefits other employers.

Green et al. report research on perceptions of 1,539 employees on different kinds of training. They found that the overall effect is neutral, 19 per cent of employees saying that training was 'more likely to make them actively look for another job' and 18 per cent saying it was less likely to do so. However, they also found the type of training and the source of sponsorship to be a significant variable. Training which is paid for by the employer is a good deal less likely to raise job mobility than that paid for by the employee or the government. Firm-specific training is also shown in the study to be associated with lower turnover than training which leads to the acquisition of transferable skills. The point is made, however, that whatever the form of training an employer can develop a workforce which is both 'capable and committed' by combining training interventions with other forms of retention initiative.

The most expensive types of training intervention involve long-term courses of study such as an MBA, or accountancy qualification. In financing such courses, employers are sending a very clear signal to the employees concerned that their contribution is valued and that they can look forward to substantial career advancement if they opt to stay. The fact that leaving will also mean an end to the funding for the course provides a more direct incentive to remain with the sponsoring employer.

IMPROVING THE QUALITY OF LINE MANAGEMENT

If it is the case that many, if not most, voluntary resignations are explained by dissatisfaction on the part of employees with their supervisors, it follows that the most effective means of reducing staff turnover in organizations is to improve the performance of line managers. Too often, it appears, people are promoted into supervisory positions without adequate experience or training. Organizations seem to assume that their managers are capable supervisors, without recognising that the role is difficult and does not usually come naturally to people. Hence it is common to find managers who are 'quick to critise but slow to praise', who are too tied up in their own work to show an interest in their subordinates and who prefer to impose their own solutions without first taking account of their staff's views. The solution is to take action on various fronts to improve the effectiveness of supervisors:

- Select people for line management roles following an assessment of their supervisory capabilities;
- Ensure that all newly appointed line managers are trained in the art of effective supervision;
- Regularly appraise line managers on their supervisory skills.

This really amounts to little more than common sense, but such approaches are the exception to the rule in most Indian organizations.

Note: Reader can visit Benchmark Electronics company's site www.bench.com for a detailed study connected to this chapter. Benchmark Electronics (Benchmark) manufactures electronics and provides services to original equipment manufacturers (OEMs) of telecommunication equipment. The company also provides to OEMs of computers and related products for business enterprises, medical devices, industrial control equipment, and testing and instrumentation products. It is headquartered in Angleton, Texas and employs 10,522 people.

10

Ending the Contract

In previous chapter we looked at situations in which employees decide to end their contracts of employment by giving their employers notice. Here we focus on circumstances when the contract is brought to an end by the employer through a dismissal of one kind or another, something that over a million employees experience in the India each year. In some cases employees are happy to leave (or at least not unhappy) such as when they are retiring or when they are due to receive a large redundancy payment. More common, however, are situations where the person dismissed is distinctly unhappy about the contract being brought to an end. When someone feels that they have been treated unfairly in terms of the reason for, or the manner of, their dismissal they can take their case to an employment tribunal. In practice, between five per cent and ten per cent of all dismissed workers who qualify do bring such claims. If someone wins their case they may ask to be reinstated, but will usually settle for a compensation payment. The size of such awards is not generally substantial (around Rs.3,000 on average), but occasionally people are awarded larger sums. Whatever the final outcome there are often additional legal costs for the employer to bear, not to mention the loss of a great deal of management time. An organization's reputation as a good employer can also be damaged by adverse publicity arising from such cases. Employers generally take careful account of the requirements of the law when dismissing employees. The alternative is to run the risk of being summoned to an employment tribunal and possibly losing the case. To a great extent the law therefore effectively determines practice in the field of dismissal.

In the India there are three forms of dismissal claim that can be brought to a tribunal. Rights associated with the law of wrongful dismissal are the longest established. A person who claims wrongful dismissal complains that the way that they were dismissed breached the terms of their contract of employment. Constructive dismissal occurs when someone feels forced to resign as a direct result of their employer's actions. In this area the law aims to deter employers from seeking to avoid dismissing people by pushing them into resignation. The third category, unfair dismissal, is by far the most common. It is best defined as a dismissal which falls short of the expectations of the law.

UNFAIR DISMISSAL

The law of unfair dismissal dates from 1971, since when it has been amended a number of times. Although new additions and the outcomes of leading cases have made it more complex than it was originally, the basic principles have stood the test of time and remain in place. Their aim was to reduce the number of claims being brought before employment tribunals by providing strong incentives for employers and employees to exhaust internal disciplinary and grievance procedures first. These regulations also adjusted the position of the law in respect of dismissals that are for justified reasons but which are carried out using an incomplete or deficient procedure.

In most circumstances the right to bring a claim of unfair dismissal applies to employees who have completed a year's continuous service with their employer on the date their contract was terminated. This allows the employer a period of 12 months to assess whether or not an individual employee is suitable before the freedom to dismiss is restricted. For a number of years until 1999 the time limit was two years. In reducing the period, the government brought an additional 2.8 million more people within the scope of unfair dismissal law.

Restrictions on qualification apply except where the reason for the dismissal is one of those listed below which are classed as 'automatically unfair' or 'inadmissible'. A further requirement is that the claim form is lodged at the tribunal office before three months have elapsed from the date of dismissal. Unless there are circumstances justifying the failure to submit a claim before the deadline, applications received after three months are ruled out of time.

When faced with a claim of unfair dismissal, and where it is not disputed that a dismissal took place, an employment tribunal asks two separate questions:

1. Was the reason for the dismissal one which is classed by the law as legitimate?
2. Did the employer act reasonably in carrying out the dismissal?

Where the answer to the first question is 'no', there is no need to ask the second because the dismissed employee will already have won his or her case. Interestingly the burden of proof shifts as the tribunal moves from considering the first to the second question. It is for the employer to satisfy the tribunal that it dismissed the employee for a legitimate reason. The burden of proof then becomes neutral when the question of reasonableness is addressed.

AUTOMATICALLY UNFAIR REASONS

Certain reasons for dismissal are declared in law to be inadmissable or automatically unfair. Where the tribunal finds that one of these was the principal reason for the dismissal, they find in favour of the claimant (i.e. the ex-employee) whatever the circumstances of the case. In practice, therefore, there is no defence that an employer can make to explain its actions that will be acceptable to the tribunal. Some of these relate to other areas of employment law such as non-discrimination, working time and the minimum wage. The list of automatically unfair reasons for dismissal has grown steadily in recent years as new employment rights have come on to the statute book; in 2004 it was as follows:

- On grounds of sex, marital status or gender reassignment;
- On racial grounds;
- On grounds of disability (unless objectively justified);
- On grounds of sexual orientation;
- On grounds of religion or belief;
- On grounds of having committed a criminal offence where the conviction is spent;
- On grounds of pregnancy or maternity;
- On grounds of being a part-time worker;
- For exercising the right to parental leave or time off for dependants;
- For carrying out duties as a safety representative;
- For carrying out duties as a pension fund trustee;

- For refusing to work on a Sunday (retail workers only);
- For taking part, or proposing to take part, in lawful trade union activity;
- For joining or refusing to join a trade union;
- For taking part in official industrial action (i.e. organized and approved by a trade union executive) during the first eight weeks that the action takes place;
- For refusing to work in unsafe conditions;
- For asserting a statutory right.

This last provision relates to the various other employment protection rights set out in statute. It is designed to ensure that no one is victimised by being dismissed (unfairly or constructively) simply because they sought to exercise their rights under employment law.

A further situation which is classed as automatically unfair is a dismissal which occurs directly as a result of a business changing hands (known as a transfer of undertakings case). Dismissals for this reason will be judged as unfair by employment tribunals unless it can be shown that the dismissals were for economic, technical or organizational reasons. Unlike the other automatically unfair dismissals, transfer of undertakings cases can only be brought by ex-employees who have completed a year's continuous service and are under the 'normal' age of retirement at the time of their dismissal.

POTENTIALLY FAIR REASONS

From an employer's perspective it is important to be able to satisfy the tribunal that the true reason for the dismissal was one of those reasons classed as potentially fair in unfair dismissal law. Only once this has been achieved can the second question (the issue of reasonableness) be addressed. The potentially fair grounds for dismissal are as follows:

- *Lack of capability or qualifications*: if an employee lacks the skill, aptitude or physical health to carry out the job, then there is a potentially fair ground for dismissal.
- *Misconduct*: this category covers the range of behaviours that we examine in considering the grievance and discipline processes: disobedience, absence, insubordination and criminal acts. It can also include taking industrial action.
- *Redundancy*: where an employee's job ceases to exist, it is

potentially fair to dismiss the employee for redundancy.

- *Statutory bar*: when employees cannot continue to discharge their duties without breaking the law, they can be fairly dismissed. Most cases of this kind follow disqualification of drivers following convictions for speeding, drunk or dangerous driving. Other common cases involve foreign nationals whose work permits have been terminated.
- Some other substantial reason: this most intangible category is introduced in order to cater for genuinely fair dismissals for reasons so diverse that they could not realistically be listed. Examples have been security of commercial information (where an employee's husband set up a rival company) or employee refusal to accept altered working conditions.
- Dismissals arising from official industrial action after eight weeks have passed.

DETERMINING REASONABLENESS

Having decided that potentially fair grounds for the dismissal exist, the tribunal then proceeds to consider whether the dismissal is fair in the circumstances. There are two questions: was the decision reasonable in the circumstances, and was the dismissal carried out in line with the procedure? When considering the first, tribunal members pay particular attention to consistency of treatment, seeking to satisfy themselves that the dismissed employee has not been treated more severely than others have been in similar circumstances. They are also required to have regard to the size and resources of the employer concerned. Higher standards are thus expected of a large PLC with a well-staffed HR department than of a small owner-managed business employing a handful of people. The former, for example, might be expected to give two or three warnings and additional training before dismissing someone on grounds of incapability. One simple warning might suffice in a small business which relied heavily on an acceptable level of performance from the individual concerned.

The significance attached to procedure has varied over the years. Until 1987 employers were able to argue successfully that although the procedure used was deficient in some respects, the outcome was not affected. Henceforth, tribunals were obliged to find dismissals unfair where the employer had not completed a proper procedure before making the final decision to dismiss. Typical procedural defects were identified as follows by Earnshaw:

- No chance given to the applicants to give an explanation;
- Dismissal without any prior disciplinary hearing;
- No procedure in cases involving senior staff;
- The procedure used did not comply with the respondent's own rules;
- Unwillingness to have a procedure because of disliking formality; and
- No chance for the applicant to rectify their shortcomings.

LACK OF CAPABILITY OR QUALIFICATIONS

The first aspect of capability relates to skill or aptitude. Although employers have the right and opportunity to test an applicant's suitability for a particular post before that individual is engaged, or before promotion, the law recognises that mistakes may be made so that dismissal can be an appropriate remedy for the error, if the unsuitability is gross and beyond redemption. In order for such a dismissal to be fair and reasonable at least one warning has to be given and a reasonable opportunity to improve before the dismissal is implemented.

Where an employee is going through a period of probation at the time of termination, the following are appropriate check questions:

1. Has the employer shown that reasonable steps were taken to maintain the appraisal of the probationer through the period of probation?
2. Was there guidance by advice or warning when it would have been useful or fair to provide it?
3. Did an appropriate person make an honest effort to determine whether the probationer came up to the required standard, after reviewing the appraisals made by supervisors and other facts recorded about the probationer?

The employer will always need to demonstrate the employee's unsuitability to the satisfaction of the tribunal by producing evidence of that unsuitability. This evidence must not be undermined by, for instance, giving the employee a glowing testimonial at the time of dismissal or by the presence of positive appraisal reports on the individual's personal file. Lack of skill or aptitude is a fair ground when the lack can be demonstrated and where the employer has not contributed to it by, for instance, ignoring it for a long period. Normally there must be the chance to state a case and/ or improve before the dismissal will be procedurally fair. Redeployment to a more suitable job is also an option employers are expected to consider before taking the decision to dismiss.

The second aspect of capability is qualifications: the degree, diploma or other paper qualification needed to qualify the individual to do the work for which they are employed. The simple cases are those of misrepresentation, where an employee claims qualifications he or she does not have. More difficult are the situations where the employee cannot acquire the necessary qualifications.

The third aspect of employee capability is health. It is potentially fair to dismiss someone on the grounds of ill health which renders the employee incapable of discharging the contract of employment. Even the most distressing dismissal can be legally admissible, provided that it is not too hasty and that there is consideration of alternative employment. Employers are expected, however, to take account of any medical advice available to them before dismissing someone on the grounds of ill health. Companies with occupational health services are well placed to obtain detailed medical reports to help in such judgements but the decision to terminate someone's employment is ultimately for the manager to take and, if necessary, to justify at a tribunal. Medical evidence will be sought and has to be carefully considered but dismissal remains an employer's decision, not a medical decision.

Normally, absences through sickness have to be frequent or prolonged in order for dismissal on the grounds of such absence to be judged fair, although absence which seriously interferes with the running of a business may be judged fair even if it is neither frequent nor prolonged. In all cases the employee must be consulted before being dismissed.

Following are the questions that have to be asked to determine the potential fairness of dismissing someone after long-term sickness:

- How long has the employment lasted;
- How long had it been expected the employment would continue;
- What is the nature of the job;
- What was the nature, effect and length of the illness;
- What is the need of the employer for the work to be done, and to engage a replacement to do it;

- If the employer takes no action, will he incur obligations in respect of redundancy payments or compensation for unfair dismissal;
- Are wages continuing to be paid;
- Why has the employer dismissed (or failed to do so); and
- In all the circumstances, could a reasonable employer have been expected to wait any longer?

A different situation is where an employee is frequently absent for short spells. Here too it is potentially reasonable to dismiss, but only after proper consideration of the illnesses and after warning the employee of the consequences if their attendance record does not improve. As is made clear by Duggan each case has to be decided on its own merits. Medical evidence must be sought and a judgement reached about how likely it is that high levels of absence will continue in the future. The fact that an employee is wholly fit at the time of his or her dismissal does not mean that it is necessarily unfair. What matters is the overall attendance record and its impact on the organization.

MISCONDUCT

The law expects employers to make a distinction between two classes of misconduct when dismissing employees or considering doing so.

- *Gross misconduct*. This occurs when an employee commits an offence which is sufficiently serious to justify summary dismissal. To qualify, the employee must have acted in such a way as to have breached either an express term of their contract or one of the common law duties owed by an employee to an employer.
- *Ordinary misconduct*. This involves lesser transgressions, such as minor breaches of rules and relatively insignificant acts of disobedience, insubordination, lateness, forgetfulness or rudeness. In such cases the employer is deemed by the courts to be acting unreasonably if it dismisses as a result of a first offence. The dismissal would only be fair if, having been formally warned at least once, the employee failed to improve his/her conduct.

Employers have a wide degree of discretion when it comes to deciding what exactly does and does not constitute gross misconduct, and this will vary from workplace to workplace. For example, a distinction can be made between smoking in an office where there is a no-smoking policy (ordinary misconduct) and smoking on the factory floor near to combustible materials (gross misconduct). While much depends on the circumstances, the tribunals also look carefully at an employer's established policies on matters of conduct:

Where the disciplinary rules spell out clearly the type of conduct that will warrant dismissal then a dismissal for this reason may be fair. Conversely, if the rules are silent or ambiguous as to whether particular conduct warrants dismissal, a dismissal for a first offence may be unfair.

It is important, therefore, for employers to set out in writing what standards of conduct they expect, to make clear what will be regarded as 'sackable misconduct', and to ensure that everyone is aware of these rules.

The second key principle in misconduct cases concerns procedure. Whether the individual is dismissed summarily for gross misconduct or after a number of warnings for ordinary misconduct, the tribunals look to see if a reasonable procedure has been used. However, these regulations do permit employers to dispense with the need for a disciplinary hearing in 'extreme' cases of gross misconduct. Here it is necessary to note the main questions that an employment tribunal asks when faced with such cases:

1. Was the accusation thoroughly, promptly and properly investigated by managers before the decision was made to dismiss or issue a formal warning?
2. Was a formal hearing held at which the accused employee was given the opportunity to state their case and challenge evidence brought forward by managers?
3. Was the employee concerned permitted to be accompanied at the hearing by a colleague or trade union representative?
4. Was the employee treated consistently when compared with other employees who had committed similar acts of misconduct in the past?

Only if the answers to all these questions is 'yes' will a tribunal find a dismissal fair. They do not, however, expect employers to adhere to very high standards of evidence gathering such as those employed by the police in criminal investigations. Here, as throughout employment law, the requirement is for the employer to act reasonably in all the circumstances, conforming to the principles of natural justice and doing what it thought to be right at the time, given the available facts.

Conversely, if an employee is found guilty by court proceedings, this does not automatically justify fair dismissal; it must still be procedurally fair and reasonable. A theft committed off duty and away from the workforce is not necessarily grounds for dismissal; it all depends on the nature of the work carried out by the employee concerned. For example, it might well be reasonable to dismiss members of staff with responsibility for cash if they commit an offence of dishonesty while off duty.

On the other hand, evidence that would not be sufficient to bring a prosecution may be sufficient to sustain a fair dismissal. Clocking-in offences will normally merit dismissal. Convictions for other offences like drug handling or indecency will only justify dismissal if the nature of the offence will have some bearing on the work done by the employee. For someone like an instructor of apprentices it might justify summary dismissal, but in other types of employment it would be unfair, just as it would be unfair to dismiss an employee for a driving offence when there was no need for driving in the course of normal duties and there were other means of transport for getting to work.

REDUNDANCY

Dismissal for redundancy is protected by compensation for unfair redundancy, compensation for genuine redundancy and the right to consultation before the redundancy takes place:

An employee who is dismissed shall be taken to be dismissed by reason of redundancy if the dismissal is attributable wholly or mainly to:

- The fact that his employer has ceased, or intends to cease, to carry on the business for the purposes of which the employee was employed by him, or has ceased, or intends to cease, to carry on that business in the place where the employee was so employed, or
- The fact that the requirements of that business for employees to carry out work of a particular kind, or for employees to carry out work of a particular kind in the place where he was so employed, have ceased or are expected to cease or diminish.

Apart from certain specialised groups of employees, anyone who has been continuously employed for two years or more is guaranteed a compensation payment from an employer, if dismissed for redundancy.

The compensation is currently assessed on a sliding scale relating to length of service, age and rate of pay per week. If the employer wishes to escape the obligation to compensate, then it is necessary to show that the reason for dismissal was something other than redundancy.

.Although the legal rights relating to redundancy have not altered for 35 years, there have been persistent problems of interpretation, different courts reaching different decisions when faced with similar sets of circumstances.

The employer has to consult with the individual employee before dismissal takes place, but there is also a separate legal obligation to consult with recognised trade unions or some other body of employee representatives where no union is recognised. If it is proposed to make more than 100 employees redundant within a three-month period, then 90 days' advance notice must be given. Having done this, the employer has a legal duty to consult on the redundancies. There is no obligation to negotiate with employees, merely to explain, listen to comments and reply with reasons. Employees also have the right to reasonable time off with pay during their redundancy notice so that they can seek other work.

One of the most difficult aspects of redundancy for the employer is the selection of who should go. The traditional approach provides that people should leave on a last-in-first-out basis, as this provides a rough-and-ready justice with which it is difficult to argue. In recent years, however, an increasing number of employers are using a mix of other criteria, including skill, competence and attendance record. A third approach involves drawing up a new post-redundancy organization structure and inviting everyone to apply for the jobs that will remain. In principle all are acceptable as far as the law is concerned provided they are carried out objectively and consistently.

Increasingly, employers are trying to avoid enforced redundancy by a range of strategies, such as not replacing people who leave, early retirement and voluntary redundancy. The large scale of redundancies in recent years has produced a variety of managerial initiatives to mitigate the effects. One of the most constructive has been a redundancy counselling or outplacement service. Sometimes this is administered by the HR department, but many organizations use external services. Contrary to some popular perception there is no legal requirement to offer such services or to ask for volunteers before carrying through a programme of compulsory redundancies.

SOME OTHER SUBSTANTIAL REASON

As the law of unfair dismissal has evolved since 1971 the most controversial area has been the category of potentially fair dismissals known as 'some other substantial reason'. Many commentators see this as a catch-all or dustbin category which enables employers to dismiss virtually anyone provided a satisfactory business case can be made. All manner of cases have been successfully defended under this heading including the following: dismissals resulting from personality clashes, pressure to dismiss from subordinates or customers, disclosure of damaging information, the dismissal of a man whose wife worked for a rival firm, and the dismissal of a landlord's wife following her husband's dismissal on grounds of capability.

The majority of cases brought under this heading, however, result from business reorganizations where there is no redundancy. These often occur when the employer seeks to alter terms and conditions of employment and cannot secure the employee's agreement. Such circumstances can result in the dismissal of the employee together with an offer of re-employment on new contractual terms. Such dismissals are judged fair provided a sound business reason exists to justify the changes envisaged. It will usually be necessary to consult prior to the reorganization but the tribunal will not base its judgment on whether the employee acted reasonably in refusing new terms and conditions.

WRITTEN STATEMENT OF REASONS

The Employment Rights Act gives employees the right to obtain from their employer a written statement of the reasons for their dismissal, if they are dismissed after completing a year's continuous service. If asked, the employer must provide the statement within 14 days. If it is not provided, the employee can complain to an employment tribunal that the statement has been refused and the tribunal will award the employee two weeks' pay if they find the complaint justified. The same right applies where a fixed-term contract is not renewed after having expired. The employee can also complain, and receive the same award, if the employer's reasons are untrue or inadequate, provided that the tribunal agrees.

Such an award is in addition to anything the tribunal may decide about the unfairness of the dismissal, if the employee complains about that. The main purpose of this provision is to enable the employee to test whether there is a reasonable case for an unfair dismissal complaint or not. Although the statement is admissible as evidence in tribunal proceedings, the tribunal will not necessarily be bound by what the statement contains. If the tribunal members were to decide that the reasons for dismissal were other than stated, then the management case would be jeopardised.

CONSTRUCTIVE DISMISSAL

When the behaviour of the management causes the employee to resign, the ex-employee may still be able to claim dismissal on the grounds that the behaviour of the employer constituted a repudiation of the contract, leaving the employee with no alternative but to resign. The employee may then be able to claim that the dismissal was unfair. It is not sufficient for the employer simply to be awkward or whimsical; the employer's conduct must amount to a significant breach, going to the root of the contract, such as physical assault, demotion, reduction in pay, change in location of work or significant change in duties. The breach must, however, be significant, so that a slight lateness in paying wages would not involve a breach, neither would a temporary change in place of work.

Some of the more interesting constructive dismissal cases concern claims that implied terms of contract have been breached, such as the employer's duty to maintain safe systems of working or mutual trust and confidence. Constructive dismissal, like unfair dismissal, dates from 1971. It too only applies to employees who have completed a year's continuous service. The cases are harder for employees to win and easier for employers to defend because of the need to establish that a dismissal has taken place, before issues of reasonableness in the circumstances are addressed. The burden of proof is on the employee to show that they were forced into resigning as a result of a repudiatory breach on the part of the employer.

COMPENSATION FOR DISMISSAL

Having found in favour of the applicant in cases of unfair or constructive dismissal, the tribunal can make two types of decision: either they can order that the ex-employee be re-employed or they can award some financial compensation from the ex-employer for the loss that the employee has suffered. Originally it was intended that re-employment should be the main remedy, although this was not previously available under earlier legislation. In practice, however, the vast majority of ex-employees (over 95 per cent) want compensation.

Tribunals will not order re-employment unless the dismissed employee wants it, and tribunals can choose between reinstatement or re-engagement. In reinstatement the old job is given back to the employee under the same terms and conditions, plus any increments, etc., to which the individual would have become entitled had the dismissal not occurred, plus any arrears of payment that would have been received. The situation is just as it would have been, including all rights deriving from length of service, if the dismissal had not taken place. The alternative of re-engagement will be that the employee is employed afresh in a job comparable to the last one (usually in a different department), but without continuity of employment. The decision as to which of the two to order will depend on assessment of the practicability of the alternatives, the wishes of the unfairly dismissed employee and the natural justice of the award taking account of the ex-employee's behaviour.

Tribunals currently calculate the level of compensation under a series of headings. First is the basic award which is based on the employee's age and length of service. It is calculated in the same way as statutory redundancy payments, and like them will have to be reviewed to ensure that it complies with age discrimination law when it is introduced:

- Half a week's pay for every year of service below the age of 22;
- One week's pay for every year of service between the ages of 22 and 41;
- One and a half weeks' pay for every year of service over the age of 41.

The basic award is limited, however, because tribunals can only take into account a maximum of 20 years' service when calculating the figure to be awarded. A maximum weekly salary figure is also imposed by the government. This was Rs. 75. The maximum basic award that can be ordered is therefore Rs.8,100. In many cases, of course, where the employee has only a few years' service the figure will be far lower. In addition a tribunal can also order compensation under the following headings:

- Compensatory awards take account of loss of earnings, pension rights, future earnings loss, etc.
- Additional awards are used in cases of sex and race discrimination and also when an employer fails to comply with an order of reinstatement or re-engagement. In the former case the maximum award is 52 weeks' pay, in the latter 26 weeks' pay.

- Special awards are made when unfair dismissal relates to trade union activity or membership. They can also be used when the dismissal was for health and safety reasons.

A tribunal can reduce the total level of compensation if it judges the individual concerned to have contributed to his or her own dismissal. For example, a dismissal on grounds of poor work performance may be found unfair because no procedure was followed and consequently no warnings given. This does not automatically entitle the ex-employee concerned to compensation based on the above formulae. If the tribunal judges them to have been 60 per cent responsible for their own dismissal the compensation will be reduced by 60 per cent. Reductions are also made if an ex-employee is judged not to have taken reasonable steps to mitigate his or her loss.

WRONGFUL DISMISSAL

In addition to the body of legislation defining unfair and constructive dismissal there is a long-standing common law right to damages for an employee who has been dismissed wrongfully.

Cases of wrongful dismissal are taken to employment tribunals where the claim is for less than Rs.25,000; otherwise they are taken to the county court. These cases are concerned solely with alleged breaches of contract. Employees can thus only bring cases of wrongful dismissal against their employers when they believe their dismissal to have been unlawful according to the terms of their contract of employment.

Wrongful dismissal can, therefore, be used when the employer has not given proper notice or if the dismissal is in breach of any clause or agreement incorporated into the contract. This remains a form of remedy that very few people use, but it could be useful to employees who do not have sufficient length of service to claim unfair dismissal and whose contracts include the right to a full disciplinary procedure. There may also be cases where a very highly paid employee might get higher damages in an ordinary court than the maximum that the tribunal can award.

RETIREMENT

The final mode of contract termination is retirement, and this has the advantage for the employer that there is usually plenty of notice, so that succession arrangements can be planned smoothly. It is now rare for people to retire abruptly after working at high pressure to the very end. Some sort of phased withdrawal is much preferred, so that the retiree adjusts gradually to the new state of being out of regular employment and with a lower level of income, while the employing organization is able to prepare a successor to take office.

Another advantage of this arrangement is that there may be 'a life after death', with the retiree continuing to work part time after retirement, or coming back to help out at peak periods or at holiday times. Many organizations go to great lengths to keep in touch with their retired personnel, often arranging Christmas parties, excursions and other events, with people returning year after year.

Early retirement has become a widespread method of slimming payrolls and making opportunities both for some people to retire early and for others to take their place. The nature of the pension arrangements are critical to early retirement strategies, as early retirements are ideally voluntary and the majority of people will accept, or volunteer for, early retirement if the financial terms are acceptable. It is not, of course, possible to draw state retirement pension until the official retirement ages of 65 for men and 60 for women, but many people will accept an occupational pension and a lump sum in their 50s if they see the possibility of a new lease of life to pursue other interests or to start their own business. According to Disney another reason is a substantial increase in the numbers who are able to claim incapacity benefit on a long-term basis. Between a fifth and a quarter of men in these age groups now claim the benefit. As a result, since the mid-1970s the proportion of men aged between 55 and 59 in the labour force has fallen from 90 per cent to 75 per cent. For those aged 60–65 participation rates have fallen from 80 per cent to under 50 per cent. By contrast, the proportion of women in these age groups undertaking paid work has risen during the same period. As a result of this trend, and a demographic context in which the population is ageing and living much longer, the government is considering proposals to push the date at which people can claim a state pension back to 70.

NOTICE

An employee qualifies for notice of dismissal on completion of four weeks of employment with an employer. At that time the employee is entitled to receive one week's notice. This remains constant until the employee has completed two years' service, after which it increases to two weeks' notice, thereafter increasing on the basis of one week's notice per additional year of service up to a maximum of 12 weeks for 12 years' unbroken service with that employer. These are minimum statutory periods. If the employer includes longer periods of notice in the contract, which is quite common with senior employees, then they are bound by the longer period.

The employee is required to give one week's notice after completing four weeks' service and this period does not increase as a statutory obligation. If an employee accepts a contract in which the period of notice to be given is longer, then that is binding, but the employer may have problems of enforcement if an employee is not willing to continue in employment for the longer period.

Neither party can withdraw notice unilaterally. The withdrawal will be effective only if the other party agrees. Therefore, if an employer gives notice to an employee and wishes later to withdraw it, this can be done only if the employee agrees to the contract of employment remaining in existence. Equally, employees cannot change their minds about resigning unless the employer agrees. Notice exists when a date has been specified. The statement 'We're going to wind up the business, so you will have to find another job' is not notice: it is a warning of intention.

Note: For a case study visit company's site of BorgWarner Inc. BorgWarner is a product leader in highly engineered components and systems for vehicle powertrain applications worldwide. The company primarily operates in the US and Europe. It is headquartered in Auburn Hills, Michigan and employs about 13,800 people. www.borgwarner.com

11

Strategic Aspects of Performance

In our opening chapters we described the shift in emphasis away from the contract of employment towards the contract for performance. Even before the development of Taylor's scientific management methods a century ago, getting the most out of the workforce has always been a predominant management preoccupation, and the management literature is full of studies on the topic. Psychologists have studied motivation and leadership, ergonomists have dismantled and reconstructed every aspect of the physical environment in which people work, industrial relations specialists have pondered power relationships and reward, while sociologists discussed the design of organizations and their social structure, and operations experts have looked for ways to engineer process improvements.

A CHANGE IN PERSPECTIVE: FROM EMPLOYMENT TO PERFORMANCE

The traditional HRM approach to enhancing individual performance has centred on the assessment of past performance and the allocation of reward – rewards were provided in exchange for performance. This has been powerfully influenced by the industrial relations history, as trade unions have developed the process of collective bargaining and negotiation.

The prime purpose of trade unions has always been to improve the terms and working conditions of their members; the union has only one thing to offer in exchange for improvements in terms and conditions, that is, some opportunity for improvement in productivity or performance. With the steadily increasing influence of unions in most industrial countries through most of the twentieth century, it was inevitable that performance improvement was something of direct interest only to management.

Performance therefore became stereotyped as something of no intrinsic interest to the person doing the work.

The influence of trade unions has altered and collective bargaining does not dominate the management agenda as much as it used to. This is the most significant feature in the general change in attitudes about what we go to work for. Managements are gradually waking up to this fact and realising that there is now scope for integration in a way that was previously unrealistic. Not only is it possible to say, 'Performance is rewarded', one can now begin to say, 'Performance is a reward.' The long-standing motivational ideas of job enlargement, job enrichment, and so forth, become more cogent when those at work are able to look for the satisfaction of their needs not only in the job, but also in their performance at the job.

Although it may seem like playing with words, this subtle shift of emphasis is fundamental to understanding the strategic approach to performance.

INFLUENCES ON OUR UNDERSTANDING OF PERFORMANCE

THE JAPANESE INFLUENCE

In the 1980s the success of Japanese companies and the decline of Western organizations encouraged an exploration and adoption of Japanese management ideas and practices in order to improve performance. Thurley described the objectives of personnel policies in Japan as performance, motivation, flexibility and mobility. Delbridge and Turnbull described type 'J' organizations (based on Japanese thinking) as characterised by commitment, effort and company loyalty. A key theme in Japanese thinking appears to be people development and continuous improvement, or 'kaizen'.

Much of this thinking and the specific management techniques used in Japan, such as JIT (just in time), have been adopted into UK organizations, often in an uncritical way and without due regard for the cultural differences between the two nations. It is only where the initiatives are developed and modified for their location that they appear to succeed.

THE AMERICAN LITERATURE

Key writers from the American 'excellence' school, Peters and Waterman, identified eight characteristics that they found to be associated with excellent companies – all American. These companies were chosen as excellent on the basis of their innovativeness and on a set of financial indicators, compared on an industry-wide basis. The characteristics they identified were:

- *A bias for action* – rather than an emphasis on bureaucracy or analysis;
- *Close to the customer* – concern for customer wishes;
- *Autonomy and entrepreneurship* – the company is split into small operational units where innovation and initiative are encouraged;
- *Productivity through people* – employees are seen as the key resource, and the value of the employees' contribution is reinforced;
- *Hands on, value driven* – strong corporate culture promoted from the top;
- *Stick to the knitting* – pursuing the core business rather than becoming conglomerates;
- *Simple form, lean staff* – simple organization structure and small HQ staffing;
- *Simultaneous loose and tight properties* – company values strongly emphasised, but within these considerable freedom and errors tolerated.

Peters and Waterman identified a shift from the importance of strategy and structural factors to style, systems, staff and skills (from the hard 's's to the soft 's's). In a follow-on book Peters and Austin identify four key factors related to excellence as concern for customers, innovation, attention to people and leadership.

However, there are problems with the research methodology used; for example, no comparison was made with companies not considered to be excellent. We do not, therefore, know whether these principles were applied to a greater extent in excellent organizations. In addition, a number of the companies quoted have experienced severe problems since the research was carried out, and there remains the problem of the extent to which we can apply the results to Indian organizations.

Whatever the reservations, the influence of this work on strategic thinking about performance remains profound. Even the use of the term 'excellence' means that there is a change of emphasis away from deadpan, objective terms such as profitability, effectiveness, value added and competitive advantage towards an idea that may trigger a feeling of enthusiasm and achievement. 'Try your best' becomes 'Go for it'.

More recently there has been considerable quantitative research in the USA that aims to identify HR practices which lead to high organizational performance, for example Huselid and Pfeffer. The HR practices identified are termed 'high performance work practices' and have encouraged similar investigations in the India to determine 'high commitment work practices'.

HRM AND THE STRATEGY LITERATURE

The HRM strategy literature provides different ways to understand the contribution of HR policies and practices to organizational performance. There are three distinct approaches to HR strategy can be identified. The universalist or best practice approach presupposes that certain HR policies and practices will always result in high performance, and the question is to identify exactly what these are. The contingency or fit approach suggests that different HR policies and practices will be needed to produce high performance in different firms depending on their business strategy and environment. Finally the resource-based view of the firm suggests that neither of these approaches is sufficient, but that every organization and its employees should be considered as unique and that the set of HR policies and practices that will result in high performance will also be unique to that firm. From this perspective no formula can be applied, and the way that people processes contribute to organizational performance can only be understood within the context of the particular firm. These three perspectives have resulted in different investigational approaches to understanding the impact of people management on organizational performance, as will become clear in the following section.

DO PEOPLE-MANAGEMENT PROCESSES CONTRIBUTE TO HIGH PERFORMANCE?

The investigations to date have had a dual purpose, the first being to seek to establish a link between people-management practices and organizational performance. In other words, does the way that people are managed affect the bottom line? The second one follows logically from this, and is: If the answer to the first question is yes, then which particular policies and practices result in high performance? Both these questions are usually investigated in parallel. A variety of different definitions of performance have been used in these studies. These range from bottom line financial performance (profitability), through productivity measures, to measurement of outcomes such as wastage, quality and labour turnover (which are sometimes referred to as internal performance outcomes). Sometimes the respondent's view of performance is used, on the basis that bottom line figures can be influenced by management accounting procedures. The studies have generally used large datasets and complex statistical analysis to determine relationships.

Some researchers argue that the performance effects of HR policies and practices are multiplicative rather than additive, and this is often termed the 'bundles' approach, and this highlights an emphasis on internal rather than external fit. In other words, a particular set of mutually reinforcing practices is likely to have more impact on performance than applying one or just some of these in isolation. Pfeffer, for example, identifies seven critical people-management policies: emphasising employment security; recruiting the 'right' people; extensive use of self-managed teams and decentralisation; high wages solidly linked to organizational performance; high spending on training; reducing status differentials; and sharing information; and he suggests that these policies will benefit every organization.

This avenue of work has a very optimistic flavour, suggesting that not only are people-management practices related to high organizational performance, but that we can identify the innovative and sophisticated practices that will work best in combination. On a practical level there are problems because different researchers identify different practices or 'bundles' associated with high performance.

There have been many criticisms of this approach, partly based on the methods used – which involve, for example, the view of a single respondent as to which practices are in place, with no account taken of how the practices are implemented. A further confusion is that some studies are at establishment level, some at corporate level, some are sector based and some are cross-sector. Each of these approaches has inbuilt problems and creates extreme difficulties for any meta-analysis of the studies so far. A further problem is causality. It could be that profitable firms use best practice people-management methods, because they can afford to since they are profitable, rather than that such methods lead to profitability. A further issue concerns the conflict between different aspects of the bundle. Such contradictions are, for example, between individualism and teamwork and between a strong culture and adaptability. Lastly, this approach ignores the business strategy of the organization.

The work we have described so far comes from a universalist/best practice perspective and an alternative way forward is to use the contingency or fit point of view, asking the question, 'Which people-management policies create high performance in which different organizational circumstances?' This approach does bring the integration with business strategy to the fore, and draws attention to sectoral differences; for example Guest has suggested that 'high performance work practices' may be effective in producing high performance in manufacturing rather than services. However, it fails to provide a more useful way forward. Attempting to model all the different factors that influence the appropriate set of HR policies and practices that lead to high performance is an extremely complex, if not impossible, task. In addition to this Purcell et al. argue that the speed of change poses a real problem for the fit approach.

In summary, the extent to which all the statistical work that has been done proves the relationship between people-management practices and organizational performance continues to be hotly contested. Reviewing the academic literature Richardson and Thompson come to the conclusion that the evidence indicates a positive relationship between innovative and sophisticated people-management practices and better business performance. Guest et al., however, recognise that although the statistical work so far provides some associations between people management and organizational performance there is a lack of convincing evidence. Guest, Hall and particularly Purcell all provide detailed expositions of the problems with the above approaches.

Purcell suggests that a more useful approach is to focus on the resource-based view of the firm, which is the third perspective on HR strategy. From this perspective each organization is a unique and complex whole, so we need to look beyond lists of HR policies and practices to explain organizational performance. We also need to consider long-term performance capability and not just short-term performance improvements. From this perspective Paauwe and Richardson argue that the move to longitudinal studies and case study work is useful, and suggest that organizational context and institutional arrangements need greater attention; Becker and Gerhart suggest that it is more likely to be the architecture of the system, not just a group of HR practices, that results in high performance, and Purcell suggests that it is how practices are implemented and change is managed that makes the difference. Hutchinson et al. term this 'idiosyncratic fit'. They collected data on 11 HR policy/

practice areas identified from previous research as being linked to high organizational performance. In testing the link between people management and performance this study differs from others in that the measures taken were ones that were the most meaningful to each organization.

Also the organizations were each visited twice over a two-and-a-half-year period so comparisons could be made over time. Their results are not clear-cut, but a major conclusion is that it is the way policies are implemented and the role of line mangers which are critical. They also acknowledge that it is difficult to disentangle the performance impact of HR policies from the performance impact of changing environmental circumstances and other changes such as technology. They do argue, however, that those organizations with a 'big idea', which expresses what the organization stands for and what it is trying to achieve, were more able to sustain their performance over the longer term. For example the big idea in Jaguar is quality and in Nationwide it is mutuality. They also found that such big ideas have five characteristics in high-performing organizations:

- *Embedded* – in policies and practices
- *Connected* – connects relationships with customers, values, culture and the way people are managed
- *Enduring* – stable, longlasting values which survive even in difficult times
- *Collective* – acts as corporate glue
- *Measured and managed* – often through the use of balanced scorecard type approaches

HOW DO HR POLICIES AND PRACTICES AFFECT PERFORMANCE?

We have sufficient evidence to claim that HR policies and practices do affect company performance, although some studies do not support this. We then need to understand better the processes which link these HR practices to business performance. As Purcell et al. point out, 'what remains unclear is what is actually happening in successful organizations to make this connection'. Currently the focus is on commitment in mediating the impact of HR policies and practices on business performance.

COMMITMENT

Commitment has been described as:

- *Attitudinal commitment* – that is, loyalty and support for the organization, strength of identification with the organization, a belief in its values and goals and a readiness to put in effort for the organization.
- *Behavioural commitment* – actually remaining with the company and continuing to pursue its objectives.

Walton notes that commitment is thought to result in better quality, lower turnover, a greater capacity for innovation and more flexible employees. In turn these are seen to enhance the ability of the organization to achieve competitive advantage. Iles, Mabey and Robertson add that some of the outcomes of commitment have been identified as the industrial relations climate, absence levels, turnover levels and individual performance. Pfeffer and Wood and Albanese argue that commitment is a core variable, and Guest suggests that: The concept of organizational commitment lies at the heart of any analysis of HRM. Indeed the whole rationale for introducing HRM policies is to increase levels of commitment so that other positive outcomes can ensue.

Fig : A Simple Model of HRM and Performance

Hence we see the adoption of the terms 'high commitment work practices' and 'high commitment management' and their linkage with high performance. Meyer and Allen argue that there is not a great deal of evidence to link high commitment and high levels of organizational performance. He is, however, cautious about identifying causal links.

Some authors, however, have argued that high commitment could indeed reduce organizational performance. Cooper and Hartley suggest that commitment might decrease flexibility and inhibit creative problem solving. If commitment reduces staff turnover, this may result in fewer new ideas coming into the organization. Staff who would like to leave the organization but who are committed to it in other ways, for example through high pay and benefits, may stay, but may not produce high levels of performance.

As well as the debate on the value of commitment to organizational performance, there is also the debate on the extent to which commitment can be managed, and how it can be managed. Guest suggests that commitment is affected by: personal characteristics; experiences in job role; work experiences; structural factors; and personnel policies.

Lastly, it is important to consider whether using commitment as a shorthand for attitudes and satisfaction is sufficient, and whether there are other important dimensions which may be lost, by focusing on commitment alone. Patterson et al. found that in addition to commitment, employee satisfaction was related to organizational performance. Purcell and his colleagues give equal prominence to job satisfaction and motivation. In their model HR policies and practices are seen to impact on employee ability/skills, motivation and incentive (in that people can be motivated to use their ability productively via intrinsic and extrinsic rewards) and opportunity. In turn these three factors have an impact on commitment, individual motivation and job satisfaction, all of which have an impact on employee discretionary behaviour which in turn impacts on performance. In relation to HR practices they found that:

- Job influence, career opportunities, job challenge, involvement in management decisions, training and line manager respect all influence employee motivation;
- Job influence, career opportunities, job challenge and teamworking all influence job satisfaction;
- Training, career opportunities, job challenge, management leadership, performance appraisal, work-life balance and communication on organizational performance all influence commitment.

MAJOR PERFORMANCE INITIATIVES

We have previously considered some HR policies and practices that have been identified as related to high performance, and have noted the idea of using practices in bundles. Many of the popular performance initiatives that companies have adopted represent similar (but not the same) bundles of HR policies and practices, and we now turn to these. There are many small initiatives every day that help to improve performance, but we are concentrating here on major strategic initiatives although the labels may, of course, mean different things in practice in different organizations. Interestingly, Guest and King found that many senior managers were not aware of the research on performance, and it is therefore unclear what is informing senior managers' choice of performance initiatives.

This brings us to the concern that too many initiatives in the same organization will give conflicting messages to employees, particularly when they are introduced by different parts of the business. There may, for example, be contradictions between the messages of total quality management ('right first time') and those of the learning organization type of approach ('it's OK to make mistakes as long as you learn from them').

The performance research to date focuses very much on the individual, but we agree with Caulkin who suggests that organizations also need to develop the capability of the organization as a whole, and to this end we include in table below three levels of initiative depending on the primary focus: organizational, team or individual. Some of them partly cover the same ground, and it would be surprising to find them in the same business at the same time.

Table: *Some Major Performance Initiatives*

Organizational Focus	Learning organization Knowledge management Organizational development Investors in people Total quality management (TQM) Performance culture Lean production Business process re-engineering Just in time (JIT) Standards: e.g. ISO9000 Customer care/orientation

Individual Focus	Performance management Performance-related pay Self-development/continuous development Empowerment
Team Focus	High-performance teams Cross-functional teams Self-regulating teams

Things That Go Wrong

The level of satisfaction with performance initiatives is typically low, so we close this chapter with a summary of the problems most often reported.

THE PROCESS/PEOPLE BALANCE

Schemes rarely strike the right balance between a people emphasis and a process emphasis. Concentrating on being brilliant at talking to the people, getting them going and talking them down gently if they don't quite make it will not suffice if there is not a clear, disciplined process that brings in the essential features of consistency and defining sensible goals. Getting the goals and measures right is a waste of time if there is not the necessary input to changing attitudes, developing skills and winning consent.

GETTING THE MEASURES RIGHT

On the basis of what gets measured gets done, it is critical that the organization selects the most useful measure of performance for the organizaton as a whole and for the individuals within it. Single measures are unlikely to be sufficiently robust. Kaplan and Norton argue convincingly that the mix of measures which an organization should use to assess its performance should be based around four different perspectives:

- *Financial measures* – such as sales growth, profits, cash flow and increased market share.
- *Customer measures* – that is, the customer perspective, which looks at, for example, delivery time, service quality, product quality.
- *Internal business measures* – cycle time, productivity, employee skills, labour turnover.

- *Innovation and learning perspective* – including such elements as ability to innovate and improve.

The focus must be on what is achieved: results are what count. At an individual level a focus on behaviour rather than results achieved can be unhelpful, leading to personality clashes, and misleading. Doing things in the right way is no substitute for doing the right things.

MANAGEMENT LOSING INTEREST

A constant axiom with any initiative is the need for endorsement from senior management. With a performance initiative there is the need to go a great deal further. First, senior managers have to accept that the initiative is something in which they have to participate continuously and thoroughly. They cannot introduce it, say how important it is and then go off to find other games to play: *studies have shown that in organizations that utilise performance management, 90 per cent of senior managers have not received performance reviews in the last two years. Clearly the problem here is that PM is not used, modelled and visibly supported at the top of the organization. Sooner or later people at lower levels catch on and no longer feel compelled to take the time to make PM work.*

The second aspect is indicated in that quotation. Performance initiatives will not work unless people at all levels either believe in them or are prepared to give them a try with the hope that they will be convinced by the practice.

THE TEAM/INDIVIDUAL BALANCE

Individuals can rarely perform entirely on their own merits; they are part of a department or team of people whose activities interact in innumerable ways. Trevor Macdonald may read the television news with a clarity and sureness that is outstanding, but it would be of little value if the lights did not work or the script contained errors. Most working people, no matter how eminent, are not solo performers to that extent. Somehow the performance initiative has to stimulate both individual and team performance, working together within the envelope of organizational objectives.

LEAVING OUT THE DEVELOPMENT PART

A key feature of managing performance is developing people so that they can perform. This is the feature that is most often not delivered. It is often the lack of follow-up on development needs that is the least satisfactory aspect of performance management systems.

IMPLEMENTING AND MANAGING THE CHANGE

If, as Purcell identifies, 'our concern should be less about the precise policy mix in the "bundle" and more about how and when organizations manage the HR side of change', then the way that large and small performance initiatives are implemented and managed is critical. While this is well-trodden ground, there is considerable evidence of attempted changes which have failed for a wide range of reasons including: trust is low; change is seen as a management fad which will go away; change has been poorly communicated and understood; change is just a way to get us to work harder for the same money.

GETTING IT RIGHT

Here are four suggestions for running a successful performance initiative:

1. Develop and promulgate a clear vision for the business as a framework for individual/team goals and targets.
2. In consultation, develop and agree individual goals and targets with three characteristics: (a) what to do to achieve the target; (b) how to satisfy the customer rather than pleasing the boss; (c) targets that are precise, difficult and challenging, but attainable, with feedback.
3. Do not begin until you are sure of: (a) unwavering commitment from the top; (b) an approach that is driven by the line and bought into and owned by middle and first-line managers; (c) a system that is run, monitored and updated by HR specialists; (d) an agreement that every development commitment or pay commitment is honoured, or a swift, full explanation is given of why not.
4. Train all participants.

Note: For further knowledge regarding this chapter reader can visit www.fredsinc.com. Fred's, Inc. (Fred's or "the company") operates a chain of discount general merchandise stores in Southeastern US. The company offer products in various categories including pharmaceuticals, apparel and linen, household goods, food and tobacco, and paper. The company is headquartered in Memphis, Tennessee and employs 9,979 people.

12

Organizational Performance: Knowledge and Learning

There was a time when performance was seen primarily in terms of individual motivation and performance. The focus has now shifted to emphasise performance of the organization as a whole. While some performance variations are the result of individual differences, ultimate organizational performance can also be significantly affected by systems, processes, structures and culture. These are outside the control of the individual employee, but can be implemented and controlled to some extent by managers. The focus of this chapter is on the whole organization and its performance, although it is inevitable that within this individual performance and team performance issues will play a part.

ORGANIZATIONAL PERFORMANCE 'INITIATIVES'

The word 'initiative' may appear inappropriate, as approaches to improving organizational performance may be seen as long-term and permanent changes in the philosophy of the organization and the way that it is managed. We use the word 'initiative' as this is usually the term used for packaging such ideas and presenting them to managers. These 'initiatives' generally involve a variety of organizational change measures, which may be structural, processual and/or cultural. Culture, in particular, has a high profile. How many times have you heard that organizations are attempting to develop a 'quality culture', a 'learning culture' or a 'knowledge-centric culture'?

Many of these initiatives overlap; for example, similarities between business process re-engineering (BPR) and total quality management (TQM), and between TQM and learning organizations have been pointed out, although there are contradictions here too. Much current research and literature demonstrates the similarity between learning organizations and knowledge management. Similar concepts are used, such as 'communities of practice'; and similar dilemmas are addressed, such as how to embed individual knowledge and learning into organizational systems and processes. Some of the same researchers investigate both areas, others link the two areas explicitly together, and conferences span both areas, for example the 2001 event in a series of conferences on organizational learning was entitled 'Organizational Learning and Knowledge Management: New Directions'.

The term 'initiative' may also be misleading in that some organsiations may display characteristics of these organizational performance strategies without ever consciously trying to implement such a strategy. A good example of this is provided by Jones who, in research on organizational twinning, claims that he might have 'discovered' a learning organization. He suggests that members of the organization may not have heard the term 'learning organization', but the way that the organization was led and managed provided the suitable conditions for a learning organization to happen naturally. This is an interesting contrast to organizations which employ the rhetoric of a learning organization but which in practice are quite different. In all of these performance initiatives, it is unfortunate that the way they have been applied does not always live up to the ideals that are promulgated.

LEARNING ORGANIZATIONS

The interest in learning organizations has been stimulated by the need to be competitive, as learning is considered to be the only way of obtaining and keeping a competitive edge. Edmonson and Moingeon put it very well when they say: To remain viable in an environment characterized by uncertainty and change, organizations and individuals alike depend upon an ability to learn.

While the concept of organizational learning has been explored for some time, the concept of the learning organization is a comparatively recent notion reflected in the literature since the late 1980s. Pedler et al. suggested that the concept of the learning organization was a response to poor organizational performance. In other words they saw it as a way of overcoming sluggishness, an excess of bureaucracy and over-control, of organizations as straitjackets frustrating the self-development efforts of individual members and failing to capitalise upon their potential.

In 1987 Pedler, Boydell and Burgoyne carried out a project entitled 'Developing the Learning Company' and interviewed staff in organizations which were pursuing learning company strategies. They asked why these strategies had been adopted, and found such reasons as the need to improve quality; the wish to become more people oriented in relation to both staff and customers; the need to encourage 'active experimentation' and generally to cope with competitive pressures in order to survive. They defined the learning organization, which they identify as a 'dream' rather than a description of current practice, as: an organization which facilitates the learning of all its members and continually transforms itself.

By the year 2003 there was still little empirical evidence of organizations that have transformed themselves like this, and in 1999 Sloman suggested that the concept of the learning organization was in terminal decline. Part of the problem, he argues, is that there is such confusion over the concept and, as Stewart notes, a lack of tangible practices to implement. While Burgoyne, and many others, such as Popper and Lipshitz , concur with the extent of confusion, Burgoyne claims that there is still considerable interest in the idea from both organizations and academics, and that our understanding of the concept needs to be developed. He recognises that much of the early thinking about the learning organization was naive, and suggests that, as the concept is developed, organizations will have more success with it. In particular, he describes the idea of becoming a learning organization as one grand project, as 'utopian and unrealistic', and he recognises the value of a more incremental approach.

Easterby-Smith and Araujo note that a number of different disciplines have made a contribution to the debate on organizational learning and learning organizations, producing a plurality of perspectives. Part of the confusion, though, lies in the practices adopted by organizations under the banner of a learning organization, rather than in the fundamental ideas. Academics and theorists may place different emphases on different aspects, but these are mutually supportive rather than conflicting. There is a common thread of a holistic approach and that organizational learning is greater than the sum of individual learning in the organization. Different organizations appear to have been inspired by some aspects of this approach and, having adopted these, they see themselves as learning organizations.

In essence they have taken some steps towards their goal, and have certainly improved the level of learning going on in the organization, but have taken a partial rather than a holistic approach. A further confusion lies in the difference between the nature of organizational learning and the learning organization, which we consider in the following section.

ORGANIZATIONAL LEARNING AND THE LEARNING ORGANIZATION

The study of organizational learning is based on the detached observation of individual and collective learning processes in the organization. The approach is critical and academic, and the focus is the nature and processes of learning, whereas Easterby-Smith and Araujo suggest that the study of learning organizations is focused on 'normative models for creating change in the direction of improved learning processes'. Much of the research on learning organizations has been produced by consultants and organizations that are involved in the process. In other words the data come from an action learning perspective and are produced by interested parties, giving, inevitably, a positive spin to what is produced. This is not to say that the learning organization perspective is devoid of theory. The study of learning organizations often focuses on organizational learning mechanisms, and these can be seen as a way of making the concept of organizational learning more concrete, and thus linking the two perspectives. Popper and Lipshitz describe organizational learning mechanisms as the structural and procedural arrangements that allow organizations to learn, in other words: that is to collect, analyse, store, disseminate and use systematically information that is relevant to their and their members' performance.

These issues are well reflected in Pedler et al.'s model of the learning organization, which we will describe shortly. Easterby-Smith and Araujo argue that the literature on the learning organization draws heavily on the concepts of organizational learning, from a utilitarian perspective, and there is some commonality in the literature, as Argyris and Schon suggest. It is generally agreed that there is a lack of critical research from both perspectives.

ORGANIZATIONAL AND INDIVIDUAL LEARNING

Although some pragmatic definitions of learning organizations centre on more and more individual learning, learning support and self-development, organizational learning is more than just the sum of individual learning in the organization. It is only when an individual's learning has an impact on and interrelates with others that organization members learn together and gradually begin to change the way things are done.

In this way mutual behaviour change is achieved which increases the collective competence, rather than just individual competence. Argyris and Schon see such learning as a change in the 'theory in use' (that is, the understanding, whether conscious or unconscious, that determines what we actually do) rather than merely a change in the 'espoused' theory (what we say we do). In other words the often unspoken rules of the organization have changed. The question of how individual learning feeds into organizational learning and transformation, and how this is greater than the sum of individual learning, is only beginning to be addressed. Viewing the organization as a process rather than an entity may offer some help here. Another perspective is that of viewing the organization as a living organizm

Argyris and Schon describe different levels, or loops, of organizational learning, which others have developed. These levels are:

- *Level 1*: Single loop learning: Learning about how we can do better, thus improving what we are currently doing. This is seen as learning at the operational level, or at the level of rules.
- *Level 2*: Double loop learning: A more fundamental level, which is concerned with 'why' questions in relation to what we are doing rather than with doing the same things better, that is, questioning whether we should be doing different things. This level is described as developing knowledge and understanding due to insights, and can result in strategic changes and renewal.
- *Level 3*: Triple loop learning: This level of learning is the hardest of all to achieve as it is focused on the purpose or principles of the organization, challenging whether these are appropriate, and is sometimes described as learning at the level of will or being.

WHAT ARE THE CHARACTERISTICS OF LEARNING ORGANIZATIONS?

There are many different approaches to describing the characteristics of a learning organization, and we shall briefly consider three of these. First, we look at the approach of Pedler et al., who identify 11 characteristics of a learning organization, grouped into five general themes.

Strategy

Two characteristics within this theme are suggested, first that a learning approach to strategy should be taken. Strategy formation, implementation, evaluation and improvement are deliberately structured as learning experiences by using feedback loops. Second, participative policy making infers that this is shared with all in the organization, and even further, that suppliers, customers and the total community have some involvement. The aim of the policy is to 'delight customers', and the differences of opinion and values that are revealed in the participative process are seen as productive tensions.

Looking in

Four characteristics are suggested within this theme – the first being informating which involves using technology to empower and inform employees, and is made widely available. They note that such information should be used to understand what is going on in the company, and so stimulate learning, rather than used to reward, punish or control. Second, there is formative accounting and control which involves designing accounting, budgeting and reporting systems to assist learning. Third, there is internal exchange which involves all internal units seeing themselves as customers and suppliers of each other. Fourth, they identify reward flexibility, which implies that the question of why some receive more money than others is a debate to be brought out into the open. They recommend that alternatives are discussed and tried out, but recognise that this is the most difficult of the 11 characteristics to put into practice.

Structures

Enabling structures suggest that roles are loosely structured in line with the needs of internal customers and suppliers, and in a way that allows for personal growth and experimentation. Internal boundaries can be flexible. For example, project groups and transient structures help to break down barriers between units, provide mechanisms for spreading new ideas and encourage the idea of change.

Looking Out

Boundary workers as environmental scanners implies that part of the role of all workers in contact with suppliers, customers and neighbours of the organization should be to participate in data collection. A second feature in this theme is intercompany learning, which entails joining with customers, suppliers and possibly competitors in training experiences, research and development and job exchanges. They also suggest that benchmarking can be used to learn from other companies.

Learning Opportunities

First, a learning climate is important, that is, one that encourages experimentation and learning from experience, questioning current ideas, attitudes and actions and trying out new ideas. Mistakes are allowed because not all new ideas will work. There is a focus on continuous improvement, and the involvement of customers, suppliers and neighbours in experimentation is suggested. A learning climate suggests that feedback from others is continually requested, is made available and is acted upon. Second, self-development opportunities for all requires resources and facilities for self-development for employees at all levels in the organization, and coaching, mentoring, peer support, counselling, feedback and so on must be available to support individuals in their learning.

Peter Senge takes a slightly different perspective. In his book about the art and practice of a learning organization he identified five vital dimensions in building organizations which can learn, which he refers to as disciplines:

- *Systems thinking*. This is an understanding of the interrelatedness between things, seeing the whole rather than just a part and concentrating on processes. In terms of organizational actions it suggests that connections need to be constantly made and that there must be consideration of the implications that every action has elsewhere in the organization.

- *Personal mastery*. This underlines the need for continuous development and individual self-development.

- *Mental models*. This is about the need to expose the 'theories in use' in the organization. These can block change and the adoption of new ideas, and can only be confronted, challenged and changed if they are brought to the surface rather than remaining unconscious.

- *Shared visions*. This is expressing the need for a common purpose or vision which can inspire members of the organization and break down barriers and mistrust. Senge argues that such a vision plus an accurate view of the present state results in a creative tension which is helpful for learning and change.

- *Team learning*. Teams are seen as important in that they are microcosms of the organization, and the place where different views and perspectives come together, which Senge sees as a productive process.

Senge acknowledges that he presents a very positive vision of what organizations can do, and recognises that without the appropriate leadership this will not happen. He goes on to identify three critical leadership roles: designer, teacher and steward. As designer the leader needs to engage employees at all levels in designing the vision, core purpose and values of the organization: design processes for strategic thinking and effective learning processes. As teacher the leader needs to help all organization members gain more insight into the organizational reality, to coach, guide and facilitate, and help others bring their theories into use. As steward the leader needs to demonstrate a sense of personal commitment to the organization's mission and take responsibility for the impact of leadership on others.

Bob Garratt concentrates on the role that the directors of an organization have in encouraging a learning organization and in overcoming learning blocks. He suggests:

- The top team concentrate on strategy and policy and hold back from day-to-day operational issues;
- Thinking time is needed for the top team to relate changes in the external environment to the internal working of the organization;
- The creation of a top team, involving the development and deployment of the strengths of each member;
- The delegation of problem solving to staff close to the operation;
- Acceptance that learning occurs at all levels of the organization, and that directors need to create a climate where this learning flows freely.

Clearly, a learning organization is not something that can be developed overnight and has to be viewed as a long-term strategy.

Easterby-Smith makes some key points about encouraging experimentation in organizations in relation to flexible structures, information, people and reward. We have discussed flexibility and information in some detail. In respect of people he argues that organizations will seek to select those who are similar to current organization members. The problem here is that such a strategy, in reinforcing homogeneity and reducing diversity, restrains the production of innovative and creative ideas. He sees diversity as a positive stimulant and concludes that organizations should therefore select some employees who would not normally fit their criteria, and especially those who would be likely to experiment and be able to tolerate ambiguity. In relation to the reward system he notes the need to reinforce rather than punish risk taking and innovation.

Critique

The initial idealism of the learning organization concept has been tempered by experiences, and more pragmatic material is gradually being developed. Popper and Lipshitz have identified four conditions under which organizational learning is likely to be productive. These are in situations where there is:

- *Valid information* – that is, complete, undistorted and verifiable information.
- *Transparency* – where individuals are prepared to hold themselves open to inspection in order to receive valid feedback. This reduces self-deception, and helps to resist pressures to distort information.
- *Issues orientation rather than a personal orientation* – that is, where information is judged on its merits and relevance to the issue at hand, rather than on the status or attributes of the individual who provides the information.
- *Accountability* – that is, 'holding oneself responsible for one's own actions and their consequences and for learning from these consequences'.

In a different approach Burgoyne provides a list of nine things that need to happen for continuous learning to become a reality.

There remains a wide range of concerns regarding the concept of the learning organization. Hawkins notes the evangelistic fervour with which learning organizations and total quality management (TQM) are recommended to the uninitiated and fears that the commercialisation of these ideas means that they become superficial. He argues that an assumption may be made that all learning is good whatever is being learned, whereas the value of learning is where it is taking us and, as Stewart points out, learning is neither objective nor neutral. Learning should be seen as the means rather than the end in itself. Learning to be more efficient at what is being done does not necessarily make one more effective; it depends on the appropriateness of the activity itself. It is not surprising therefore that there is a lack of evidence linking learning organization strategies with financial performance.

Nor does the literature cover adequately the barriers to becoming a learning organization – for example, the role of politics within the organization. If learning requires sharing of information, and information is power, then how can individuals be encouraged to let go of the power they have? There has also been a lack of attention to emotion, ethics and human irrationality. Harris, for example, demonstrates how the potential for learning in her retail bank case studies was constrained by the overwhelming desire to maintain continuity in the organization.

In particular, both Senge and Garratt have high expectations of the leaders of organizations. To what extent are these expectations realistic, and how might they be achieved? The literature of learning organizations has a clear unitarist perspective – the question of whether employees desire to be involved in or united by a vision of the organization needs to be addressed. The question of willing participation was also raised by Harris when she found that contractors were unwilling to share their learning when leaving the organization, even though this expectation was built into their contracts. For a useful critique of the assumptions behind learning organizations. In addition, the full complexity of the ideas implicit in the words 'learning organization' requires more explanation.

The problems in implementing learning organization prescriptions has led Sun and Scott to suggest that attention needs to refocus on organizational learning in order really to understand how individual learning can be transformed into collective learning, and they suggest some useful ways forward. An alternative development is that of the 'living company' which extends the learning organization concept. Another focus has been the more recent attention to knowledge management which is generally presented in a more practical/applicable manner, and yet as we have previously suggested has some similar foundations to the learning organization.

KNOWLEDGE MANAGEMENT

KNOWLEDGE AND ITS PERCEIVED VALUE

Knowledge is increasingly viewed as a critical organizational resource which provides competitive advantage. As the speed of change gets faster organizations increasingly need innovations, new ideas and new ways of doing things to keep ahead of the competition, and they constantly need to know what their competitors and customers are doing. Increasing organizational knowledge is seen to underpin this. In addition knowledge-based organizations, such as consultancies and finance companies, are growing. The growth of knowledge work and the increasing number of knowledge workers has been well reported. Examples of knowledge workers would be research and development staff, legal, IT, accounting and other professionals. But, although the prevalence of knowledge work still accounts for only a minority of workers in the India, it would be a mistake to see knowledge as relevant just to such a narrow range of staff. We take the view in this chapter that knowledge is important for everyone in the organization.

Providing a definition of knowledge is surprisingly difficult, and there are many different perspectives in the literature. For an academic debate about the nature of knowledge see Tsoukas and Vladimirou. At a simple level we can say that data are raw facts, that analysis and contextualisation of raw data so that they become something meaningful produce information, and that knowledge is more than information in that it has been reflected on and processed to the extent that it can be applied and is with the person who needs to apply it. Explicit knowledge, sometimes referred to as operational knowledge, or 'know what' type knowledge, can be codified and stored for others to access. Examples here might be competitors' price changes, new competitor products, customer buying patterns and changes in employment legislation.

However, most knowledge is more complex than this, it is something which resides in a person's head and we are often unaware of what we know until we come to use it. This is usually referred to as tacit knowledge, or 'know how' type knowledge. This is made up of our accumulated experiences about how things are done, how problems can be solved, what works, what doesn't and in what contexts and under what conditions. An example of this might be a fireman who during a fire would be able to work out when a backdraught would be likely to occur and could then make sure the immediate area is clear of people. Working this out involves a series of decision processes about the current conditions of the fire and comparing this with previous experiences when backdraughts have occurred. This is usually done intuitively. For anyone else to use this knowledge it needs to be made explicit, which is recognised by many as difficult, and by some as unachievable. Knowledge management initiatives may cover either or both types of knowledge.

Knowledge in itself is not enough as it has to be accessed, applied appropriately and used to enhance the organization's ability to achieve its objectives. Thus for knowledge to be of value it needs to be turned into action. Given this, it is not surprising that attention has been focused on how to generate knowledge, how to share knowledge and how to reuse it – in other words knowledge management.

MANAGING KNOWLEDGE

Knowledge management has been variously defined and the term is ambiguous. In this chapter we will use a definition suggested by Scarbrough and Swan: defined broadly and inclusively to cover a loosely connected set of ideas, tools and practices centring on the communication and exploitation of knowledge in organizations.

Our understanding of what knowledge is will have implications for the way we try to manage it. Early approaches to knowledge management focused on IT systems as a means of codifying an individual's knowledge, storing it and making it available to others in the organization. This somewhat simplistic approach was based on the concept that knowledge is an abstract objective truth which can be easily recorded and manipulated, separately from the person who created the knowledge. The resultant activity led to a proliferation of organizational databases, search programmes, yellow pages type directories, intranets and extranets. An example of an extranet is provided by Hunter et al. in the context of a legal firm which offered professional knowledge in this format to valued clients as part of the service that they paid for. While this may be useful for the explicit knowledge referred to above, and is the focus of much research work in the area, it has very limited value.

The alternative perspective is that knowledge is personal and socially constructed. In other words, knowledge is an ongoing interpretation of the external world, as suggested by Blackler: knowledge to be ... pragmatic, partial, tentative and always open to revision – it is no more, and no less, than a collective interpretation.

This perspective suggests that codifying knowledge and using IT systems to store and share it is inadequate. Instead attention needs to be focused on 'communities of interest' – in other words the way in which individuals with a common interest network to share knowledge and spark off new ideas. A second focus is on the way that knowledge becomes embedded into systems, processes and culture within the organization.

This perspective requires that individuals need to be willing to share their knowledge, and since knowledge is power, there can be no assumptions that individuals will comply. To this end encouraging and perhaps facilitating various types of networking would be more appropriate. Trust in the organization is critical here as sharing knowledge may involve admitting to failures and what has been learned from them and giving bad news. Project write-ups and reports may also be used in trying to make tacit knowledge explicit, especially when individuals holding the knowledge may leave the organization. An example of this is a Department Head in a university who was aware that a valued member of staff teaching a very specialist area was about to retire and instigated a project to document their teaching content and methods so that their particular knowledge would not be lost to the university.

Kermally identifies a range of knowledge management initiatives, based on Nonaka and Takeuchi's model of how organizational knowledge can be created. Kermally suggests that to develop knowledge through socialisation activities such as brainstorming, informal meetings, conversations, coaching, mentoring, interacting with customers, on-the-job training and observation may be helpful; to develop knowledge through externalisation, databases, exchange of best practices, building models, after-action reviews and master classes would be helpful; for a combined approach, conferences, publications and electronic libraries are suggested; and for knowledge internalisation, feedback from customers, facilitation skills and development counselling would be helpful.

The barriers to knowledge management have been variously identified as the culture of the organization, the risk of admitting to failure, lack of incentive to change, resistance to ideas and learning from other contexts, internal competition and individual reward practices. Factors identified as encouraging knowledge management are an organization which engenders trust and openness, a knowledge-centric culture, defined roles and responsibilities in knowledge management, support through the performance management system (such as targets about sharing knowledge and team/organizational rewards), building on informal practices which already exist.

It has been suggested that organizations need to make all their knowledge management activities explicit in order to justify the investment made and demonstrate the organization's commitment to knowledge.

ROLES IN KNOWLEDGE MANAGEMENT

Evans notes that there is still much confusion about the responsibility for and accountabilities in knowledge management, and Lank suggests three new organizational roles intended to promote knowledge management:

- *The knowledge architects*: Lank suggests that these are senior, strategic roles such as Chief Knowledge Officer and involve, among other things, working out which knowledge is critical and how it will be shared, how technology could be used, how people will be trained, how they will be rewarded for collabourative working.
- *The knowledge facilitators*: These are the people who run processes to help knowledge flow, for example company journalists who write up customer case studies and project reviews; librarians who develop indexes for storage and retrieval of information; information service providers who provide an internal consultancy service to find and deliver information to staff – including external and internal information; webmasters who develop the company intranet; and learning facilitators who can facilitate post-event reviews to elicit lessons learned.
- *The knowledge aware*: These include all employees, who have a responsibility to share their own expertise and knowledge, who will participate in post-event reviews, and who act to reinforce the value of collabouration.

There are two critical roles missing here – the line manager and the HR specialist. MacNeil makes a convincing case for the importance of the line manager in knowledge management which she suggests has been overlooked to date. She identifies the line manager's contribution as creating a positive learning climate, encouraging open exchange, reinforcing that making mistakes is acceptable and that it is helpful to share errors. Although she does note that there are questions about the extent to which line managers have the skills to facilitate knowledge management.

Given a broader understanding of knowledge as above, then knowledge management is inevitably bound up with human resource management in overcoming barriers and in proactively supporting knowledge management. HR professionals may, for example, utilise facilitation skills in supporting knowledge management, or they align human resource activities with knowledge management needs.

KNOWLEDGE MANAGEMENT AND HUMAN RESOURCE MANAGEMENT

MacNeil goes on to suggest that there has been a lack of research on the links between HRM and knowledge management, yet Lengnick-Hall and Lengnick-Hall suggest that knowledge facilitator is a key HR role. They suggest that HR has a key role in: developing the motivation, competencies, value orientation, and knowledge of the firm's strategic intent to use knowledge to enhance organizational capabilities.

In more detail they recommend that HR managers need to design organizational structures and processes that promote knowledge diffusion, contribute to designing user-friendly systems for accessing knowledge and training people in their use, develop a knowledge-centric culture, provide mechanisms for people to share knowledge – for example allowing teams to work together long enough to develop

knowledge together and then move people around the organization to cross-fertilise.

Scarbrough and Carter asked their sample of researchers in the knowledge management area what implications their work had for HRM, and found that:

- 27 per cent claimed there were implications for recruitment and selection policy;
- 63 per cent claimed there were implications for training and development in the workplace;
- 27 per cent claimed there were implications for rewards and appraisal;
- 77 per cent claimed there were implications for organizational and cultural change policy and practice.

At a strategic level Scarbrough and Carter identify five different perspectives in the work on knowledge management and draw out the implications that each has for HRM:

- *Best practice perspective*: Encouraging employees to share knowledge and cooperate with knowledge management initiatives.

If commitment is required in order that individuals are prepared to share their knowledge and remain with the organization then 'best practice' HRM will be important to generate that commitment.

- *Knowledge work perspective*: Managing knowledge work and knowledge workers. Such workers may have distinctive needs in terms of motivation, job challenge, autonomy, careers and so on. These will need to be addressed by HR policies.
- *Congruence perspective*: Increasing performance by aligning HRM and knowledge management practices.
- *Human and social capital perspective*: This involves the development of human and social resources in the organsisation. This both underpins the success of knowledge management initiatives and mobilises longer-term capabilities.
- *Learning perspective*: This perspective incorporates two different approaches. First is the notion of communities of learning, discussed above, which draws attention to the way tacit knowledge is developed and shared in practitioner groups. Second, there is organizational learning which focuses on how learning can be embedded in organizational routines and processes to improve organizational performance.

Note: Reader can visit OfficeMax, Inc. site www.officemax.com for a detailed study of connected to this chapter. OfficeMax (formerly Boise Cascade Corporation) is engaged in the distribution of office products. The company operates in the US, Puerto Rico, the US Virgin Islands, Mexico, Canada, Australia and New Zealand. It is headquartered in Naperville, Illinois and employs 33,000 people; this figure includes 11,000 part-time employees.

13

Individual Performance Management

The treatment of individual performance in organizations has traditionally centred on the assessment of performance and the allocation of reward. Performance was typically seen as the result of the interaction between individual ability and motivation.

Increasingly, organizations recognise that planning and enabling performance have a critical effect on individual performance. So, for example, clarity of performance goals and standards, appropriate resources, guidance and support from the individual's manager all become central.

PERFORMANCE MANAGEMENT AND PERFORMANCE APPRAISAL

APPRAISAL SYSTEMS

Traditionally performance appraisal systems have provided a formalised process to review the performance of employees. They are typically designed on a central basis, usually by the HR function, and require each line manager to appraise the performance of their staff, usually on an annual basis. This normally requires the manager and employee to take part in a performance review meeting. Elabourate forms are often completed as a record of the process, but these are not living documents, they are generally stored in the archives of the HR department, and the issue of performance is often neglected until the next round of performance review meetings.

The nature of what is being appraised varies between organizations and might cover personality, behaviour or job performance. These areas might be measured either quantitively or qualitatively. Qualitative appraisal often involves the writing of an unstructured narrative on the general performance of the appraisee. Alternatively, some guidance might be given as to the areas on which the appraiser should comment. The problem with qualitative appraisals is that they may leave important areas unappraised, and that they are not suitable for comparison purposes.

Coates argues that what is actually measured in performance appraisal is the extent to which the individual conforms to the organization. Some traditional appraisal was based on measures of personality traits that were felt to be important to the job. These included traits such as resourcefulness, enthusiasm, drive, application and other traits such as intelligence. One difficulty with these is that everyone defines them differently. Raters, therefore, are often unsure of what they are rating, leaving more scope for bias and prejudice. Another problem is that since the same scales are often used for many different jobs, traits that are irrelevant to an appraisee's job may still be measured.

Other approaches concentrate on linking ratings to behaviour and performance on the job. So performance may be reviewed against key aspects of the job or major headings on the job description. Specific methods of linking ratings with behaviour at work have been developed such as behaviourally anchored rating scales (BARS) and behavioural observation scales (BOS) although evidence suggests that these are not widely used.

Another method of making appraisal more objective is to use the process to set job objectives over the coming year and, a year later, to measure the extent to which these objectives have been met. The extent to which the appraisee is involved in setting these objectives varies considerably. When a competency profile has been identified for a particular job, it is then possible to use this in the appraisal of performance. Many appraisal systems combine competency assessment with assessment against objectives or job accountabilities.

Lastly, performance may be appraised by collecting primary data via various forms of electronic surveillance system. There are increasing examples of how activity rates of computer operators can be recorded and analysed, and how the calls made by telephone sales staff can be overheard and analysed. Sewell and Wilkinson describe a Japanese electronics plant where the final electronic test on a piece of equipment can indicate not only faults but the individual operator responsible for them. On another level some companies test the performance of their sales staff by sending in assessors acting in the role of customer, often termed 'mystery shoppers'.

In a recent survey 79 out of 96 very large employers appraised all employees. But while performance appraisal has gradually been applied to wider groups of employees, beyond managers and professionals, there are also concerns that appraisal systems are treated as an administrative exercise, are ineffective, and do little to improve performance of employees in the future. A further problem with such systems is the lack of clarity of purpose. The Employment Studies Institute suggests that appraisal is a victim of its own expectations, in that it is expected to deliver in too many areas. Systems may focus on development, identifying future potential, reward, identifying poor performers, or motivation. In systems where appraisal results were linked to reward the manager was placed in the position of an assessor or judge. Alternatively some systems focused on support or development, particularly in the public sector. These provided a better opportunity for managers to give constructive feedback, for employees to be open about difficulties, and for plannning to improve future performance. Many systems try to encompass both approaches. However, as these approaches conflict, the results are typically unsatisfactory.

The effectiveness of appraisal systems hinges on a range of different factors. Research by Longenecker in the USA sheds some light on this. In a large-scale survey and focus groups he found that the three most common reasons for failure of an appraisal system were: unclear performance criteria or an ineffective rating instrument (83 per cent); poor working relationships with the boss (79 per cent); and that the appraiser lacked information on the manager's actual performance (75 per cent). Other problems were a lack of ongoing performance feedback (67 per cent) and a lack of focus on management development/improvement (50 per cent). Smaller numbers identified problems with the process, such as lack of appraisal skills (33 per cent) and the review process lacking structure or substance (29 per cent).

We would add that ownership of the system is also important. If it is designed and imposed by the HR function there may be little ownership of the system by line managers. Similarly, if paperwork has to be returned to the HR function it may well be seen as a form-filling exercise for someone else's benefit and with no practical value to performance within the job. More fundamentally Egan argues that the problem with appraisal not only relates to poor design or implementation, but is rooted deeply in the basic reaction of organizational members to such a concept. There is an increasing body of critical literature addressing the role and theory of appraisal. These debates centre on the underlying reasons for appraisal and the social construction of appraisal. This literature throws some light on the use and effectiveness of performance appraisal in organizations.

PERFORMANCE MANAGEMENT SYSTEMS

While many appraisal systems are still in existence and continue to be updated, performance management systems are increasingly seen as the way to manage employee performance, and have incorporated the appraisal/review process into this. Such systems offer the advantage of being tied closely into the objectives of the organization, and therefore the resulting performance is more likely to meet organizational needs. The systems also represent a more holistic view of performance. Performance appraisal or review is almost always a key part of the system, but is integrated with performance planning (linking an individual's objectives to business objectives) to ensure that employee effort is directed towards organizational priorities: support for performance delivery (via development plans, coaching and ongoing review) to enable employee effort to be successful, and that performance is assessed and successful performance rewarded and reinforced.

The conceptual foundation of performance management relies on a view that performance is more than ability and motivation. It is argued that clarity of goals is key in enabling the employee to understand what is expected and the order of priorities. In addition goals themselves are seen to provide motivation, and this is based on goal setting theory originally developed by Locke in 1968 and further developed with practical applicability. Research to date suggests that for goals to be motivating they must be sufficiently specific, challenging but not impossible and set participatively. Also the person appraised needs feedback on future progress.

The other theoretical base of performance management is expectancy theory, which states that individuals will be motivated to act provided they expect to be able to achieve the goals set, believe that achieving the goals will lead to other rewards and believe that the rewards on offer are valued.

Given such an emphasis on a link into the organization's objectives it is somewhat disappointing that Bevan and Thompson found no correlation between the existence of a performance management system and organizational performance in the private sector. So performance management, such as HR systems and processes, still remains an act of faith. As with appraisal systems, some performance management systems are development driven and some are reward driven.

There are many different definitions of performance management and some have identified it as 'management by objectives' under another name. There are, however, some key differences. Management by objectives was primarily an off-the-peg system which was bought in and generally involved objectives being imposed on managers from above. Performance management tends to be tailor-made and produced inhouse (which is why there are so many different versions), with an emphasis on mutual objective setting and on ongoing performance support and review. The term, therefore, remains beyond precise definition, and rightly so, as it is critical that the system adopted fits with the culture and context of the organization. As well as the right sort of culture, the right sort of leadership is needed together with a focus on the right priorities. Interestingly, though, Williams notes that performance management can be used as a tool of culture change.

Characteristics of performance management systems:

- Top-down link between business objectives and individual objectives (compared with performance appraisal where there may be no objectives, or objectives not explicitly linked to business objectives)
- Line manager driven and owned (rather than being owned by the HR function, as typically with performance appraisal)
- A living document where performance plans, support and ongoing review are documented as work progresses, and prior to annual review (rather than an archived document retrieved at appraisal time to compare achievement with intentions)
- Performance is rewarded and reinforced

STAGES IN A PERFORMANCE MANAGEMENT SYSTEM

BUSINESS MISSION, VALUES, OBJECTIVES AND COMPETENCIES

There is an assumption that before it is able to plan and manage individual performance the organization will have made significant steps in identifying the performance required of the organization as a whole. In most cases this will involve a mission statement so that performance is seen within the context of an overriding theme. Bevan and Thompson found that performance management organizations were more likely than others to have an organizational mission statement and to communicate this to employees. In addition many organizations will identify the strategic business objectives that are required within the current business context to be competitive and that align with the organization's mission statement.

Many organizations will also identify core values of the business and the key competencies required. Each of these has a potential role in managing individual performance. Organizational objectives are particularly important, as it is common for such objectives to be cascaded down the organization in order to ensure that individual objectives contribute to their achievement.

PLANNING PERFORMANCE: A SHARED VIEW OF EXPECTED PERFORMANCE

Individual objectives derived from team objectives and an agreed job description can be jointly devised by manager and employee. These objectives are outcome/results oriented rather than task oriented, are tightly defined and include measures to be assessed. The objectives are designed to stretch the individual, and offer potential development as well as meeting business needs. It is helpful to both the organization and the individual if objectives are prioritised. Many organizations use the 'SMART' acronym for describing individual objectives or targets:

- Specific
- Measurable
- Appropriate
- Relevant
- Timed

It is clearly easier for some parts of the organization than others to set targets. There is often a tendency for those in technical jobs, such as computer systems development, to identify purely technical targets, reflecting the heavy task emphasis they see in their jobs. Moving staff to a different view of how their personal objectives contribute to team and organizational objectives is an important part of the performance management process. An objective for a team leader in systems development could be: To complete development interviews with all team members by end July 2010.

Clearly, the timescale for each objective will need to reflect the content of the objective and not timescales set into the performance management system. As objectives are met, managers and their staff need to have a brief review meeting to look at progress in all objectives and decide what other objectives should be added, changed or deleted. Five or six ongoing objectives are generally sufficient for one individual to work on at any time.

The critical point about a shared view of performance suggests that handing out a job description or list of objectives to the employee is not adequate. Performance expectations need to be understood and, where possible, to involve a contribution from the employee. For example, although key accountabilities may be fixed by the manager, they will need to be discussed. Specific objectives allow for and benefit from a greater degree of employee input as employees will have a valid view of barriers to overcome, the effort involved and feasibility. Expressing objectives as a 'what' statement rather than a 'how' statement gives employees the power to decide the appropriate approach once they begin to work on the issue. Incorporating employee input and using 'what' statements are likely to generate a higher degree of employee ownership and commitment. However, difficulties have been experienced with purely 'what' objectives as there may be appropriate and inappropriate ways of achieving an objective. For example, a manager with an objective to ensure that another department agrees to a plan of action could achieve this in different ways. The manager may pressure susceptible members of the other department and force agreement through without listening to the other department's perspective. This may alienate the other department and damage future good relations. Alternatively the manager could adopt a collabourative approach so that the needs of both departments are met, providing a sound basis for future cooperation between the departments. More sophisticated systems now incorporate the 'how' as well.

Planning the support, development and resources necessary for employees to achieve their objectives is imperative. Without this support it is unlikely that even the most determined employees will achieve the performance required.

Concerns have been expressed over restricting the objectives to those which specify output targets, and there is now evidence of increasing use of input targets, such as developing a critical competency which is valued by the organization and relevant to the achievement of objectives. Williams argues that as individuals cannot always control their results it is important to have behavioural targets as well as output targets. It is also recommended that there is a personal development plan which would again underpin the achievement of objectives.

DELIVERING AND MONITORING PERFORMANCE

While the employee is working to achieve the performance agreed, the manager retains a key enabling role. Organizing the resources and off-job training is clearly essential. So too is being accessible. There may well be unforeseen barriers to the agreed performance which the manager needs to deal with, and sometimes the situation will demand that the expected performance needs to be revised. The employee may want to sound out possible courses of action with the manager before proceeding, or may require further information. Sharing 'inside' information that will affect the employee's performance is often a key need, although it is also something that managers find difficult, especially with sensitive information. Managers can identify information sources and other people who may be helpful.

Ongoing coaching during the task is especially important. Managers can guide employees through discussion and by giving constructive feedback. They are in a position to provide practical job experiences to develop the critical skills and competencies that the employee needs, and can provide job-related opportunities for practice. Managers can identify potential role models to employees, and help to explain how high achievers perform so well.

Although it is the employee's responsibility to achieve the performance agreed, the manager has a continuous role in providing support and guidance, and in oiling the organizational wheels.

Ongoing review is an important activity for employees to carry out in order to plan their work and priorities and also to highlight to the manager well in advance if the agreed performance will not be delivered by the agreed dates. Joint employee/ manager review is essential so that information is shared. For example, a manager needs to be kept up to date on employee progress, while the employee needs to be kept up to date on organizational changes that have an impact on the agreed objectives. Both need to share perceptions of how the other is doing in their role, and what they could do that would be more helpful.

These reviews are normally informal, although a few notes may be taken of progress made and actions agreed. They need not be part of any formal system and therefore can take place when the job or the individuals involved demand, and not according to a pre-set schedule. The purpose of the review is to facilitate future employee performance, and provide an opportunity for the manager to confirm that the employee is 'on the right track', or redirect him or her if necessary. They thus provide a forum for employee reward in terms of recognition of progress. A 'well done' or an objective signed off as completed can enhance the motivation to perform well in the future. During this period evidence collection is also important. In the Scottish Prison Service line managers maintain a performance monitoring log of their team members' positive and negative behaviours in order to provide regular feedback and to embed the practice on ingoing assessment. Employees are expected to build up a portfolio of evidence of their performance over the period to increase the objectivity of reviews and to provide an audit trail to back up any assessment ratings. It is also during this part of the cycle that employees in many organizations can collect 360-degree feedback to be used developmentally and as part of an evidence base.

FORMAL PERFORMANCE REVIEW/ASSESSMENT

Regular formal reviews are needed to concentrate on developmental issues and to motivate the employee. Also, an annual review and assessment is needed, of the extent to which objectives have been met which may well affect pay received. In many organizations employees are now invited to prepare an initial draft of achievement against objectives. Some organizations continue to have overall assessment ratings which have to conform to a forced distribution. So if there were a five-point rating scale percentages would be set requiring each team/department to have, say, 10 per cent of employees on the top point, 20 per cent on the next point, and so on. Some organizations encourage employees to give upward feedback to their managers at this point in the cycle.

REWARD

Many systems still include a link with pay, but Fletcher and Williams point to some difficulties experienced. Some public and private organizations found that the merit element of pay was too small to motivate staff, and sometimes seen as insulting. Although performance management organizations were more likely than others to have merit or performance-related pay, some organizations have regretted its inclusion. Armstrong and Baron report that staff almost universally disliked the link with pay, and a manager in one of their case study companies reported that 'the whole process is an absolute nightmare'. There are other forms of reward than monetary and the Institute of Employment Studies found that there was more satisfaction with the system where promotion and development, rather than money, was used as a reward for good performance.

IMPLEMENTATION AND CRITIQUE OF PERFORMANCE MANAGEMENT

Performance management needs to be line driven rather than HR driven, and therefore mechanisms need to be found to make this happen. The incorporation of line managers alongside HR managers in a working party to develop the system is clearly important as it not only takes account of the needs of the line in the system design, it also demonstrates that the system is line led. Training in the introduction and use of the system is also ideally line led, and Fletcher and Williams give us an excellent example of an organization where line managers were trained as 'performance management coaches' who were involved in departmental training and support for the new system. However, some researchers have found that line managers are the weak link in the system.

Bevan and Thompson found incomplete take-up of performance management, with some aspects being adopted and not others. They noted that there was a general lack of integration of activities. This is rather unfortunate as one of the key advantages of performance management is the capacity for integration of activities concerned with the management of individual performance. This problem is still apparent. Hendry et al. reported the comments of Phil Wills from GrandMet, that there is still little understanding of what an integrated approach to performance management means. While alignment is critical, some organizations do not understand whether their HR processes are aligned or pulling in different directions. Williams suggests that there is still confusion over the nature of performance management.

Performance management seems to suffer from the same problems as traditional appraisal systems. Armstrong and Baron report, for example, that over half the respondents to their survey feel that managers give their best ratings to people that they like, and over half the managers surveyed felt that they had not received sufficient training in performance management processes. They also report that the use of ratings was consistently derided by staff and seen as subjective and inconsistent. Performance ratings can be seen as demotivating, and forced distributions are felt to be particularly unfair.

In terms of individual objective setting linked to organizational performance objectives, there are problems when strategy is unclear and when it evolves. Rose also reports a range of problems, particularly the fact that SMART targets can be problematic if they are not constantly reviewed and updated, although this is a time-consuming process. Pre-set objectives can be a constraining factor in such a rapidly changing business context, and they remind us of the trap of setting measurable targets, precisely because they are measurable and satisfy the system, rather than because they are most important to the organization. He argues that a broader approach which assesses the employee's accomplishments as a whole and their contribution to the organization is more helpful than concentrating on pre-set objectives. Williams also notes that there is more to performance than task performance, such as volunteering and helping others. He refers to this as contextual performance; it is sometimes referred to as collegiate behaviour.

A further concern with SMART targets is that they inevitably have a short-term focus, yet what is most important to the organization is developments which are complex and longer term, which are very difficult to pin down to short-term targets. In this context systems which also focus on the development of competencies will add greater value in the longer term. Armstrong and Baron do note that a more rounded view of performance is gradually being adopted, which involves the 'how' as well as the 'what', and inputs such as the development of competencies. There is, however, a long way to go adequately to describe performance and define what is really required for organizational success.

THE NATURE OF 360-DEGREE FEEDBACK

This approach to feedback refers to the use of the whole range of sources from which feedback can be collected about any individual. Thus feedback is collected from every angle on the way that the individual carries out their job: from immediate line manager; peers; subordinates; more senior managers; internal customers; external customers; and from individuals themselves. It is argued that this breadth of feedback provides superior feedback to feedback from the line manager's perspective only, since the latter will only be able to observe the individual in a limited range of situations, and Atwater and his colleagues suggest that 360-degree feedback provides a better way to capture the complexities of performance. Individuals, it is argued, will find feedback from peers and subordinates compelling and more valid, and Edwards and Ewen maintain that: No organizational action has more power for motivating employee behaviour change than feedback from credible work associates.

Such all-round feedback enables the individual to understand how they may be seen differently (or similarly) by different organizational groups, and how this may contrast with their own views of their strengths and weaknesses. This provides powerful information for the development of self-awareness. While 360-degree feedback may be collected using informal methods, as shown in the Window on practice box on Humberside Tec, the term itself is a registered trade mark, and refers to a very specific method of feedback collection and analysis which was devised in the United States, and they suggest that 'simplistic, informal approaches to multi-source assessment are likely to multiply rather than reduce error'. However, informal approaches to 360-degree feedback are sometimes used quite successfully as an alternative to a survey questionnaire and statistical analysis. The formal process is a survey approach which involves the use of a carefully constructed questionnaire that is used with all the contributors of feedback. This questionnaire may be bought off the peg, providing a well-tested tool, or may be developed internally, providing a tool which is more precisely matched to the needs of the organization. Whichever form is used, the essence is that it is based on behavioural competencies, and their associated behaviours. Contributors will be asked to score, on a given scale, the extent to which the individual displays these behaviours.

Using a well-designed questionnaire, distributed to a sufficient number of contributors and employing appropriate sophisticated analysis, for example specifically designed computer packages which are set up to detect and moderate collusion and bias on behalf of the contributors, should provide reliable and valid data for the individual. The feedback is usually presented to the individual in the form of graphs or bar charts showing comparative scores from different feedback groups, such as peers, subordinates, customers, where the average will be provided for each group, and single scores from line manager and self. In most cases the individual will have been able to choose the composition of the contributors in each group, for example which seven subordinates, out of a team of 10, will be asked to complete the feedback questionnaire.

But beyond this the feedback will be anonymous as only averages for each group of contributors will be reported back, except for the line manager's score. The feedback will need to be interpreted by an internal or external facilitator, and done via a face-to-face meeting. It is generally recommended that the individual will need some training in the nature of the system and how to receive feedback, and the contributors will need some training on how to provide feedback. The principle behind the idea of feedback is that individuals can then use this information to change their behaviours and to improve performance, by setting and meeting development goals and an action plan.

Reported benefits include a stronger ownership of development goals, a climate of constructive feedback, improved communication over time and an organization which is more capable of change as continuous feedback and improvement have become part of the way people work.

DIFFICULTIES AND DILEMMAS

As with all processes and systems there needs to be clarity about the purpose. Most authors distinguish between developmental uses, which they identify as fairly safe and a good way of introducing such a system, and other uses such as to determine pay awards. There seems to be an almost universal view that using these data for pay purposes is not advisable, and in the literature from the United States there is clearly a concern about the legal ramifications of doing this. Ward provides a useful framework for considering the different applications of this type of feedback, and reviews in some detail other applications such as using 360-degree feedback as part of a training course to focus attention for each individual on what they need to get out of the course. Other applications he suggests include using 360-degree feedback as an approach to team building, as a method of performance appraisal/management, for organization development purposes and to evaluate training anddevelopment. Edwards and Ewen suggest that it can be used for nearly all HR systems, using selection, training and development, recognition and the allocation of job assignments as examples.

As well as clarity of purpose, confidentiality of raters is very important with most approaches to 360-degree feedback, and this can be difficult to maintain with a small team, as Hurley suggests. Thus raters may feel uncomfortable about being open and honest. The dangers of collusion and bias need to be eliminated, and it is suggested that the appropriate software systems can achieve this, but they are of course expensive, as are well-validated off-the-peg systems. Follow-up is critical and if the experience of 360-degree feedback is not built on via the construction of development goals and the support and resources to fulfil these, the process may be viewed negatively and may be demotivating.

London et al. report concerns about the way systems are implemented, and that nearly one-third of respondents they surveyed experienced negative effects. Atwater and his colleagues found some negative reactions such as reduced effort, dissatisfaction with peers who provided the feedback and a lower commitment to colleagues. Fletcher and Baldry note that there are contradictions in the results from 360-degree feedback so far, and they suggest that further research is needed on how feedback affects self-esteem, motivation, satisfaction and commitment. The DTI suggests that sufficient resources need to be devoted to planning a system and that it should be piloted before general use. Clearly, 360-degree feedback needs to be handled carefully and sensitively and in the context of an appropriate organizational climate so that it is not experienced as a threat. The DTI suggests that there needs to be a climate of openness and trust for 360-degree feedback to work. Atwater et al. suggest that to counteract any negative effects it is important to prepare people for making their own ratings and on how they can provide honest and constructive feedback to others, ensure confidentiality and anonymity of raters, make sure the feedback is used developmentally and owned by the person being rated (for example they may be the only person to receive the report), provide post-feedback coaching and encouragement and encourage people to follow up the feedback they have received.

Note: For a case study visit company's site of Ryder System, Inc. www.ryder.com. Ryder System (Ryder) is engaged in the provision of transportation, logistics and supply chain management solutions worldwide. It also undertakes maintenance of commercial trucks, tractors and trailers. The company primarily operates in the US. It is headquartered in Miami, Florida and employs 28,000 people.

14

Team Performance

The appointments pages of Personnel Management, People Management and other periodicals have since the early 1990s been littered with advertisements from rganisations that are seeking 'proactive', 'natural', 'enthusiastic', 'genuine' and 'effective' team players, who 'enjoy' or 'have a preference for' working in a team environment, and who are 'committed' to team working. The report of the 1998 Workplace Employee Relations survey acknowledged that teamworking is central to new forms of work organization, Geary and Dobbins suggest that teams are repeatedly identified as an aspect of post-industrial society and we could say that 'the team is now the norm at work'. Yet again, however, a gap between rhetoric and reality has been identified due to unevenness of current practices.

PURPOSE, NATURE AND IMPACT OF TEAMWORK

While it is generally accepted that teamworking has increased, there are continued debates about the prevalence of teamwork, its definition and the advantages and disadvantages of this way of working.

Determining the prevalence of teamwork is extremely difficult because of differences in the definition used and the criteria applied. Teamwork is frequently seen as an aspect of high-performance work systems, in which case the focus is on lean production teams/semi-autonomous teams, usually in the production sector. However, teams are used in a much wider context than this, as we shall explore later. Even in this narrower context there is much debate about what might constitute a team. In teamworking surveys lists of team characteristics are typically used and only if the organization being surveyed ticks off a sufficient percentage of these is it considered that teamworking exists. In addition, for an organization to be identified as being based on teamworking, there has to be a specified percentage of employees, or employees in the largest employee group organized by team. Benders and others provide an excellent discussion of the definitions used in teamworking surveys across a range of European countries.

In spite of a more critical perspective being taken of late, teamwork is still used and introduced as a way of empowering employees and facilitating the development of their full potential in order to enhance organizational performance. A heavy emphasis on teamwork usually corresponds with 'flatter' organizations, which have diminished status differentials, and reduced staffing. Teamwork, of course, is not a recent idea, and the autonomous working groups of the 1960s and 1970s are its clear forerunners. The similarities are increasing responsibility, authority and a sense of achievement among group members. The protagonists of autonomous working groups were also intent on improving the quality of working life of employees by providing a wider range of tasks to work on (job enrichment) and a social environment in which to carry them out. The emphasis currently is quite different. While it is argued that team members will gain intrinsic rewards from autonomy, job satisfaction, identification with work and greater skills development, performance is the unvarying aim. Higher performance is expected due to increased flexibility and communication within teams, increased ownership of the task and commitment to team goals. Some of the most famous autonomous working groups at Volvo in Sweden have now been disbanded because their production levels were too low compared with other forms of production. Current teams are designed to outperform other production methods, and Natále et al., for example, argue that they are fundamental to continuous corporate improvement. They are also seen as critical in the development of a learning organization.

There remain many strong supporters of teamwork and many organizations committed to this approach, although it is also criticised as management control by another means and has often failed to improve performance. Van den Beukel and Molleman found a range of unintended consequences of teamwork, and others have reported loss of skills, work intensification and peer pressure as problems. Butcher and Bailey, for example, note that teamwork has not always achieved the desired result, and Attaran and Nguyen found that flexible structures, such as teamwork, have sometimes been abandoned in favour of returning to more traditional approaches. Not only have organizations begun to consider whether teamwork will produce the expected productivity gains, employees who have experienced teamwork have sometimes viewed it as unsuccessful and feel less optimistic about it than previously. Part of the problem may also be unrealistic expectations. Very often performance dips when teamwork is introduced, and the performance improvements only come later on. Teamwork is not a 'quick fix', as has been noted by many of those who have been involved. Part of the problem may also be that, as Church notes, there has been a tendency to think that teamwork is a solution for all our problems. Thus teamwork has undoubtedly been used in some situations where it was inappropriate, or where there was insufficient support to make it effective.

So, what is a team? How does it differ from all the other groups in organizations? A team can be described as more than the sum of the individual members. In other words, a team demands collabourative, not competitive, effort, where each member takes responsibility for the performance of the team rather than just their own individual performance. The team comes first, the individual comes second, and everything the individual member does is geared to the fulfilment of the team's goals rather than their individual agenda. If you think of a football team, a surgical team or an orchestra, it is easier to see how each member is assigned a specific role depending on their skills and how individuals use their skills for the benefit of the team performance rather than selectively using them for personal achievement. In a football game, for example, a player making a run towards the goal would pass to another player in a better position to score rather than risk trying to score themselves for the sake of personal glory.

Moxon defines a team as having a common purpose; agreed norms and values which regulate behaviour; members with interdependent functions and a recognition of team identity. Katzenbach and Smith and Katzenbach have also described the differences that they see between teams and work-groups, and identify teams as comprising individuals with complementary skills, shared leadership roles, mutual accountability and a specific team purpose, among other attributes. In organizations this dedication only happens when individuals are fully committed to the team's goals. This commitment derives from an involvement in defining how the goals will be met and having the power to make decisions within teams rather than being dependent on the agreement of external management. These are particularly characteristics of self-managing teams.

Organizational teams differ, though, in terms of their temporary or permanent nature, the interchangeability of individual members and tasks and the breadth of tasks or functions held within the team:

- *Timespan*. Some teams are set up to solve a specific problem, and when this has been solved the team disbands. Other teams may be longer term and project based, and may disband when the project is complete. Some teams will be relatively permanent fixtures, such as production teams, where the task is ongoing.
- *Leadership*. Some teams are based on shared responsibility, although a leader may emerge, and this leader may change depending on the task. Other teams will have a hierarchically appointed leader.
- *Interchangeability*. Teams differ in the range of specific skills that are required and as to whether there is an expectation that all members will learn all skills. In some production teams interchangeability of skills is key, and all members will have the potential and will be expected to learn all skills eventually. In other types of team, for example cross-functional teams (surgical teams, product development teams), each member is expected to bring their specialist skills to use for the benefit of the team, and they are not expected to be able to learn all the skills of each other member.
- *Task and functional range*. Many production teams will often be designed to cover a whole task and within this there will be a wide range of activities. This clearly differs from the traditional line form of production where the tasks are broken down and segmented. Other teams will span a range of functions – for example cross-functional teams involving, say, research, development, marketing and production staff.

In this chapter we shall go on to look at the characteristics of four broad types of team: production or service teams; cross-functional management teams; problem-

solving teams; and departmental teams. We then look at what factors affect teams' performance and what can be done to improve team effectiveness, as these matters are currently of critical concern.

BROAD TEAM TYPES

PRODUCTION AND SERVICE TEAMS

It is producton and service teams that are often referred to as self-managing teams, self-managing work teams or self-directed teams. They are typically given the authority to submit a team budget, order resources as necessary within budget, organize training required, select new team members, plan production to meet predefined goals, schedule holidays and absence cover and deploy staff within the team. There is a clear emphasis on taking on managerial tasks that would previously have been done by a member of the managerial hierarchy. These managerial tasks are delegated to the lowest possible organizational level in the belief that these tasks will be carried out in a responsible manner for the benefit of the team and the organization. The payoff from this self-management has been shown in Monsanto, for example, to be a 47 per cent increase in productivity and quality over four years. These teams are often used in such areas as car production and the production of electrical and electronic equipment. Teams will be based around a complete task so that they perform a whole chunk of the production process and in this way have something clear to manage. For example, the team will normally include people with maintenance skills, specific technical skills and different types of assembly skills so that they are self-sufficient and not dependent on waiting for support from other parts of the organization. The ultimate aim is usually for all members to have all the skills needed within the team, in other words to be multiskilled.

There are, however, two major variations of such teams. In some teams there is a hierarchically distinct team leader, and these are sometimes referred to as lean teams, compared with teams where everyone is on an equal level. Doorewaard et al. distinguish between 'hierarchical teams' and 'shared responsibility teams', making the point that in the hierarchical teams, team autonomy does not mean team member autonomy. They go on to say that a lot of so-called autonomous teams are lean teams and there is not much autonomy for team members as responsibility is in the hands of the team leader. In shared-responsibility teams a leader may emerge, or the leadership may vary according to the nature of task, resting with whoever has the most appropriate skills to offer. Leaders, in both forms of team, will need to take on managerial tasks such as planning, organizing, supporting individuals, presenting information and representing the team to the rest of the organization. The way that the leader carries out these activities and involves others in them will clearly have an impact on the effectiveness of the team. Where leadership is static the leader's role is often defined in terms of a coaching rather than a directing role.

The nature of self-management also has an impact on the role of managers outside the team. Traditionally these managers would carry out the tasks described above and would monitor and control the performance of the team. If these tasks are no longer appropriate, what is the role of the manager – is there a role at all? It will come as no surprise that the formation of self-managed teams is seen as a threat to some managers. However, Casey comments that 'self-managed teams do not deny the role of manager, they redefine it'. He also notes that the management of the team is a balance between responsibility within the team and management without, rather than an all-or-nothing situation. He suggests a move towards 90 per cent within the team in a self-management situation rather than nearer 30 per cent in a traditional management situation.

Where there are self-managed teams the role of the traditional manager outside the team changes to adviser and coach, as they have now delegated most of their responsibilities for directly managing the team. These managers become a resource to be called on when needed in order to enable the team to solve their own problems.

The self-managing team concept has much to offer in terms of increasing employee ownership and control and thereby releasing their commitment, creativity and potential. There are, of course, potential problems with this approach too. These include the difficulty of returning to traditional systems once employees have experienced greater autonomy; resistance from other parts of the organization; and peer pressure and its consequences. We would also add resistance from team members too. Let us look at some of these in more detail.

RESISTANCE FROM OTHER PARTS OF THE ORGANIZATION

As self-managing teams have clear knock-on effects for other parts of the organization these other parts will react. If traditional managers do not give direction and control over to the team an immediate conflict is set up as to 'who makes the decisions around here'; if they fail to support and coach, the team may feel abandoned and insecure. In general, the climate of the organization needs to be supportive in terms of the value placed on individual autonomy and learning. Marchington points out that it is unrealistic to assess teamworking in isolation from management's perceived commitment to employees and their approach to the employment relationship as a whole. There are situations also where the rhetoric of the organization is about delegating responsibility to the team, but where management fail to give up ownership of the task.

RESISTANCE WITHIN THE TEAM

Individuals who have spent many years being told what to do may need some time to take this responsibility for themselves. However, for locations which want to make the transition, the importance of team selection of newcomers and of selecting skills relevant to a team environment as well as essential technical skills will be key. Salem, Lazarus and Cullen note that the most often cited individual characteristics for a team environment are 'interpersonal skills, self-motivation, ability to cope with peer pressure, level of technical/administrative experience, communication skills and the ability to cope with stress'. Other characteristics that have been noted elsewhere include the ability to deal with ambiguous situations and cope with conflict in a constructive way. Team members may feel resistant due to fear of loss of valued skills, but this seldom actually happens.

PEER PRESSURE

The byproducts of peer pressure have been identified as lower absence levels, due to an awareness that colleagues have to cover for them; and a higher production rate so as not to let colleagues down. However, intense peer pressure can lead to stress and destroy many of the perceived benefits of team involvement from the employees' perspective. It is argued that peer pressure makes team members active participants in their own work intensification, as they develop rules to monitor behaviour in the team. Ezzamel and Willmott found that social loafing within the team (i.e. not pulling your weight) provoked other team members to act as supervisors, when team performance was related to rewards, adding yet more pressure.

CROSS-FUNCTIONAL MANAGEMENT TEAMS

Cross-functional management teams are very different from the teams described above, and members are more likely to retain other roles in the organization. Typically they will see themselves as members of their function, whether it be marketing, research, sales, development and members of a specific project team as well. In fact the term 'project' (for example as in 'projects for change') rather than 'team' is being used increasingly to minimise any negative connotations of the word 'team'. Very often the project team will manage the development of a particular product, such as a computer package, a drug, a piece of electrical equipment from creation to sales. Members may be allocated to the team by their home function for all or part of their time. In fact many cross-functional teams are virtual teams, and although they may work closely together, they are rarely physically together. Henry and Hartzler define virtual teams as 'groups of people who work closely together even though they are geographically separated and may reside in different time zones in different parts of the world'. It is in this context that technology comes into its own – video conferencing, for example. However, Bal and Grundy argue that all too often the emphasis is the technology, rather than the all-important human processes.

The thinking behind a cross-functional team is that each member brings with them the expertise in their own function and the dedication to the team task around a certain product or project. By bringing individuals together as a team the project gains through the commitment of team members to a task that they feel that they own. Bringing these individuals together enables the development of a common language and the overcoming of departmental boundaries. Such teams are a key feature of a matrix organization where individuals may be, simultaneously, members of a functional department and a product-based team, frequently with two direct line managers.

Meyer expresses the importance of measures of performance for cross-functional teams, and sees process measures as key rather than just measures of achievements. His argument is that process measures help the team to gauge their progress, and identify and rectify problems. It follows from this that the performance measures used need to be designed by the team and not imposed on them from senior management, as the team will know best what measures will help them to do their job. Inevitably these measures will need to be designed against a strategic context set by higher management. Meyer describes a good example of the problems that can result if managers try to control the performance measurement process rather than empowering team members.

The process of agreeing their own performance measures will also enable the team to identify different assumptions and perceptions that each team member holds, and generate discussion on the exact goals of the team. All this is helpful in bringing the team together, generating a common language and ensuring that everyone is pulling in the same direction.

One special form of cross-functional management team is the top management team of the organization. Clearly, this team is different in that it is permanent and not project based, but its members still need to work as a team rather than a collection of individuals. Katzenbach and

Smith note that it is more difficult to get this group to work together as a team as they are more likely to be individualist than are team members elsewhere in the organization. Directors often still see themselves as representatives of their function rather than members of a team, and thus will be more likely to defend their position and attempt to influence each other than to pull together. Katzenbach suggests that strong executive leadership and true teamwork require different, but equally important disciplines, which need to be integrated rather than being seen as alternatives. Garratt asks three key questions of top teams to assess whether they are truly direction-giving teams. He asks about regular processes, outside formal meetings, to discuss what is going on in the organization and what possibilities exist; to what extent the team involve themselves in unstructured visioning before grappling with the practical matters of plans and budgets; and to what extent they assess individual contributions and the skills and resources owned within the team. He finds little evidence of any of these activities taking place.

FUNCTIONAL TEAMS

Functional teams, as the name implies, are made up of individuals within a function. For example, the training section of the HR department may well be referred to as the training team – different groups of nurses on a specific ward are sometimes divided into, say, the 'red' team and the 'blue' team. Sales staff for a particular product or region may refer to themselves as the 'games software sales team' or the 'north west sales team'. Some of the rationale behind this is to give the customer, internal or external, an identified set of individuals to liaise with. Given that these will be a smaller set than those in the whole department, they will be able to gain a much closer knowledge of particular customers and a better understanding of customer needs. The extent to which these are really teams as opposed to groups of individuals will vary enormously.

PROBLEM-SOLVING TEAMS

Problem-solving teams may be within a function or cross-functional. Within-function teams may typically be in the form of quality circles where employees voluntarily come together to tackle production and quality issues affecting their work. Unfortunately, many of these teams have had little impact and it has not been possible to implement recommended changes and improvements, owing to the retention of management control. Other within-function problem-solving teams may consist of specially selected individuals who will be involved in the implementation of a major development within the function or department. For example, the implementation of performance management may be supported by specific coaches in each department who carry out related training, offer counselling and advice and who tailor organization policy so that it meets department needs. These coaches may become the departmental performance management team.

Cross-functional problem-solving teams may be brought together to solve an identified and specific organizational problem, and will remain together for a short period until that problem has been solved. They differ from cross-functional management teams as their role is not to manage anything, but rather to collect and analyse data and perspectives and develop an understanding of the nature of the problem. From this they will make recommendations on how to solve the problem which are then passed on to higher management. Usually their remit ends here, and they have little or no involvement in implementation. Team members will retain their normal work role at the same time as being a team member.

TEAM EFFECTIVENESS

For a team to be effective its members need a clear and agreed vision, objectives and set of rules by which they will work together. Proehl, for example, identifies the need for a clear project purpose, which members agree is worthy. In addition, he found that clear project boundaries, deadlines and specific follow-up activities by a designated co-ordinator were all important to team effectiveness.

Team members will need to feel able to be open and honest with each other and be prepared to confront difficulties and differences. It is also important for members to be able to tolerate conflict and be able to use this in a collabourative way in the achievement of the team's objectives. Some researchers have commented upon the size of the team and suggest it should be small enough, say no more than 20, for communications to be feasible. Others have suggested that proximity is important in maintaining communications and team spirit.

We have previously mentioned support from management as being critical to team success. Edwards and Wright note from their case study the problems caused by managers who interfere with team autonomy. Next we explore the key issues of selection, training and development, assessment and reward in relation to team effectiveness.

SELECTING TEAM MEMBERS

The effectiveness of a team largely depends on the appropriateness of the team members. For self-managing teams there is a strong lobby for newcomers to be appointed by the team themselves, and indeed some would argue that unless this happens the team is not truly self-managing. Other case studies suggest that team members, whether selected by the team or by others, are chosen very carefully in the likeness of the team and with the 'right attitudes'. For all teamwork Katzenbach and Smith identify three critical selection criteria: technical or functional expertise, problem-solving and decision-making skills and interpersonal skills, and it also seems that successful teams have team members with high levels of emotional intelligence.

Another approach to selection of team members is to gain an understanding of the team roles that they are best able to play, so that the team is endowed with a full range of the roles that it will need to be effective. Meredith Belbin, through extensive research and the evolution of his original ideas, has identified nine team roles which are important to a team and which individuals may have as strengths or weaknesses. The absence of some or many of these roles can cause problems in team effectiveness. Too many individuals playing the same type of role can cause undue friction in the team and again damage effectiveness. The key is achieving a balance. These team roles are as follows:

- *Coordinator*. This person will have a clear view of the team objectives and will be skilled at inviting the contribution of team members in achieving these, rather than just pushing his or her own view. The coordinator (or chairperson) is self-disciplined and applies this discipline to the team. They are confident and mature, and will summarise the view of the group and will be prepared to take a decision on the basis of this.

- *Shaper*. The shaper is full of drive to make things happen and get things going. In doing this they are quite happy to push their own views forward, do not mind being challenged and are always ready to challenge others. The shaper looks for the pattern in discussions and tries to pull things together into something feasible which the team can then get to work on.

- *Plant*. This member is the one who is most likely to come out with original ideas and challenge the traditional way of thinking about things. Sometimes they become so imaginative and creative that the team cannot see the relevance of what they are saying. However, without the plant to scatter the seeds of new ideas the team will often find it difficult to make any headway. The plant's strength is in providing major new insights and ideas for changes in direction and not in contributing to the detail of what needs to be done.

- *Resource investigator*. The resource investigator is the group member with the strongest contacts and networks, and is excellent at bringing in information and support from the outside. This member can be very enthusiastic in pursuit of the team's goals, but cannot always sustain this enthusiasm.
- *Implementer*. The individual who is a company worker is well organized and effective at turning big ideas into manageable tasks and plans that can be achieved. Such individuals are both logical and disciplined in their approach. They are hardworking and methodical but may have some difficulty in being flexible.
- *Team worker*. The team worker is the one who is most aware of the others in the team, their needs and their concerns. They are sensitive and supportive of other people's efforts, and try to promote harmony and reduce conflict. Team workers are particularly important when the team is experiencing a stressful or difficult period.
- *Completer*. As the title suggests, the completer is the one who drives the deadlines and makes sure they are achieved. The completer usually communicates a sense of urgency which galvanises other team members into action. They are conscientious and effective at checking the details, which is a vital contribution, but sometimes get 'bogged down' in them.
- *Monitor evaluator*. The monitor evaluator is good at seeing all the options. They have a strategic perspective and can judge situations accurately. The monitor evaluator can be overcritical and is not usually good at inspiring and encouraging others.
- *Specialist*. This person provides specialist skills and knowledge and has a dedicated and single-minded approach. They can adopt a very narrow perspective and sometimes

fail to see the whole picture.

An individual's potential team roles can be interpreted from some of the psychometric tests used in the normal selection procedure. They can also be assessed in a different way. Belbin designed a specific questionnaire to identify the individual's perceived current team role strengths (that is, the roles they have developed and are actually playing). This is particularly helpful for development within the current team, but may be less useful for selection purposes. Although helpful, current team role strengths may not be automatically transferred into another team situation.

TEAM LEADER AND MANAGER TRAINING

Both team leaders and senior managers begin to play new roles in team situations. Team leaders suddenly find themselves with a host of new responsibilities for the support of team members and the planning and organizing of team activities, responsibilities for which they have little experience and often no training. Similarly managers will need some training support in moving from a directive, controlling role to a coaching and counselling role. Training needs to encompass not only new skills but an opportunity to discuss the changing philosophy of the organization and to encourage attitude change. Support in understanding the nature of involvement, empowerment and participation will also be relevant.

TEAM MEMBER TRAINING

Whether or not the team has an appointed leader all team members will need some training support in working in a different environment with different rules about what they should and should not be doing. Being more involved and taking on more responsibility, and sometimes leading activities, will require some initial training support. Attaran and Nguyen suggest that training in problem solving, communications and time management is important. Applebaum et al. recommend training in conflict management. Further training in new technical skills can often be handled within the team once at least one member has the required knowledge and has gained some training skills themselves.

TEAM DEVELOPMENT

Blau suggests that the current interest in team building is due to the fact that many teams are not working effectively. Teams can be developed in many different ways, and perhaps one of the most critical is early development through the task itself. For example, teams can develop by jointly describing the core purpose of the team, visualising the future position that they are aiming to achieve, developing the rules and procedures they will use, performance measures and so on. If the team are given some support to do this, perhaps a facilitator from the HR function or externally, they can not only develop vital guidelines but also gain an understanding of a way of working things out together, a process which they can use by themselves in the future.

Teams can also develop by looking at the way they have been working since they came together. One way of doing this is by completing a team roles questionnaire to identify the strengths and weaknesses of each member. This will help to promote a better understanding of why things happen as they do, and also pave the way for some changes. On this basis some individuals can develop their potential in team roles that they are not presently using, but for which they have some preference, and in this way a better balance may be struck, making the team more effective. Another process is to review what the team as a whole are good at and bad at, what different individuals can do to enable others to carry out their tasks more effectively, and what improvements can be made in the way that the team organizes itself. Simple suggestions can be surprisingly effective, such as: 'It would really help me if you gave me a list of telephone numbers where I can leave a message for you when I need to get hold of you urgently' (cross-functional team); and 'I don't understand why we need to lay the figures out in this way and it really gets my back up – will someone take some time out to explain it to me?' Rubin, Plovnick and Fry identified four major problem areas in relation to group effectiveness – goals, roles, processes and relationships – and these four can be used to provide a framework for team development activities.

Other less direct methods of development involve working through simulated exercises as a team, such as building a tower out of pieces of paper, and learning from this how the team operate and what they could do to operate better. Outdoor training is also used to good effect in team situations, where the team tackle new, and perhaps dangerous, activities in the outdoors. Typically, some activities involve learning to trust and to depend on each other in a real and risky situation, and the learning from this, and the trust developed, can then be transferred back into the work situation.

The approach taken to team building needs to be appropriate to the stage of development of the team. Tuckman identified four stages of team development – forming, storming, norming and performing. Forming centres on team members working out what they are supposed to be doing, and trying to feel part of it. At this stage they are quite likely to be wary of each other and hide their feelings. Storming is the stage where members are prepared to express strongly held views, where there is conflict and competition and where some push for power while others withdraw. The norming stage is characterised by a desire to begin to organize themselves. Members actually begin to listen to each other, become more open and see problems as belonging to the whole group. Performing is where a sense of group loyalty has developed and where all contribute in an atmosphere of openness and trust. Proehl identifies the importance of mutual respect, and Ingram and Descombe found in their research that camaraderie was very important in getting the work done.

RECOGNITION AND REWARD

Like individuals, teams need some form of recognition and reward for their efforts. Recognition may be in the form of articles in company newsletters or local papers about team successes, inscribing the team name on the product or monetary rewards. A sense of team identity is often encouraged by the use of team T-shirts, coffee mugs and other usable items. It is most important that other reward systems in the organization, say based on individual contribution, do not cut across the reinforcement for team performance. Kerrin and Oliver, for example, found contradictions between the team structure of work and an individual focus in terms of reward. For example, workers did not put improvement ideas directly to the team, but submitted them to the company suggestion scheme instead as they could gain monetary awards from this. Also when new processes were suggested they did not voice their concerns about the problems they foresaw – instead they waited until the process was implemented and then put suggestions into the suggestion scheme. For teams where the longer-term objective is for all members to acquire the whole range of skills, a payment system which pays for skills gained rather than job done will be important.

ARE TEAMS ALWAYS THE RIGHT ANSWER?

Team-based work seems set to increase – on the premise that it will improve organizational commitment and performance. The three difficult issues that will need to be tackled are that not all employees will feel comfortable or perform their best in a team-based situation; that teamwork is not always the best approach; and that not all teams are effective teams. Critics of a team environment suggest that it can have a downward levelling effect, that it stunts creativity and is generally limiting. Generating the essential openness, trust and commitment is also a potential difficulty, and decision making can become a lengthy process. Where teams have been introduced inappropriately the result has been lower productivity, poorer decisions and increased dissatisfaction, as noted by Applebaum et al., and this finding conflicts with all the case examples of performance improvement due to the use of teams. These contradictory reports may be explained, as Edwards and Wright suggested, by the many different types of teams that are set up, and by the impact of different organizational environments.

Note: For a detailed example of this chapter visit Big 5 Sporting Goods Corporation site. Big 5 Sporting Goods Corporation (Big 5) is a retailer of sporting goods and accessories. The company primarily operates in the US. It is headquartered in El Segundo, California and employs 8,900 people; this figure includes part-time employees. www.big5sportinggoods.com

15

Leadership and Motivation

Leadership and motivation are two of the most loaded and misunderstood words in management. Individual managers are often seduced by concepts of leadership that show them to be knights in shining armour with superhuman qualities and (this is the really dangerous bit) adoring followers. The followers rarely have that view of their managers. Motivation is often constructed in the same way, 'How can I motivate the members of my team?', although this ignores the mainsprings of motivation, which are in the performer rather than in the manager of the performer.

We must not, however, underestimate the importance of leadership, motivation and the link between the two. There are indeed sometimes needs for individual leaders who have outstanding personal qualities and who achieve extraordinary change in their business, sometimes more subtle leadership qualities are more important, and there are infinitely more roles which call on different and more modest leadership skills, which can be learned and which are equally important, even if they do not merit shining armour and a white charger.

Understanding of both leadership and motivation was well developed in the second half of the twentieth century and it is this work which is the basis of our understanding and analysis today. The one major addition of recent years has been an appreciation of the impact of changing circumstances of contemporary business and the role of women. All of the twentieth-century studies and theories were based on two complementary assumptions; first, the business norm was of large, stable organizations steadily getting bigger; second, management was almost exclusively a male activity, with male norms. This led to explanations and suggestions based on those two givens. We now see a weakening of both these assumptions. Effective businesses are not necessarily large, growing organizations and there are many more women in the workforce and in management positions within it. Although charismatic leaders (a predominantly male concept) are still needed in some situations, empowering leaders are increasingly required. We reach this at the close of the chapter, but we can only get there by starting further back.

LEADERSHIP AND MANAGEMENT

Northouse suggests that there are four components that characterise leadership: that leadership is a process; it involves influence; it occurs within a group context; and it involves goal attainment. This corresponds with Shackleton's definition, which we shall use as a working definition for the remainder of the chapter: Leadership is the process in which an individual influences other group members towards the attainment of group or organizational goals.

This definition is useful as it leaves open the question of whether leadership is exercised in a commanding or a facilitative manner. It does suggest, however, that the leader in some way motivates others to act in such a way as to achieve group goals.

The definition also makes no assumptions about who is the leader; it may or may not be the nominal head of the group. Managers, therefore, may or may not be leaders, and leaders may or may not be managers. Some authors distinguish very clearly between the nature of management and the nature of leadership but this draws on a particular perspective, that of the transformational leader, and we will consider this in the section on whether the organization needs heroes. This is a school of thought that concentrates on the one leader at the top of the organization, which is very different from organizations and individuals who use the terms manager and leader interchangeably with nothing more than a vague notion that managers should be leaders. Indeed, any individual may act as a manager one day and a leader the next, depending on the situation.

The flow of articles on leadership continues unabated, but it would be a mistake to think that there is an ultimate truth to be discovered; rather, there is a range of perspectives from which we can try to make sense of leadership and motivation. Grint puts it well when he comments that: What counts as leadership appears to change quite radically across time and space.

In the following three sections we will look at three questions which underlie virtually all the work on leadership. First, what are the traits of a leader, or an effective leader? Second, what is the 'best' leadership style or behaviour? Third, if different styles are appropriate at different times, what factors influence the desired style?

WHAT ARE THE TRAITS OF LEADERS AND EFFECTIVE LEADERS?

Trait approaches, which were the earliest to be employed, seek to identify the traits of leaders – in other words what characterises leaders as opposed to those who are not leaders. These approaches rest on the assumption that some people were born to lead due to their personal qualities, while others are not. It suggests that leadership is only available to the chosen few and not accessible to all. These approaches have been discredited for this very reason and because there has been little consistency in the lists of traits that research has uncovered. However, this perspective is frequently resurrected.

Kilpatrick and Locke, in a meta-analysis, did seem to find some consistency around the following traits: drive to achieve; the motivation to lead; honesty and integrity; self-confidence, including the ability to withstand setbacks, standing firm and being emotionally resilient; cognitive ability; and knowledge of the business. They also note the importance of managing the perceptions of others in relation to these characteristics. Northouse provides a useful historical comparison of the lists of traits uncovered in other studies. Perhaps the most well-known expression of the trait approach is the work relating to charismatic leadership. House, for example, describes charismatic leaders as being dominant, having a strong desire to influence, being self-confident and having a strong sense of their own moral values. We will pick up on this concept of leadership in the later section on heroes.

In a slightly different vein Goleman carried out a meta-analysis of leadership competency frameworks in 188 different companies. These frameworks represented the competencies related to outstanding leadership performance. Goleman analysed the competencies into three groups: technical, cognitive and emotional, and found that, in terms of the ratios between each group, emotional competencies 'proved to be twice as important as the others'. Goleman goes on to describe five components of emotional intelligence:

- *Self-awareness*: this he defines as a deep understanding of one's strengths, weaknesses, needs, values and goals. Self-aware managers are aware of their own limitations.

- *Self-regulation*: the control of feelings, the ability to channel them in constructive ways. The ability to feel comfortable with ambiguity and not panic.
- *Motivation*: the desire to achieve beyond expectations, being driven by internal rather than external factors, and to be involved in a continuous striving for improvement.
- *Empathy*: considering employees' feelings alongside other factors when decision making.
- *Social skill*: friendliness with a purpose, being good at finding common ground and building rapport. Individuals with this competency are good persuaders, collabourative managers and natural networkers.

Goleman's research is slightly different from previous work on the trait approach, as here we are considering what makes an effective leader rather than what makes a leader (irrespective of whether they are effective or not). It is also different in that Goleman refers to competencies rather than traits. There is some debate over whether competencies can be developed in people. The general feeling is that some can and some cannot. Goleman maintains that the five aspects of emotional intelligence can be learned and provides an example in his article of one such individual. In spite of his argument we feel that it is still a matter for debate, and as many of the terms used by Goleman are similar to those of the previous trait models of leadership, we have categorised his model as an extension of the trait perspective. To some extent his work sits between the trait approach and the style approach which follows. It is interesting that a number of researchers and writers are recognising that there is some value in considering a mix of personality characteristics and behaviours, and in particular Higgs links this approach to emotional intelligence.

Rajan and van Eupen also consider that leaders are strong on emotional intelligence, and that this involves the traits of self-awareness, zeal, resilience and the ability to read emotions in others. They argue that these traits are particularly important in the development and deployment of people skills. Heifetz and Laurie similarly identify that in order for leaders to regulate emotional distress in the organization, which is inevitable in change situations, the leader has to have 'the emotional capacity to tolerate uncertainty, frustration and pain'. Along the same lines Goffe identifies that inspirational leaders need to understand and admit their own weaknesses (within reason); sense the needs of situations; have empathy and self-awareness.

LEADERSHIP STYLES AND BEHAVIOURS

Dissatisfaction with research on leadership that saw leadership as a set of permanent personal characteristics that describe the leader led to further studies that emphasised the nature of the leadership process – the interaction between leader and follower – aiming to understand how the leaders behave rather than what they are. The first such studies sought to find the 'best' leadership style; from this perspective leadership comprises an ideal set of behaviours that can be learned. Fulop et al. suggest that Douglas McGregor's work, The Human Side of Enterprise, can be understood from this perspective. McGregor argued that American corporations managed their employees as if they were work-shy, and needed constant direction, monitoring and control (theory 'x'), rather than as if they were responsible individuals who were willing and able to take on responsibility and organize their own work (theory 'y'). McGregor argued that the underlying assumptions of the manager determined the way they managed their employees and this in turn determined how the employees would react. Thus if employees were managed as if they operated on theory 'x' then they would act in a theory 'x' manner; conversely if employees were managed as if they operated on theory 'y' then they would respond as theory 'y' employees would respond. The message was that management style should reinforce theory 'y' and thus employees would take on responsibility, be motivated by what they were doing and work hard. Although the original book was written over forty years ago, this approach is being revisited and it fits well with the empowering or post-heroic approach to leadership that we discuss later in the chapter. Another piece of research from the style approach is that by Blake and Mouton, who developed the famous 'Managerial Grid'. The grid is based on two aspects of leadership behaviour. One is concern for production, that is, task-oriented behaviours such as clarifying roles, scheduling work, measuring outputs; the second is concern for people, that is, people-centred behaviour such as building trust, camaraderie, a friendly atmosphere. These two dimensions are at the heart of many models of leadership. Blake and Mouton proposed that individual leaders could be measured on a nine-point scale in each of these two aspects, and by combining them in grid form they identified the four leadership styles presented in Table below.

Table: Blake and Mouton's four leadership styles

High concern for people	High concern for people
Low concern for production	High concern for production
Country Club management	Team management
Low concern for people	Low concern for people
Low concern for production	High concern for production
Impoverished management	Authority-compliance management

such studies, which are well substantiated by evidence, suggest that leadership is accessible for all people and that it is more a matter of learning leadership behaviour than of personality characteristics. Many leadership development courses have therefore been based around this model. However, as Northouse argues, there is an assumption in the model that the team management style (high concern for people and high concern for production; sometimes termed 9,9 management) is the ideal style; and yet this claim is not substantiated by the research. This approach also fails to take account of the characteristics of the situation and the nature of the followers.

Much of the recent work on the notion of transformational/heroic leadership, and empowering/post-heroic leadership, similarly assumes that what is being discussed is the one best way for a leader to lead, and we return to this leadership debate later on.

Do Leaders Need Different Styles for Different Situations?

A variety of models, sometimes termed contingency models, have been developed to address the importance of context in terms of the leadership process, and as a consequence these models become more complex. Many, however, retain the concepts of production-centred and people-centred behaviour as ways of describing leadership behaviour, but use them in a different way. Hersey and Blanchard developed a model which identified that the appropriate leadership style in a situation should be dependent on their diagnosis of the 'readiness', that is, developmental level or maturity, of their followers. The model is sometimes referred to as 'situational leadership', and works on the premise that leaders can 'adapt their leadership style to meet the demands of their environment'. Readiness of followers is defined in terms of ability and willingness. Level of ability includes the experience, knowledge and skills that an individual possesses in relation to the particular task at hand; and level of willingness encompasses the extent to which the individual has the motivation and commitment, or the self-confidence, to carry out the task. Having diagnosed the developmental level of the followers, Hersey and Blanchard suggest that the leader then adapts their behaviour to fit. They identify two dimensions of leader behaviour: task behaviour, which is sometimes termed 'directive'; and relationship behaviour, which is sometimes termed 'supportive'. Task behaviour refers to the extent to which leaders spell out what has to be done. This includes 'telling people what to do, how to do it, when to do it, where to do it, and who is to do it'. On the other hand, relationship behaviour is defined as 'the extent to which the leader engages in two-way or multi-way communication. The behaviours include listening, facilitating and supporting behaviours'. The extent to which the leader emphasises each of these two types of behaviour results in the usual two-by-two matrix. The four resulting styles are identified, as shown in Table below.

Table: Hersey and Blanchard's four styles of leadership

High relationship behaviour	High relationship behaviour
Low task behaviour	High task behaviour
Followers are able, but	Followers are unable,
unwilling or insecure	bùt willing or confident
Supportive (participating)style	Coaching (selling) style
Low relationship behaviour	Low relationship behaviour
Low task behaviour	High task behaviour
Followers are both able	Followers are unable and
and willing or confident	unwilling or insecure
Delegation style	Directing (telling) style

Other well-known contingency models include Fielder's contingency model where leadership behaviour is matched to three factors in the situation: the nature of the relationship between the leader and members, the extent to which tasks are highly structured and the position power of the leader. The appropriate leader behaviour (that is, whether it should be task oriented or relationship oriented) depends on the combination of these three aspects in any situation. Fielder's model is considered to be well supported by the evidence. The research was based on the relationship between style and performance in existing organizations in different contexts.

Table: Six leadership styles reported by Goleman

Coercive style	Leader demands immediate compliance
Authoritative style	Leader mobilises people towards a vision
Affiliative style	Leader creates emotional bonds and harmony
Democratic style	Leaders use participation to build consensus
Pacesetting style	Leader expects excellence and self-direction from followers
Coaching style	Leader develops people for the future

Goleman goes on to consider the appropriate context and impact of each style, and argues that the more styles the leader uses the better. We have already reported Goleman's work on emotional intelligence, and he links this with the six styles by suggesting that leaders need to understand how the styles relate back to the different competencies of emotional intelligence so that they can identify where they need to focus their leadership development.

One of the differences between the contingency models we have just discussed and the 'best' style models is the implications for development. The Blake and Mouton model suggests leaders can be developed to lead in the one best way. The Hersey and Blanchard model, and most other contingency models, stress the flexibility of the leader – to learn to lead differently with different employees depending on their needs; hence the leader should learn many styles and learn to diagnose the needs of their employees. Fielder's model, however, emphasises matching the leader to the context (a selection decision), rather than developing leaders in the context.

DO WE REALLY NEED HEROES?

A different approach to understanding leadership is transformational leadership, which focuses on the leader's role at a strategic level, so there is a concentration on the one leader at the top of the organizaton. There is a wide range of literature in this vein, most of it written in the 1980s. Since that time the academic literature may have moved on but the image of the transformational leader still remains widely attractive. While this is a different approach it links back to our original three questions about leadership. Transformational leadership shows elements of the trait approach, as leaders are seen to 'have' charisma, which sets them apart as extraordinary and exceptional, and they are also seen to use a set of 'ideal' behaviours, with the assumption in many writings that this is the 'best' approach.

The leader is usually characterised as a hero, although Steyrer proposes that there are other charismatic types such as the father figure, the saviour and the king. Such leaders appear to know exactly what they are doing and how to 'save' the organization from its present predicament (and consequently such leadership is found more often when organizations are in trouble). Leaders involve followers by generating a high level of commitment, partly due to such leaders focusing on the needs of followers and expressing their vision in such a way that it satisfies these needs. They communicate high expectations to followers and also the firm belief that followers will be able to achieve these goals. In this way the leader promotes self-confidence in the followers and they are motivated to achieve more than they ordinarily expect to achieve. In terms of behaviours, perhaps the most important is the vision of the future that the leader offers and that they communicate this and dramatise this to the followers. Such leaders are able to help the followers make sense of what is going on and why as well as what needs to be done in the future. It is from this perspective that the distinction between management and leadership is often made. Bennis and Nanus, for example, suggest leadership is path finding while management is path following; and that leadership is about doing the right thing whereas management is about doing things right. Kotter identified leaders as establishing a direction (whereas managers plan and budget); leaders align people with the vision (whereas managers organize things); leaders motivate and inspire (whereas managers control and solve problems); and leaders encourage change (whereas managers encourage order and predictability). Other writers analysing leadership from this perspective include Tichy and Devanna and Bass, and there is a wide research base to support the findings. The approach does have a great strength in taking followers' needs into account and seeking to promote their self-confidence and potential, and the idea of the knight in shining armour is very attractive and potentially exciting – Tichy and Devanna, for example, present the process of such leadership as a three-act drama. However, in spite of the emphasis on process there is also an emphasis on leadership characteristics which harks back to the trait approach to leadership, which has been characterised as elitist. There is also the ethical concern of one person wielding such power over others.

Maybe we should ask whether organizations really require such leaders. A very different conception of leadership is now offered as an alternative, partly a reaction to the previous approach, and partly a response to a changing environment. This is termed empowering or post-heroic leadership, and could be described as the currently favoured ideal way to lead.

Fulop et al. identify factors in a rapidly changing turbulent environment which by the 1990s dilute the appropriateness of concentrating on the one leader at the top of the organization. These factors include: globalisation making centralisation more difficult; technology enabling better sharing of information; and change being seen as a responsibility of all levels of the organization – not just the top. They also note a dissatisfaction with corporate failures, identify few transformational leaders as positive role models, suggest that such a model of male authoritarian leadership is less relevant, and in particular that the macho leader with all the answers does not necessarily fit well with the encouragement of creativity and innovation. In addition they suggest that increasing teamwork and an increasing emphasis on knowledge workers mean that employees will be less responsive now to a transformational leader. The emphasis has therefore moved away from understanding the traits and style of the one leader at the top of the organization who knows how to solve all the organization's problems, to how empowering or post-heroic leaders can facilitate many members of the organization in taking on leadership roles. In this context Applebaum et al. comment that female leadership styles are more effective in today's team-based consensually driven organizations. Many commentators speak of leaders with integrity and humility, the ability to select good people and to remove barriers so they can fulfil their potential and perform.

The leader becomes a developer who can help others identify problems as opportunities for learning, and who can harness the collective intelligence of the organization, and Fulop et al. note that this means in practice that they encourage the development of a learning organization.

This changing perspective on leadership is well demonstrated by a survey on leadership skills reported by Rajan and van Eupen. The research is based on interviews with 49 top business leaders, 50 HR directors and a postal questionnaire of 375 companies in the service sector. They asked what were the most important leadership skills during the period 1995–7 and compared the results with those of a similar survey conducted in the late 1980s. The change in skills base shown in Table below reflects very well the change in the idealised leadership role and the increasing importance of facilitative people-related skills. They also note the prediction that the future will require an equal balance of traditionally masculine and feminine personality traits.

Higgs argues that leaders need a combination of skills and personality:

envisioning, engaging, enabling, enquiring and developing skills are needed, together with authenticity, integrity, will, self-belief and self-awareness.

Top Five Skills in Order of Importance

1995–7	1 Ability to inspire trust and motivation
	2 Visioning
	3 Ability, willingness and self-discipline to listen
	4 Strategic thinking
	5 Interpersonal communication skills
Late 1980s	1 Strategic thinking
	2 Entrepreneurial skills
	3 Originality
	4 Flair
	5 Problem-solving skills

From a slightly different perspective Heifetz and Laurie propose six guiding principles of post-heroic leadership, and they conclude that leadership is about learning and that the idea of having a vision and aligning people to this is bankrupt. The idea of one leader at the top creating major changes in order to solve a one-off challenge is no longer appropriate, as organizations now face a constant stream of adaptive challenges, and leadership is required of many in the organization, not just one person at the top. They argue that employees should be allowed to identify and solve problems themselves and learn to take responsibility. The role of the leader is to develop collective self-confidence. As Grint puts it, 'the apparent devolvement (or desertion – depending on your perspective) of responsibility has become the new standard in contemporary models of leadership'.

These visions of leadership are very attractive but they do require a dramatic change in thinking for both leaders and followers. For leaders there is the risk of giving away power, learning to trust employees, developing new skills, developing a different perspective of their role and overriding self-interest. For followers there is the challenge of taking responsibility – which some may welcome, but others shun. Yet, if sustained competitive advantage is based on human capital and collective intelligence, it is difficult to relegate this perspective to 'just an ideal'.

While empowering leaders have been shown to fit with the current climate we may sometimes need heroic leaders. Kets de Vries makes the point that heroic leadership will never die as change makes people anxious and we need heroic leaders to calm them down, but since no one can live up to the expectations of heroic leaders, they will eventually become a disappointment. We conclude with the thought that there is no one best way – different leaders and different leader behaviours are needed at different times.

LEADERSHIP AND MOTIVATION

All leadership models are based on the assumption that one person can motivate another to act, and we have looked at different explanations of how leaders may do this – based on their traits, their employment of the one best leadership style or their use of a style which matches (in some ways) the needs of their followers, and is responsive (in some ways) to the context. We have also explained how the leader may be reconceptualised as heroic (transformational leader) and as empowering or post-heroic.

Some interconnections can be made between these theories and motivation theories. It is not our purpose here to recount any motivation theories in detail. Below we identify some of the key concepts addressed in motivation theories and suggest which leadership perspectives tap into these concepts:

- *Expectancy has an impact on motivation*. We have already mentioned McGregor's model and his argument that if you treat people as responsible and self-motivated then they will act in a responsible and motivated manner. In addition Vroom's expectancy theory of motivation recognises that in the process of motivation the extent to which the individual feels they can realistically achieve the target will have an influence on whether they are motivated even to try. In respect of transformational leadership it is argued that followers can be inspired to achieve beyond the normal, partly because the leader has high expectations of the followers and in addition the leader expresses the belief that the followers are capable of achieving these great things. From a different perspective the post-heroic leader concept is based on trusting organization members to play their part, trusting them with information and expecting them to use this wisely for the good of the organization.
- *Social needs are important*. Maslow, Mayo and McClelland,

among others, highlight the need for affiliation as a motivational factor. Some leadership models specifically respond to this, for example Blake and Mouton ('one best style' theory), Hersey and Blanchard and Fielder (contingency theory) all use 'concern for people' in some form as one of the key aspects of their leadership models. The concept of post-heroic leadership concerns involving those who may previously have been excluded, and concerns the impact of their leadership on individuals. In addition this perspective concentrates on the importance of learning and acting collectively.

- *Importance of the work itself.* Maslow, Herzberg, and Hackman and Oldham, for example, all underline the way in which individuals are motivated to seek and may achieve satisfaction through their jobs. Herzberg, for example, identifies how opportunities for achievement, recognition, responsibility, autonomy, challenging tasks and opportunities for development may all be motivational. In some ways, Hersey and Blanchard's model addresses these needs in their 'delegation' style. In the post-heroic model many people in the organization need to be involved in meeting adaptive challenges, in working out solutions and in contributing to vision building and many need to take on the responsibility of leadership. This is very different from the transformational leadership model in which the leader at the top of the organization is seen to have all the responsibility.
- *Recognising different people are motivated by different things.* Expectancy theory, previously mentioned, also identifies that different individuals value different things and hence have different motivational needs. In the process of motivation, only those things that the individual values will spur them to act. Contingency models of leadership take this on board to some extent. From a different perspective the transformational leader develops an interpretation of the world, or narrative, that plays to the followers' needs. However, while post-heroic leadership identifies that different people may play a different part, there is an assumption that all will be prepared to be involved, to share information and to develop themselves in line with the needs of the organization.
- *Social influences on motivation.* Recent work in the area of motivation suggests that motivations are socially or culturally

determined, and to a limited extent the transformational leader ties into this as they reinterpret the world for their followers.

In spite of the links between leadership and motivation theories, there are many aspects of motivation that the leadership theories ignore. For example, some people have less internal energy and drive than others and less need for growth. Also, individuals with high levels of energy and drive may satisfy these outside the work environment. While we may try to motivate people externally the greatest power for motivation comes from within and is therefore under the control of the individual rather than another. The best we can say is that leaders can enhance followers' motivation by the way they treat them, and at worst leaders may neutralise the motivational energy in their followers. There will always be some factors on which leaders have no impact whatsoever.

The job of a manager in the workplace is to get things done through employees. To do this the manager should be able to motivate employees. But that's easier said than done. Motivation practice and theory are difficult subjects, touching on several disciplines.

Human nature can be very simple, yet very complex too. An understanding and appreciation of this is a prerequisite to effective employee motivation in the workplace and therefore effective management and leadership.

Quite apart from the benefit and moral value of an altruistic approach to treating colleagues as human beings and respecting human dignity in all its forms, research and observations show that well motivated employees are more productive and creative. The inverse also holds true.

DEFINITION

Many individuals wrongly view motivation as a personal trait—that is, some individuals have it, and others do not. But *motivation* is defined as the force that causes an individual to behave in a specific way. Simply put, a extremely motivated person works hard at a task; an unmotivated person doesn't. Managers frequently have difficulty motivating employees. But motivation is really an internal process. It is the result of the interaction of a person's needs, his or his power to make choices about how to meet those needs, and the environment created by management that appropriates these needs to be met and the choices to be made. Motivation isn't something that a manager can "do" to an individual.

THEORIES

Motivation is a composite phenomenon. Numerous theories attempt to explain how motivation works. In management circles, probably the most popular explanations of motivation are based on the needs of the individual. The fundamental needs model, referred to as content theory of motivation, highlights the specific factors that motivate an individual. Though these factors are found within an individual, things outside the individual can affect him or his as well. In short, all individuals have needs that they want satisfied. Some are *basic needs,* such as those for food, sleep, and water—needs that deal with the physical aspects of behaviour and are regarded unlearned. These needs are biological in nature and relatively stable. Their influences on behaviour are generally obvious and therefore easy to identify.

Secondary needs, alternatively, are psychological, which means that they are learned mainly through experience. These demands vary importantly by culture and by individual. Secondary needs consist of internal states, such as the wish for power, achievement, and love. Identifying and interpreting these needs is more difficult because they are founded in a variety of ways. Secondary needs are accountable for most of the behaviour that a supervisor is concerned with and for the rewards a person seeks in an establishment. Numerous theorists, comprising Abraham Maslow, Frederick Herzberg, David McClelland, and Clayton Alderfer, have furnished theories to help explain motives as a source of motivation.

Abraham Maslow's theory of hierarchy need

The great management scientists Abraham Maslow defined **need** as a physiological or psychological deficiency that a person feels the obsession to satisfy. This demand can produce tensions that can influence a person's work attitudes and behaviours. Maslow formed a theory based on his definition of need that proposes that humans are encouraged by multiple demands and that these needs exist in a hierarchical order. His premise is that only an unsatisfied need can influence behaviour; a satisfied motive isn't a motivator.

Maslow's theory is based on these two principles:

- **Deficit principle:** A satisfied need no more motivates behaviour because individuals act to satisfy deprived needs.

- **Progression principle:** The five needs he identified exist in a hierarchy, which means that a need at any stage only comes into play after a lower-level need has been satisfied.

In his theory, Maslow identified five levels of human needs. Table below illustrates these five levels and provides suggestions for satisfying each need.

Higher Level Needs	**To Satisfy, Offer:**
Self-actualization needs	Creative and challenging work Participation in decision making Task flexibility and autonomy
Esteem needs	Responsibility of an important task Promotion to higher position task Praise and recognition from boss
Lower Level Needs Social needs	***To Satisfy, Offer:*** Friendly co-workers Interaction with customers Pleasant supervisor
Safety needs	Safe working conditions Task security Base compensation and benefits
Physiological needs	Rest and refreshment breaks Physical comfort on the task Reasonable work hours

Though research has not asserted the strict deficit and progression principles of Maslow's theory, his ideas can help managers understand and satisfy the demands of employees.

Herzberg's two-factor theory

Frederick Herzberg offers another framework for understanding the motivational significances of work environments.

In his two-factor theory, Herzberg identifies two sets of factors that affect motivation in the workplace:

- **Hygiene factors** let in salary, task security, working conditions, organizational policies, and technical quality of supervision. Though these factors don't motivate employees, they can cause dissatisfaction if they are missing. Something as simple as adding music to the office place or implementing a no-smoking policy can make individuals less dissatisfied with these faces of their work. Nevertheless, these improvements in hygiene factors don't inevitably increase satisfaction.

- **Satisfiers** or **motivators** include such things as responsibility, accomplishment, growth opportunities, and feelings of recognition, and are the key to job satisfaction and motivation. For example, managers can find out what individuals actually do in their jobs and make improvements, therefore increasing job satisfaction and performance.

Following Herzberg's two-factor theory, managers involve to ensure that hygiene factors are adequate and then build satisfiers into jobs.

Alderfer's ERG theory

Clayton Alderfer's ERG (Existence, Relatedness, Growth) theory is rested on Maslow's hierarchy of needs theory. To begin his theory, Alderfer collapses Maslow's five levels of demands into three categories.

- **Existence needs** are desires for physiological and material well-being. (In terms of Maslow's model, existence needs include physiological and safety needs).
- **Relatedness needs** are desires for satisfying interpersonal relationships. (In terms of Maslow's model, relatedness corresponds to social needs).
- **Growth needs** are desires for continued psychological growth and development. (In terms of Maslow's model, growth needs include esteem and self-realization needs).

This approach proposes that unsatisfied needs motivate behaviour, and that as lower level needs are satisfied, they become less important. Higher level needs, although, become more important as they are satisfied, and if these needs aren't met, a person may move down the hierarchy, which Alderfer calls the *frustration-regression principle.* What he means by this term is that an already satisfied lower level need can become reactivated and determine behaviour when a higher level need cannot be satisfied. As a result, managers ought to provide opportunities for workers to capitalize on the importance of higher level demands.

McClelland's acquired needs theory

David McClelland's acquired needs theory recognizes that everyone prioritizes demands differently. He also believes that individuals aren't born with these needs, but that they are really learned through life experiences. McClelland identifies three specific needs:

- **Need for achievement** is the drive to excel.
- **Need for power** is the wish to cause others to behave in a way that they would not have behaved otherwise.
- **Need for affiliation** is the wish for friendly, close interpersonal relationships and conflict avoidance.

McClelland associates each demand with a distinct set of work preferences, and managers can help tailor the environment to meet these needs.

High achievers differentiate themselves from others by their desires to do things better. These individuals are strongly inspired by task situations with personal responsibility, feedback, and an intermediate degree of risk. Additionally, high achievers frequently exhibit the following behaviours:

- Seek personal responsibility for finding solutions to problems.
- Want rapid feedback on their performances in order that they can tell easily whether they are improving or not.
- Set moderately challenging aims and perform best when they perceive their probability of success as 50-50.

An individual with a high need of power is likely to follow a path of continued promotion over time. Individuals with a high need of power frequently demonstrate the following behaviours:

- Enjoy being in charge.
- Want to influence others.
- Prefer to be placed into competitive and position-oriented situations.
- Tend to be more concerned with prestige and gaining influence over others than with effectual performance.

Individuals with the motive for affiliation seek companionship, social approval, and satisfying interpersonal relationships. Individuals needing affiliation exhibit the following behaviours:

- Take a special interest in work that provides companionship and social approval.
- Strive for friendship.
- Prefer cooperative situations rather than competitive ones.
- Desire relationships involving a high degree of mutual understanding.
- May not make the best managers because their wish for social approval and friendship may complicate managerial decision making.

Interestingly enough, a high need to attain doesn't inevitably lead to being a good manager, especially in large organizations. Individuals with high achievement needs are generally interested in how well they do personally and not in influencing others to do well. Alternatively, the best managers are high in their needs for power and low in their needs for association.

Equity theory

As per the equity theory, based on the work of J. Stacy Adams, workers compare the reward potential to the effort they must expend. Equity exists when workers perceive that rewards equal efforts.

But employees just do not look at their potential rewards, they consider the rewards of others as well. Inequities occur when individuals feel that their rewards are inferior to the rewards offered to other persons sharing the same workloads.

Employees who feel they are being covered inequitably may show the following behaviours:

- Put less effort into their jobs.
- Ask for better treatment and/or rewards.
- Find ways to make their work seem better by comparison.
- Transfer or quit their jobs.

The equity theory makes a good point: Individuals act as per their perceptions. What a manager thinks is irrelevant to an employee because the real issue is the way an employee perceives his or her situation. Rewards perceived as equitable ought to have positive results on job satisfaction and functioning; those rewards perceived as inequitable may produce task dissatisfaction and make performance problems. Every manager needs to see that any negative consequences from equity comparisons are annulled, or at least minimized, when rewards are allocated. Informed managers anticipate perceived negative inequities when especially visible rewards, such as pay increases or promotions, are allocated. Instead of letting equity concerns get out of hand, these managers carefully communicate the intended values of rewards being given, clarify the performance appraisals upon which these rewards are based, and suggest appropriate comparison points.

Expectancy theory

Victor Vroom brought in one of the most widely consented explanations of motivation. Very simply, the expectancy theory says that an employee will be inspired to exercise a high level of effort when he believes that:

- Effort will lead to a good performance appraisal.
- A good appraisal will lead to organizational rewards.
- The organizational rewards will satisfy his personal aims.

The key to the expectancy theory is an understanding of an individual's aims and the relationships between attempt and performance, between performance and rewards, and finally, between the rewards and individual aim satisfaction. When an employee has a high level of expectancy and the reward is attractive, motivation is generally high.

Hence, to motivate workers, managers must strengthen workers' perceptions of their efforts as both possible and worthy, clarify expectations of performances, tie rewards to performances, and make a point that rewards are desirable.

Reinforcement theory

The theory of reinforcement is based on E. L. Thorndike's law of effect, simply looks at the relationship between behaviour and its consequences. This theory focuses on modifying an employee's on-the-task behaviour through the appropriate use of one of the following four techniques:

- **Avoidance** is an attempt to show an employee what the consequences of improper behaviour will be. If an employee doesn't engage in improper behaviour, he or she will not experience the consequence.

- **Extinction** is fundamentally ignoring the behaviour of a subordinate and not providing either positive or negative reinforcement. Classroom teachers frequently use this skill when they ignore learners who are "acting out" to get attention. This proficiency ought to only be used when the supervisor perceives the behaviour as temporary, not typical, and not dangerous.
- **Positive reinforcement** rewards desirable behaviour. Positive reinforcement, such as a pay raise or promotion, is provided as a reward for positive behaviour with the purpose of increasing the probability that the required behaviour will be repeated.
- **Punishment** (threats, docking pay, suspension) is an effort to decrease the likelihood of a behaviour recurring by applying negative consequences.

The reinforcement theory has the following significances for management:

- Learning what is acceptable to the establishment determines inspired behaviour.
- Managers who are trying to motivate their employees ought to be sure to tell individuals what they are doing wrong and be careful not to reward all individuals at the same time.
- Managers must tell individuals what they can do to receive positive reinforcement.
- Managers must be sure to administer the reinforcement as closely as possible to the occurrence of the behaviour.
- Managers must recognize that failure to reward can also modify behaviour. Employees who believe that they deserve a reward and don't receive it will frequently become disillusioned with both their manager and company.

Goal-setting theory

The goal-setting theory was brought in the late 1960s by Edwin Locke, who proposed that intentions to work toward an aim are a major source of work motivation. Aims, in essence, tell employees what needs to be done and how much effort ought to be expanded. Generally, the harder the aim, the higher the level of performance expected. Managers can set the aims for their employees, or employees and managers can develop aims together. One advantage of employees participating in aim setting is that they may be more likely to work toward an aim they aided to accomplish.

No matter who sets the aim, however, employees do better when they get feedback on their progress. Additionally to feedback, four other factors act upon the aims-performance relationship:

- The employee must be committed to the aim.
- The employee must believe that he is capable of performing the job.
- Jobs involved in achieving the aim ought to be simple, familiar, and independent.
- The aim-setting theory is culture bound.

If the aim-setting theory is followed, managers need to work with their employees in determining aim objectives in order to provide targets for motivation. Additionally, the aims that are based ought to be specific rather than general in nature, and managers must furnish feedback on performance.

PHILOSOPHIES AND MOTIVATION

Management philosophy can set the foundation for a positive work climate and influence a manager's approach to motivation. The way a manager views employees and communicates with employees affects their behaviour.

Two most popular theories are Douglas McGregor's Theory X and Theory Y, which talk about how managers produce self-fulfilling prophecies based on how they treat their employees. Another theory by Chris Argyris centres on what he refers to as the *mature worker.* In his book, *Personality and Establishment,* Argyris contrasts the management practices discovered in conventional organizations with the demands and capabilities of the mature adult personality.

For instance, the concept of work specialization is supposed to make individuals work more efficiently because the works are much defined. Argyris believes that this concept may actually be counterproductive because it will limit an employee from reaching self-actualization.

Like McGregor, Argyris is concerned about how managers treat individuals. He believes that if managers treat their employees in a positive manner—as accountable adults—their employees will be more productive. However, Argyris takes this conception one step further. He believes that mature workers want additional responsibilities, a variety of jobs, and the power to participate in decisions. If not, he believes that the outcome will be employee absenteeism, apathy, and even alienation.

STRATEGIES

To some extent, a high level of employee motivation is deduced from effectual management practices. To develop inspired employees, a manager must treat individuals as people, empower workers, provide an efficient reward system, redesign jobs, and produce a flexible workplace.

Empowerment

Empowerment occurs when individuals in an establishment are given autonomy, authority, trust, and encouragement to attain a job. Empowerment is designed to unshackle the worker and to retrace a task the worker's responsibility.

In an attempt to empower and to change some of the old bureaucratic ideas, managers are encouraging corporate intrapreneurships. Intrapreneurship promotes employees to pursue new ideas and gives them the authority to promote those ideas. Obviously, intrapreneurship isn't for the timid, because old structures and processes are ploughed upside down.

Reward system

Managers frequently use rewards to reinforce employee behaviour that they want to go forward. A *reward* is a work outcome of positive value to the individual. Organizations are rich in rewards for individuals whose performance achievements help meet organizational objectives. Individuals receive rewards in one of the following two ways:

- **Extrinsic rewards** are outwardly administered. They are valued outcomes given to someone by another person, normally a supervisor or higher level manager. Common workplace examples are pay bonuses, promotions, time off, special assignments, office fixtures, awards, verbal praise, and so forth. In all cases, the motivational stimulus of extrinsic rewards originates outside the individual.
- **Intrinsic rewards** are self-administered. Think of the

"natural high", a person may experience after completing a task. That person feels good because he has a feeling of competency, personal development, and self-control over his work. In contrast to extrinsic rewards, the motivational stimulus of intrinsic rewards is internal and does not depend on the actions of other individuals.

To prompt behaviour, the establishment needs to provide an effectual reward system. An effectual reward system has four elements:

- Rewards need to satisfy the fundamental demands of all employees.
- Rewards need to be comprised in the system and be comparable to ones offered by a competitive establishment in the same area.
- Rewards need to be available to individuals in the same positions and be distributed fairly and equitably.
- The overall reward system needs to be multifaceted. Because all individuals are different, managers must provide a range of rewards—pay, time off, recognition, or promotion. Additionally, managers ought to provide many different ways to earn these rewards.

This last point deserves to be noted. With the widely developing trend toward empowerment in industry, many employees and employers are beginning to view conventional pay systems as inadequate. In a conventional system, individuals are paid as per the positions they hold, not the contributions they make. As organizations adopt approaches built upon teams, customer satisfaction, and empowerment, workers need to be paid differently. Many organizations have already responded by designing many pay plans, designed by employee design teams, which base rewards on technique levels. Rewards demonstrate to employees that their behaviour is reserve and ought to be repeated. If employees do not feel that their work is valued, their motivation will decay.

Motivation in jobs

Many individuals go to work every day and go through the same, half-hearted activities to perform their jobs. These individuals frequently refer to this condition as burnout. But smart managers can do something to improve this condition before an employee becomes bored and loses motivation. The concept of *task redesign,* which requires knowledge of and concern for the human qualities individuals bring with them to the establishment, applies motivational theories to the structure of work for amending productivity and satisfaction.

When redesigning jobs, managers look at both task scope and task depth. Redesign efforts may include the following:

- **Task enlargement.** Frequently referred to as *horizontal task loading,* task enlargement increases the form of jobs a task comprises. Though it does not increase the quality or the challenge of those jobs, task enlargement may reduce some of the monotony, and as an employee's boredom decreases, his or his work quality generally increases.
- **Task rotation**. This practice assigns individuals to different jobs or jobs to different individuals on a temporary basis. The idea is to add form and to expose individuals to the dependence that one task has on other jobs. Task rotation can encourage higher levels of contributions and renew interest and enthusiasm. The establishment benefits from a cross-trained manpower.
- **Task enrichment.** Also called *vertical task loading*, this application comprises not only an increased variety of jobs, but also provides an employee with more responsibility and authority. If the skills needed to do the task are skills that match the jobholder's abilities, task enrichment may improve morale and performance.

Flexibility creation

Today's employees evaluate personal time. Because of family wants, a conventional nine-to-five workday may not work for many individuals. Hence, flextime, which permits employees to set and control their own work hours, is one way that organizations are accommodating their employees' needs. Here are some other options organizations are trying as well:

- A **compressed workweek** is a form of flextime that allows a full-time task to be completed in less than the standard 40-hour, five-day workweek. Its most common form is the 4/40 schedule, which gives employees three days off each week. This schedule benefits the individual through more leisure time and lower commuting costs. The establishment ought to gain through lower absenteeism and improved performance. Of course, the danger in this type of scheduling is the possibility of increased fatigue.

- **Task sharing** or **twinning** occurs when one full-time task is split between two or more persons. Task sharing frequently involves each person working one-half day, but it can also be done on weekly or monthly sharing arrangements. When jobs can be split and shared, organizations can gain by hiring talented individuals who would otherwise be unable to work full-time. The qualified employee who is also a parent may not want to be in the office for a full day but may be willing to work a half-day. Though adjustment problems occasionally occur, the arrangement can be good for all concerned.
- **Telecommuting,** occasionally called *flexiplace,* is a work arrangement that allows at least a portion of scheduled work hours to be completed outside of the office, with work-at-home as one of the options. Telecommuting frees the jobholder from necessitating to work fixed hours, wearing special work attire, enduring the normal constraints of commuting, and having direct contact with supervisors. Home workers frequently demonstrate increased productivity, report fewer distractions, enjoy the freedom to be their own boss, and appreciate the profit of having more time for themselves.
- Naturally, when there are positives, there are also negatives. Many home workers feel that they work too much and are isolated from their family and friends. Additionally to the feelings of isolation, many employees feel that the want of visibility at the office may outcome in the loss of promotions.

Note: For a very good case study regarding this topic, reader can visit company's website of Ford Motor Company *www.ford.com*. Ford Motor (Ford) is one of the largest automotive manufacturers in the world. It manufactures and distributes automobiles across six continents. The company's automotive vehicle brands include Ford, Lincoln, Mercury and Volvo. The company primarily operates in the US and Europe. It is headquartered in Dearborn, Michigan, and employed 213,000 people.

16

Managing Absence and Attendance

For organizations to achieve their optimum performance the extent to which employees are absent from their place of work clearly needs to be minimised. Absence has always been a matter of concern to all employers, and methods for reducing it have frequently focused on disciplinary or punitive measures. More recently absence has been framed in a more positive discourse, and the focus is now on what organizations can do to promote attendance and rehabilitation of employees with long-term absence.

THE ORGANIZATIONAL CONTEXT

Barham and Leonard question the accuracy of data in absence surveys. They argue that given the low response rates to such surveys, there is no evidence to suggest that the survey findings are representative of the whole population. In addition it is found that the much management absence is not recorded. It is likely that respondents are those with better absence information. On this basis they argue that absence costs to the organization are underestimated.

It has been found that over 90 per cent of organizations in their survey considered absence to be a significant cost to the organization, but less that half monitored this cost. The average cost was reported to be Rs.567 per year per employee. Barham and Leonard suggest that estimating the costs of absence is complicated, and that the estimate needs to include not only the direct costs (i.e., paying salary and benefits for a worker who is not there), but also indirect costs such as organizing replacement staff, overall reductions in productivity and administrative costs. Bevan, reporting research from the Employment Studies Institute, suggests that there is virtually no robust data on direct and indirect costs of absence and that most employers underestimate the true costs of sickness absence, particularly in respect of long-term sickness. Costing currently does not distinguish between short-term and long-term sickness. Using case study research Bevan reports that long-term sickness costs account for between 30 per cent and 70 per cent of absence costs. He goes on to argue, on the basis of this research, that even the most sophisticated companies are not well equipped to calculate such costs.

PROCESS AND CAUSES OF ABSENCE

It has been found that 81 per cent of organizations collected data on the causes of absence, with the public sector being more likely to do this. The most frequent stated causes of absence are minor illness for short-term absence and back pain (for manual workers) and stress (for non-manual workers) for long-term absence. The increase in stress as a cause may well be partly due to the fact that this is now a more legitimate reason for non-attendance than previously. It is important to bear in mind that recorded causes of absence in organizations will be those causes which employees perceive the organization to view as legitimate.

The causes of absence are complex and interrelated and a process approach is generally agreed to be the most useful way of understanding absence behaviour, although there are criticisms that such models are not supported by the evidence. One of the most widely quoted models is from Rhodes and Steers and in our view this is the most useful of the process models.

The Rhodes and Steers model not only includes content information on the causes of absence but also incorporates a range of interdependent processes. In essence the model focuses on attendance motivation and the ability to attend in terms of resulting attendance behaviour.

Rhodes and Steers suggest that attendance motivation is directly affected by two factors: satisfaction with the job and pressure to attend. Pressure to attend may result from such factors as market conditions. Examples include the likelihood that there will be redundancies at their workplace and how easy it would be to get another job; incentives to attend, such as attendance bonuses; work-group norms on what is acceptable in the work-group and the effects of absence on other group members; personal work ethic producing internal pressure to attend based on beliefs about what is right; and commitment to the organization through an identification with the beliefs and values of the organization and an intention to remain with the organization. On this basis threat of redundancies, attendance bonuses, team structures where team members have to cover the workload of an absent member, a personal ethic about the need to attend work wherever possible, and feelings of loyalty to the organization should all promote the motivation to attend.

Rhodes and Steers suggest that satisfaction with the job is determined by the job situation and moderated by employee values and job expectations. Factors in the job situation are identified as job scope and level of responsibility and decision making; role stress such as work overload, underload, difficult working conditions or hours; work-group size; leadership style of their immediate manager, particularly the openness of the relationship and how easy it is to discuss and solve problems jointly; strength of relationships with co-workers; and the opportunity for promotion. On this basis higher levels of responsibility and the opportunity to make decisions in relation to job demands, balanced workload and good working conditions, small work group size, an open relationship with immediate manager, good relationships with colleagues and the opportunity for promotion should all improve attendance motivation.

However job satisfaction is moderated by the values and expectations of the employee. Such values and expectations are shaped by both personality and personal characteristics and life experiences, but can also change during the course of one's life. The extent to which the job matches up with expectations and values will have a bearing on job satisfaction; a close match is more likely to lead to satisfaction than a mismatch.

Personality and personal characteristics influence expectations and values and job satisfaction. We have previously referred to the influence of age and sex on absence rates. Length of service has also been identified as having an influence.

However, none of these relationships is clear-cut, and different pieces of research often produce different findings. There is most evidence for suggesting that younger workers and female workers have the highest rates of absence, and it is argued that younger workers value free time to a greater extent than older workers.

This brings us to the last influence on attendance, which is the ability to attend. This influence is interposed between attendance motivation and actual attendance. For example an employee could be highly motivated to attend, but may have insurmountable transportation difficulties, family or domestic responsibilities, or may be genuinely ill. In these cases motivation to attend does not result in attendance.

MANAGING FOR ATTENDANCE

The complex interrelationship of the causes of absence needs to be taken into account in its management. Many organizations have introduced policies for managing absence that focus on minimising short-term rather than long-term absence. The role of sickness in long-term absence has been given little priority in the past, as has the issue that short-term absence, if badly handled, can lead to long-term absence. Typically long-term absence and short-term absence require different approaches. Attendance management policies need to take into account causes of absence, which may be identified by patterns of absence and by enabling individuals to be open about why they are not at work. Measures range from proactive methods intended to reduce the risk of ill health; measures intended to reduce spells of absence and those intended to reduce the length of absence. Typically there is a mix of processes both to discourage absence and positively to encourage attendance, but these work differently with those on long- and short-term sickness absence.

Whatever approach is chosen, there is a great need for consistency in the construction and implementation of absence management policies and procedures, not only in terms of ensuring fairness and as a support for any disciplinary action taken, but also in terms of providing employees with clear expectations about how absence will be tackled, and promoting an attendance culture. While different approaches work in different sectors and with different types of staff, there is a strong argument that the policies themselves need to be consistent in any organization, to encourage employee acceptance and line manger support. For example Dunn and Wilkinson report the difficulties that a line manager in a production company experienced due to the fact that manufacturing staff were subject to more stringent absence procedures than other staff in the company.

Lack of consistency in implementation also weakens any policy and procedures. The role of the line manager is key and there is much emphasis on giving the line manager ownership of absence and attendance issues, with support from HR. Whatever policies and procedures are set up it is critical that the line manger feels ownership of these and applies them in practice. James and his colleagues found that two-thirds of their interviewees in a long-term absence management study noted that there were problems in the way that line managers carried out their responsibilities. Managers frequently did not follow the guidelines in matters such as ongoing contact with absent employees, and consequently HR did not know what was going on and often had to step in and manage cases. James and his colleagues found that managers' behaviour resulted from time pressures, lack of awareness of what the procedure was and lack of training.

It has been found that some measures to manage absence actually increase absence, so monitoring any new policies and procedures is critical. In terms of implementing a new absence strategy, the advice given by Huczynski and Fitzpatrick still holds good. The ALIEDIM process they suggest comprises the following stages:

- Assess the absence problem
- Locate the absence problem
- Identify and prioritise absence causes
- Evaluate the current absence control methods
- Design the absence control programme
- Implement the absence control programme
- Monitor the effectiveness of the absence control programme

The mix of policies and methods chosen will be specific to the needs of the individual organization. Below are some of the most frequently used approaches to managing absence. Some are most appropriate for short-term absence, and some better suited to long-term absence, others meet the needs of both.

ACCURATE RECORDS

Managing absence is almost impossible without an accurate picture of current absence levels and patterns in terms of the identification of areas of high absence and the most common reasons for absence in the organization. It is found that aggregate information about sickness absence rates was collected by 84 per cent of survey respondents, but such data collection was carried out more often in the public sector and manufacturing industry than in the rest of the private sector. Prior to its review of absence Carlsberg-Tetley did not have an accurate picture of sickness absence. Although some records were kept, absence was inconsistently measured and recorded, so there was no reliable information about level of absence and patterns. This was their first task in tackling absence. They decided to adopt the 'Bradford factor' method for scoring absence where both frequency of absence spells and absence duration are used but with the weight being given to the former.

Absence reports are frequently produced by HR and sent to line managers – and such reports will often include details of employees where trigger points have been hit and where intervention is required by the line manager. However, Dunn and Wilkinson found that the attention line managers gave to these reports varied, and some managers never even looked at the reports, because they did not agree that this was the best way to manage staff. As one manager commented, 'I know my staff well enough not to need these reports ... at the end of the day it all comes down to good management and knowing your staff'. Some managers argued that the reports were of little use because the employees they managed often worked long hours (beyond contract) and came in at weekends. It was felt that to punish such employees, who were clearly committed to the company, because they had reached certain absence levels was unreasonable, and would be counter-productive.

ABSENCE REVIEW AND TRIGGER POINTS

In order to focus attention on those with less satisfactory absence records many organizations identify trigger points in terms of absence spells or length, or Bradford factor scores which indicate that action is needed when an individual's absence record hits the trigger. Such policies for reviewing absence appear to be critical in absence reduction, and 77 per cent of organizations reporting a decrease in absence levels put this down to tightened policies for reviewing absence. However, such trigger points may be well known to employees, and Connex found that some employees were able to manipulate the system and regularly have absence levels just below the trigger point. To overcome this some organizations have a rolling year, rather than, say, a calendar year or a financial year, against which absence levels are assessed – on the grounds that it will be much more difficult for employees to keep track of their absence levels and manipulate the system. In fact Dunn and Wilkinson found organizations where the trigger system was avoided because it was felt that it would encourage employees to take off time until they were just under the trigger limit. While the role of these groups varies, they are frequently used to review all absences and identify those who have hit trigger points which will then require intervention, such as an absence review meeting with the employee.

ABSENCE TARGETS AND BENCHMARKING

Many organizations have absence targets phrased in terms of a reduction on current absence levels or a lower absence level to attain. However, it has been found that although 90 per cent of the organizations they surveyed believed that absence levels could be reduced, only around half of these had set targets for this, and only around 50 per cent benchmarked their absence levels against other organizations. An alternative approach, used by some organizations, is to give managers absence targets for their group, and tie this into their performance review and performance payments. This is the approach used in Connex. Such overall and local targets need to be carefully used, however, so as not to give the impression to employees that absence is not allowed.

TRAINING AND SUPPORT FOR LINE MANAGERS

Most organizations recognise that line managers play a key role in making absence procedures work and in reducing absence levels, and training is usually available when a new absence system is introduced. Connex has introduced a creative form of training. The company takes managers to an employment tribunal to view an absence-related case so that managers will understand the consequences of not dealing fairly and consistently with employees when they have to deal with similar situations at work.

However, there is evidence that further training is needed. Both James et al. and Dunn and Wilkinson found managers who could not understand how 'sickness' could be managed, were scared of dealing with the situation and were embarrassed about asking personal questions about an employee's state of health.

ABSENCE NOTIFICATION PROCEDURES

Many organizations specify that when employees phone in as absent they must phone themselves, rather than asking another person to phone on their behalf. Many also specify that the employee must speak to their direct line manager or nominated representative. This means that such a telephone conversation can be the first stage of the absence management process. The conversation is welfare based and the intention is that the manager is able to ask about the nature of the problem and the anticipated date of return to work. Some organizations, make every effort to offer alternative work. For example, a telephone operator who cannot do telephone work with a sore throat may be able to do other work, and managers are asked to bear this in mind when employees phone in sick and to try to encourage the employees to come in, where appropriate, to carry out other tasks. This telephone conversation is also seen as an important tool in reducing the length of the absence.

BETTER UNDERSTANDING OF THE CAUSES OF ABSENCE

Analysis of absence data can show the primary causes of absence in any particular organization and this may help employers develop absence management methods relevant to the most frequent causes. However, as we have said, the reasons employees give for absence will be those that the organization considers legitimate, and further investigation may be necessary.

Organizations can encourage individuals to be open about the real cause for their absence, for example a minor illness may be used as an excuse to cover for caring responsibilities, a stressful working environment or alcohol or drug problems. However, this is easier said than done. The employer has a feeling that the explanation may be partly related to issues of stress and the nature and organization of the work. Helping employees to feel they can trust the employer sufficiently to admit the real cause of absence means that absence can then effectively be tackled by providing the appropriate form of support. Another key tool is risk assessment, so, for example, some organizations will assess the risk of back pain or stress and then training can be provided to meet identified needs.

ONGOING CONTACT DURING ABSENCE

Maintaining contact during absence is considered by many organizations as a method of reducing length of absence, demonstrating to the employee that the organization is interested in them, and maintaining employee motivation. In some organizations it is the line manager who will keep in touch, and in others, such as Walter Holland and Son, there are liaison officers who fulfil this role. Contact may be by telephone, and with longer periods of absence may involve home visits. The council recommends one visit per month in working hours and considers this is reasonable in terms of the need to demonstrate 'respect for private and family life', and the wish to avoid putting pressure on employees to return to work too early.

RETURN TO WORK INTERVIEWS AND FORMAL ABSENCE REVIEWS

Return to work interviews are increasingly used as a key part of attendance procedures. It has also been reported that these interviews are regarded as the most effective way of managing short-term absence. For some organizations these interviews are mandatory, even following a single day's absence, but there is frequently some flexibility about the nature of the interview depending on the circumstances. In general the purposes of such interviews are identified as to: welcome the employee back and update them on recent events; check that the employee is well enough to resume normal duties and whether any further organizational support is needed; reinforce the fact that the employee has been missed and that attendance is a high priority in the organization; and review the employee's absence record. Dunn and Wilkinson found managers in their research who said that there was not time to concentrate on return to work interviews, as the practicalities of getting the job done were more critical. They also found a view among line managers that they were just so glad to get the employee back that they did not want to 'rock the boat'. Where formal absence reviews are held these need to be handled with sensitivity and tact, and care needs to be taken so that the interview does not become recriminatory or accusatory.

USE OF DISCIPLINARY PROCEDURES

If someone is genuinely ill and unable to work as a result, disciplinary action whether threatened or real is unlikely to bring about a return to work. It would not be desirable from the point of view of the employee or the employing organization were this to be the case. There are, however, situations in which people who are too ill to work have to be dismissed. This is never a pleasant task, but it often falls to the HR manager to carry it out. The key is to make sure that the dismissal is carried out in a legally sound manner.

- Dismissing someone who is unable to work because of ill health is potentially fair under unfair dismissal law.
- It is necessary to warn the individual concerned that they may be dismissed if they do not return to work and to consult with them ahead of time to establish whether a return in the foreseeable future is feasible.
- It is necessary to act on whatever medical advice is available.

- In larger organizations, except where a person's job is very specialised or senior, it is normally considered reasonable to refrain from dismissing a sick employee for at least six months.
- In any case no dismissal should occur if the employee falls under the definition of 'disabled'. In these cases an employee should only be dismissed once the employer is wholly satisfied that no reasonable adjustments could be made to accommodate the needs of the sick employee so as to allow them to return to work.

Where someone is persistently absent for short periods of time, the course of action taken will depend on whether or not there is a genuine underlying medical condition which explains most of the absences. If so, the matter should be handled in the same way as cases of long-term absence due to ill health outlined above. If not, then it is feasible for the employer to take a tougher line and to threaten disciplinary action at an earlier stage. It is quite acceptable in law to dismiss someone whose absence record is unacceptably high, provided they have been warned ahead of time and given a fair opportunity to improve their attendance. It is also necessary to treat different employees in a consistent fashion. Taking disciplinary action in the form of issuing a formal warning is therefore credible and likely to be successful.

ABSENCE LEVELS AND PERFORMANCE ASSESSMENTS

Some organizations have communicated to employees the message that attendance levels are a measure of their performance so they are included in annual assessments. Dunn and Wilkinson found that in the three retail companies in their case sample, employees were assessed via a separate rating category on their absence levels. In addition employees with unacceptable absence levels would not be put forward for transfers or promotion. The Metropolitan Police service considers absence records as an indication of reliability, although it does not wish to give the message that absence is not permitted.

ATTENDANCE BONUS AND REWARDS

Some organizations pay bonuses direct to employees on the basis of their attendance records. For example Connex will pay a quarterly attendance bonus of Rs.155 at the end of each 13-week period for full attendance and an additional lump sum of Rs.515 if an employee has had no sickness absence during a full calendar year. In addition Connex sends out letters commending employees for improving their absence record. The company considers that its absence scheme is a success as 80 per cent of eligible employees now qualify for payments. However, some managers do not support attendance bonuses as they feel that employees are already paid to turn up, and they are effectively being paid twice. Connex also found managers who felt that attendance bonuses were a signal to employees that managers cannot control the work environment themselves and that they have relinquished all responsibility for managing absence. On the other hand, Dunn and Wilkinson found that managers felt attendance bonuses were unfair as they penalised those employees who were genuinely ill.

OCCUPATIONAL HEALTH SUPPORT AND HEALTH PROMOTION

A number of organizations carry out pre-employment screening to identify any potential health problems at this stage. Others screen employees for general fitness and for potential job hazards, such as working with radiation, or VDUs. General screening may involve heart checks, blood tests, eye tests, well-woman/man clinics, ergonomics and physiotherapy, and discussions about weight and lifestyle, such as smoking, drinking and fitness levels. The value of such screening is that problems can be identified at an early stage so that the impact on sickness absence will be minimised. In some organizations positive encouragement will be given to employees to follow healthy lifestyles, such as healthy eating, giving up smoking, taking up exercise routines.

Physiotherapists, counsellors and psychologists are often employed, and the occupational health role may include remedial fitness training and exercise therapy for those recovering from an illness. Stress counselling is increasingly being provided and if this is offered as part of an employee assistance programme can reduce the liability in stress-related personal injury cases. Also training in stress management may be offered.

James and his colleagues found that the role of occupational health was ambiguous and problematic. Their respondents suggested that while occupational health worked on behalf of the employer, they tended to see themselves as representing employee interests. They also found that employees were very sceptical about visiting occupational health workers as they saw it as the first step in the termination of their employment.

CHANGES TO WORK AND WORK ORGANIZATION

Many employers appear to offer flexible working hours, part-time work and working from home. Employers also sometimes consider offering light duties or redeployment. However, James and his colleagues found that operational factors often limited what was possible. In the three manufacturing organizations they visited it was not always feasible to offer light duties or make adjustments to the workplace. They also found that other departments were reluctant to accept someone who was being redeployed after sickness, partly because they felt the employee might have lost the work habit, and also because there might be problems with pay if the levels of the old and new job differed. They also noted that might be no budget to pay for adaptations to equipment or purchase further equipment.

PRACTICAL SUPPORT

There are many ways in which the employer can provide practical support to minimise sickness absence. Many organizations have experienced frustrations while employees are on waiting lists for diagnostic procedures and operations. In order to speed up medical treatment that employees need some organizations are prepared to pay the medical costs for employees where there is a financial case to do this. Training in areas such as stress management and time management may help employees minimise feelings of stress, and childcare support may simplify childcare arrangements.

Note: For a case study visit company's site of Save Mart Supermarkets. www.savemart.com. Save Mart Supermarkets (Save Mart), a privately held company, operates supermarkets and grocery stores in California and Nevada. The company also provides grocery retail services. It is headquartered in Modesto, California.

17

Strategic Aspects of Development

There seems to be general agreement that training and development is a good thing, and that it increases productivity, but the question is 'how much?' It is even difficult to show a causal link between HR development and organizational performance, partly because such terms are difficult to define precisely, and partly because the payoff from development may not be seen in the short term. It is also difficult to tie down performance improvements to the development itself and to understand the nature of the link. For example, is performance better because of increased or different HR development, because the reward package has improved or because we have a clearer set of organizational and individual objectives? If there is a link with HR development initiatives, is it that employees have better skills, or that they are better motivated, or that they have been selected from a more able group of candidates attracted to the organization as it offers a high level of development?

In spite of these difficulties it is important to identify the contribution of HR development to business success, and wider measures for assessing business success, beyond the standard financial indicators, make this more feasible, as, for example, suggested by Kaplan and Norton. While the search for 'evidence' goes on, the current climate encourages high levels of attention to HR development, which is increasingly seen not only as a route to achieving business strategy, but also as a means of building core competence over the longer term to promote organizational growth and sustained competitive advantage. Global competition and a fast pace of change have emphasised the importance of the human capital in the organization, and the speed and ways in which they learn.

In addition, levels and sophistication of training and development have received considerable attention in the context of the 'new psychological contract' and the need to promote employability. There is some evidence that employee demand for training and development is increasing and that unions are beginning to engage in bargaining for development. Opportunities for training and development may be a vital tool in recruitment and retention, and considered to be a reward when promotion or monetary rewards are less available. However, Stewart and Tansley found significant structural and cultural barriers to formal and informal learning in organizations; in particular lack of time was identified as an issue.

THE NATIONAL PICTURE

Employee development has traditionally been seen as a cost rather than an investment in India, although this is certainly changing in some organizations. It has been argued that Indian organizations give little support to training and development compared with our European partners. This lack of investment in training and development has been identified as a major factor in Britain's economic performance, and it has been argued that without such investment we will be trapped in a low wage, low skills economy. Our national training framework is voluntarist, with the government's role limited to encouraging training rather than intervening, as in many other countries.

More recently it has been argued, however, that it is not a lack of investment in training that is the problem but the way such investment is distributed, that is, who it is spent on and the content of the training. It is generally agreed that training spend is unevenly distributed.

Thomson explains that broader development is concentrated on those at the beginning of their careers and those in more senior and specialist posts, rather than part-timers and those with fewer qualifications to begin with. In the aerospace and pharmaceuticals businesses, defined as high skills sectors, Lloyd found a conflict of interests between employees' desire for training and development and managerial short-term aims, lack of accreditation of skills, structured development focused on key employees, access to training being dependent on individual initiative, senior managers viewing training as a minor issue to be dealt with by lower-level managers and insufficient resources. She suggests that there was under-investment and lack of support for flexibility and employability. Westwood concludes that while we do not do as much training as in Europe, we do spend a lot of money on training that doesn't last very long and on the people who may not need it. In terms of training content there is evidence to suggest that much training is related to induction and particularly health and safety, and it has been argued that this does nothing to drive the development of a knowledge-based economy.

Some view the solution to this problem as increasing state intervention, as many view voluntarism as having a limited effect. It is argued that potential intervention would not mean a return to the levy system, but, for example, statutory rights for paid study leave and employer tax credits. These reward employers with state funding for giving employees time off for training, and the scheme is being expanded.

However, there is another school of thought that suggests the problem lies with the demand side of the equation rather than the supply side. In other words the problem is not with government initiatives and measures to encourage training, development and learning but with the way that skills are used and jobs are constructed, and hence the employer demand for training, development and learning.

All this suggests that we still have a situation in which the majority of organizations are using a reactive strategy: training only in response to the immediate short-term demands of the business, rather than being considered a strategic issue.

ORGANIZATIONAL STRATEGY AND HR DEVELOPMENT STRATEGY

For training and development to be effective in terms of business success there is a well-rehearsed argument that it should be linked up front with business strategy. McClelland's research is one of many studies that show that organizations generally do not consider development issues to be part of their competitive strategy formulation, although he found that those that do so identified it to be of value in gaining as well as maintaining competitive advantage. Miller, writing specifically of management development, points to a lack of fit between business strategy and development activity. Pettigrew and others did find, though, that development issues receive a higher priority when they are linked to organizational needs and take a more strategic approach. Miller makes the point that although at the organizational level it is difficult to identify quantitatively the direct impact of strategic investment in development, this impact is well supported by anecdotal evidence and easily demonstrated at the macro-level.

Those organizations that do consider HR development at a strategic level usually see it as a key to implementing business strategy in a reactive way. Luoma categorises this approach as a 'needs driven' approach, where the purpose of the HR development strategy is to identify and remedy skill deficiencies in relation to the organizational strategy. Luoma suggests that in many articles this is 'implicitly referred to as the only way of managing strategic HRD'. Miller, for example, has demonstrated how management development can be aligned with the strategic positioning of the firm, and this can be seen as coming within the broad remit of such approaches as a needs-driven approach.

Luoma, however, identifies a second approach to HR development strategy which is an 'opportunistic approach', where the impetus is external rather than internal. This would include applying leading ideas on development to the organization in a more general way, rather than specifically in relation to meeting the current business objectives. Such ideas may be developed from benchmarking, case studies, networking and the academic and practitioner press. Such ideas could include content and method, for example the development of a corporate university, and the concept of developing non-employees who perhaps work for suppliers or who are contracted to the organization. The abilities thus developed may indeed be relevant in achieving business objectives, but they may also be relevant in developing abilities and behaviours which may be the source of future competitiveness. Thus they may also be a means of achieving culture change and/or facilitating the strategy process itself by constructing it as a learning process. In this approach the learning potential of all employees will be emphasised, and the HR development strategy may meet reactive needs in implementation of business strategy, but may also be proactive in influencing the formation of future business strategy.

The third approach to the strategy link suggested by Luoma is based on the concept, of organizational capability as the key to sustained competitive advantage, the resource-based view of the firm. This approach is proactive in that it focuses on the desired state of the organization as defined in its future vision. Within this would come the interest in anticipatory learning, which has been attracting some interest, where future needs are predicated and development takes place in advance.

While he recognises the value of competency frameworks in respect of individual development he does point out that these neglect such features as experience and the networks and range of personal contacts, both of which are key to the development of core organizational competencies which are key to developing uniqueness.

In a slightly different but compatible approach McCracken and Wallace develop a redefinition of strategic HR development, based on an initial conception by Garavan. They suggest nine characteristics of a strategic approach to HR development, which are that:

- HR development shapes the organization's mission and goals, as well as having a role in strategy implementation.
- Top management are leaders rather than just supporters of HR development.
- Senior management, and not just HR development professionals, are involved in environmental scanning in relation to HR development.
- HR development strategies, policies and plans are developed, which relate to both the present and future direction of the organization, and the top management team are involved in this.
- Line managers are not only committed and involved in HR development, but involved as strategic partners.
- There is strategic integration with other aspects of HRM.
- Trainers not only have an expanded role, including facilitation and acting as organizational change consultants, but also lead as well as facilitate change.
- HRD professionals have a role in influencing the organizational culture.
- There is an emphasis on future-oriented cost effectiveness and results, in terms of evaluation of HR development activity.

They suggest that each of these aspects needs to be interrelated in an open system. In the following sections we will address some of these characteristics in more detail.

THE EXTERNAL LABOUR MARKET AND HR STRATEGIC INTEGRATION

The external availability of individuals with the skills and competencies required by the organization will also have an impact on employee development strategy. If skilled individuals are plentiful, the organization has the choice of whether, and to what extent it wishes, to develop staff internally. If skilled individuals are in short supply, then internal development invariably becomes a priority. Predicting demographic and social changes is critical in identifying the extent of internal development required and also who will be available to be developed. In-depth analysis may challenge traditionally held assumptions about who will be developed, how and to what extent. For example, the predicted shortage of younger age groups in the labour market, coupled with a shortage of specific skills, may result in a strategy to develop older rather than younger recruits. This poses potential problems about the need to develop older workers some of whom may learn more slowly. What is the best form of development programme for employees with a very varied base of skills and experiences?

Another critical issue is that of redeployment of potentially redundant staff and their development to provide skills that are in short supply. Prediction of skills availability is critical, as for some jobs the training required will take years rather than months. Realising in January that the skills required in August by the organization will not be available in the labour market is too late if the development needed takes three years!

The external labour market clearly has a big impact on employee development strategy, so it is important that there is effective integration between HR development strategy, other aspects of human resource strategy and overall organizational strategy.

Where there is a choice between recruiting required skills or developing them internally, given a strategic approach, the decision will reflect on the positioning of the organization and its strategy.

From a slightly different perspective, the impact of the organization's development strategy on recruitment and retention, either explicit or implicit, is often underestimated. There is increasing evidence to show that employees and potential employees are more interested in development opportunities, especially structured ones, than in improvements in financial rewards. Development activity can drive motivation and commitment, and can be used in a strategic way to contribute towards these. For these ends, publishing and marketing the strategy is key, as well as ensuring that the rhetoric is backed up by action. There is also the tricky question of access to and eligibility for development. If it is offered only very selectively, it can have the reverse of the intended impact.

However, not all employees see the need for, or the value of, development and this means that reward systems need to be supportive of the development strategy. If we want employees to learn new skills and become multiskilled, it is skills development we need to reward rather than the job that is currently done. If we wish employees to gain vocational qualifications, we need to reflect this in our recruitment criteria and reward systems. Harrison notes that these links are not very strong in most organizations.

Other forms of reward, for example promotions and career moves, also need to reflect the development strategy; for example, in providing appropriate, matrix, career pathways if the strategy is to encourage a multifunctional, creative perspective in the development of future general management. Not only do the pathways have to be available, they also have to be used, and this means encouraging current managers to use them for their staff.

Finally, an organization needs to reinforce the skills and competencies it wishes to develop by appraising those skills and competencies rather than something else. Developmentally based appraisal systems can clearly be of particular value here. Mabey and Iles note that a strategic approach to development differs from a tactical one in that a consistent approach to assessment and development is identified with a common skills language and skills criteria attached to overall business objectives. They also note the importance of a decreasing emphasis on subjective assessment. To this end many organizations have introduced a series of development centres, similar to the assessment centres, but with a clear outcome of individual development plans for each participant related to their current levels of competence and potential career moves, and key competencies required by the business.

TRAINING AND DEVELOPMENT ROLES

Salaman and Mabey identify a range of stakeholders in strategic training and development, each of which will have different interests in, influence over and ownership of training and development activities and outcomes. They identify senior managers as the sponsors of training and development, who will be influenced by professional, personal and political agendas; and business planners as the clients who are concerned about customers, competitors and shareholders. Third, they identify line managers who are responsible for performance, coaching and resources; and fourth, participants who are influenced by their career aspirations and other non-work parts of their lives. HRM staff are identified as facilitators who are concerned with best practice, budget credibility and other HR strategy. Lastly, training specialists are identified as providers, who are influenced by external networks, professional expertise and educational perspectives. The agendas of each of these groups will overlap on some issues and conflict on others. We have already noted how McCracken and Wallace have redefined the roles of top managers, line managers and HR professionals so that they are all more proactively involved in HRD strategy.

Most organizational examples suggest that the formation of training and development strategy is not something that should be 'owned' by the HR/HRD function. The strategy needs to be owned and worked on by the whole organization, with the HR/HRD function acting in the roles of specialist/expert and co-ordinator. The function may also play a key role in translating that strategy into action steps. The actions themselves may be carried out by line management, the HR/HRD function or outside consultants. Stewart and Tansley suggest that the immediate and medium-term contribution of HRD professionals should focus on developing the competence and motivation of managers to manage learning and development. They confirm that such professionals need to act as facilitators and not instructors, and have a focus on the process and design of development rather than its content.

Involvement from line management in the delivery of the training and development strategy can have a range of advantages. Top management have a key role in introducing and promoting strategic developments to staff, for example, creating an organization-wide competency identification programme; setting up a system of development centres or introducing a development-based organizational performance management system. Only if management carry out this role can employees see and believe that there is a commitment from the top. At other levels line managers can be trained as trainers, assessors and advisers in delivering the strategy. This is a mechanism not only for getting them involved, but also for tailoring the strategy to meet the real and different needs of different functions and departments.

External consultants may be used at any stage. They may add to the strategy development process, but there is always the worry that their contribution comes down to an offering of their ready-packaged solution, with a bit of tailoring here and there, rather than something which really meets the needs of the organization. It is useful to have an outside perspective, but there is an art in defining the role of that outside contribution.

In delivery, external consultants may make a valuable contribution where a large number of courses have to be run over a short period. The disadvantages are that they can never really understand all the organizational issues, and that they may be seen as someone from outside imposing a new process on the organization.

Note: For a very good case study regarding this topic, reader can visit company's website of Safeway Inc. Safeway is a food and drug retailer. The company operates in the US and Canada. It is headquartered in Pleasanton, California and employs about 197,000 people; this figure includes part-time employees. www.safeway.com

BIBLIOGRAPHY

A. A. Alchian, "Reliability of Progress Curves in Airframe Production," *Econometrica*, 1963.

A. D' Innocenzio, "Wal-Mart's Town Becomes New Address for Corporate America," *Associated Press,* September, 2003.

A. Holeck, "Griffith, Ind. , Native Takes Over as Steel Plant Manager," *The Times*, Munster, IN, May, 2003.

A. Klein, "A Merger Taken AO-111," *Washington Post,* October, 2002

A. Maitland and K. Rollins, "The Two-in-a-Box World of Dell," *Financial Times*, London, March, 2003.

A. Neely, "Dysfunctional Performance through Dysfunctional Measures," *Cost Management*, 2003.

A. Park and P. Burrows, "What You Don't Know about Dell," *Business-Week,* November, 2003.

A. Sinclair, "Approaches to Organizational Culture and Ethics," *Journal of Business Ethics*, 1993.

A. Taylor, "Detroit Buffs Up," *Fortune,* February, 2004.

A. D. Chandler, *Strategy and Structure: Chapters in the History of the Industrial Enterprise*, Cambridge, MA: MIT Press, 1962.

A. P. Sloan, *My Years at General Motors*, New York: Bantum Books, 1996.

A. R. Malekazedeh and A. Nahavandi, "Making Mergers Work by Managing Cultures," *Journal of Business Strategy,* May-June 1990.

B. Bremner and C. Dawson, "Can Anything Stop Toyota?" *Business-Week.* November, 2003.

B. Darrow, "James Goodnight, Founder and CEO, SAS Institute," *Computer Reseller News,* December, 2005.

B. Kabanoff and J. Daly, "Espoused Values in Organisations," *Australian Journal of Managemen,* 2002.

B. McConnell and J. Huba, *Creating Customer Evangelists*, Chicago: Dearborn Trade Publishing, 2003.

B. J. Pine, *Mass Customization: The New Frontier in Business Competition*, Boston: Harvard Business School Press, 1993.

C . W. L. Hill, M. A. Hitt, and R. E. Hoskisson, "Declining U. S. Competitiveness: Reflections on a Crisis," *Academy of Management Executive,* 1988.

C. Bartlett, *Philips versus Matsushita: A New Century, a New Round,* Harvard Business School, 2005.

C. Daniels, "Does This Man Need a Shrink?" *Fortune,* February, 2001.

C. A. Bartlett and S. Ghosha, *Managing across Borders*, Boston: Harvard Business School Press, 1989.

C. A. Schorg, C. A. Raiborn, and M. F. Massoud, "Using a 'Cultural Audit' to Pick M&A Winners," *Journal of Corporate Accounting & Finance,* May-June 2004.

C. K. Swank, "The Lean Service Machine," *Harvard Business Review,* October, 2003.

C. R. Gentry, "Off the Clock. " *Chain Store Age,* February 2003.

C. R. Littler, R. Wiesner, and R. Dunford, "The Dynamics of Delayering," *Journal of Management Studies,* 2003.

C. W. L. Hill and R. E. Hoskisson, "Strategy and Structure in the Multi-product Firm," *Academy of Management Review*, 1988.

C. W. L. Hill, "The Role of Corporate Headquarters in the Multidivisional Firm," in *Fundamental Issues in Strategy Research,* ed. R. Rumelt, D. J. Teece, and D. Schendel, Cambridge, MA: Harvard Business School Press, 1994.

C. W. L. Hill, M. A. Hitl, and R. E. Hoskisson, "Declining US. Competitiveness: Reflections on Crisis," *Academv of Management Executive,* 1988.

C. W. L. Hill, M. A. Hitt, and R. E. Hoskisson, "Cooperative versus Competitive Structures in Related and Unrelated Firms," *Organization Science*, 1992.

Competitive Advantage," *Strategic Management Journal,* 1995.

D. Bertsimas and S. de Boer, "Dynamic Pricing and Inventory Control for Multiple Products," *Journal of Revenue and Pricing Management,* January, 2005.

D. Miller, "Relating Porter's Business Strategies to Environment and Structure," *Academy of Management Journal*, 1988.

D. Naidier, M. Gerstein, and R. Shaw, *Organization Architecture*, San Francisco: Jossey-Bass, 1992.

D. Roth, "My Job at The Container Store," *Fortune,* January, 2000.

D. Welch and K. Kerwin, "Detroit Tries It the Japanese Way," *Business Week,* January, 2004.

D. M. Wiegand and E. S. Geller, "Connecting Positive Psychology and Organization Behavior Management," *Journal of Organization Behavior Management,* 2004-2005.

E. H. Schein, "The Role of the Founder in Creating Organizational Culture," *Organizational Dynamics*, , Summer, 1983.

G. Callioni et al. , "Inventory Driven Costs," *Harvard Business Review,* March, 2005.

G. Morgan, *Images of Organization*, Beverly Hills, CA: Sage Publications, 1986.

G. P. Hattrup and B. H. Kleiner, "How to Establish a Proper Span of Control for Managers," *Industrial Management*, 1993.

H. Luft, J. Bunker, and A. Enthoven, "Should Operations Be Regionalized?" *New England Journal of Medicine*, 1979.

J. Batsell, "Cost Cutting, Inventory Control Help Boost Nordstrom's Quarterly Profit: *Knight Ridder Tribune News*, February, 2002.

J. Birkinshaw, N. Hood, and S. Jonsson, "Building Firm Specific Advantages in Multinational Corporations: The Role of Subsidiary Initiatives," *Strategic Management Journal*, 1998.

J. Bowles, "Is American Management Really Committed to Quality?" *Management Review,* April 1992.

J. Child, "Strategies of Control and Organization Behavior," *Administrative Science Quarterly*, 1973.

J. Child, Organization: *A Guide to Problems and Practice*, Harper & Row; London, 1984.

J. Davidson, "The Business of Ethics. " *Working Woman,* February, 1998.

J. Galbraith, *Designing Complex Organizations*, Reading, MA: Addison-Wesley, 1972.

J. H. Gilmore and BJ. Pine II, "The Four Faces of Mass Customization," *Harvard Business Review,* January-February, 1997.

J. Hewett, "Office Politics," *Australian Financial Review,* September, 2003.

J. Kirn and R. M. Burton, "The Effects of Uncertainty and Decentralization on Project Team Performance," *Computational & Mathematical Organization Theory*, 2002.

J. McCarthy and E. Montalbano, "Microsoft Reshuffies the Deck," InfoWorld , September 2005.

J. Muller, "The Little Car That Could," *Forties,* December, 2003.

J. S. Ott, *The Organizational Culture Perspective*, Pacific Grove, CA: Brooks/Cole, 1989.

J. Schlosser, "Cashing In on the New World of Me," *Fortune,* December, 2004

J. Van Maanen, "Breaking In: Socialization to Work," in *Handbook of Work, Organization, and Society,* ed. R. Dubin, Chicago: Rand McNally, 1976.

J. Welsh and J. Byrne, *Jack: Straight from the Gut*, Warner Books: New York, 2001.

J. A. Byrne, "Jack: A Close Look at How America's #1 Manager Runs GE," *Business Week,* June, 1998.

J. D. Thompson, *Organizations in Action*, New York: McGraw-Hill, 1967.

J. J. van Muijen, "Organizational Culture," in *A Handbook of Work and Organizational Psychology: Organizational Psychology,* 2nd ed. , ed. P. J. D. Drenth, H. Thierry, and C. J. de Wolff, East Sussex, UK: Psychology Press, 1998.

J. M. Stopforf and L. T. Wells, *Strategy and Structure of the Multinational Enterprise*, New York: Basic Books, 1972.

J. P. Womack, D. T. Jones, and D. Roos, *The Machine That Changed the World,* New York: Macmillan, 1990.

J. Z. DeLorean, *On a Clear Day You Can See General Motors*, Grosse Pointe, MI: Wright Enterprises, 1979.

K. Brooker and J. Schlosser, "The Un-CEO," *Fortune,* September, 2002.

K. Eisenhardt, "Control: Organizational and Economic Approaches," *Management Science*, 1985.

K. B. Clark and S. C. Wheelwright, *Managing New Product and Process Development*, New York: Free Press, 1993.

K. M. Eisenhardt, "Making Fast Strategic Decisions in High Velocity Environments," *Academy of Management Journal*, 1989.

L, Worrall and C. Cooper, "Managers, Hierarchies, and Perceptions," *Journal of Managerial Psychology*, 2004.

L. Kim, "The Dynamics of Samsung's Technological Learning in Semi-conductors," *California Management Review*, 1997.

L. Lavelle, "A Payday for Performance," *Business Week,* April, 2005.

M Doehrman, "Anthropologists-Deep in the Corporate Bush," *Daily Record*, Kansas City, MO, July, 2005.

M. Alvesson, *Understanding Organizational Culture*, London: Sage, 2002.

M. Cooke, "Humiliation as Motivator?" *Meetings A Conventions*, July 2001.

M. Dell, *Direct from Dell: Strategies That Revolutionized an Industry*, New York: Harper Collins, 1999.

M. Fan, "Cary, N. C. , Software Firm Posts Steady Growth without IPO," *San Jose Mercury News,* July, 2001.

M. Goold and A. Campbell, "Structured Networks: Toward the Well-Designed Matrix," *Long Range Planning,* October, 2003.

M. Hammer, "Deep Change: How Operational Innovation Can Transform Your Company," *Harvard Business Review,* April 2004.

M. Hammer, "Process Management and the Future of Six Sigma," *MIT Sloan Management Review,* Winter 2002.

M. Weber, *Economy and Society,* trans. and ed. G. Roth and C. Wittich, New York: Bedminster Press, 1968/1921.

M. A. Schilling and C. W. L. Hill, "Managing the New Product

Development Process," *Academy of Management Executive*, August 1998.

M. R. Louis, "Surprise and Sensemaking: What Newcomers Experience in Entering Unfamiliar Organizational Settings," *Administrative Science Quarterly,* 1980.

M. S. Granovetter, "The Strength of Weak Ties," *American Journal of Sociology*, 1973.

N. Greenwood, *Implementing Flexible Manu-facturing Systems*, New York: Halstead Press, 1986.

N. M. Ashkanasy, "The Case for Culture," in *Debating Organization,* ed. R. Westwood and S. Clegg, Maiden, MA: Black-well, 2003.

O. Port and G. Smith, "Quality," *Business-Week,* November, 1992.

O. E. Wiliamson, *The Economic Institutions of Capitalism*, New York: Free Press, 1985.

O. E. Williamson, *Markets and Hierarchies: Analysis and Anti-Trust Implications*, New York: Free Press, 1975.

P. Nemetz and L. Fry, "Flexible Manufacturing Organizations: Im-plications for Strategy Formulation," *Academy of Management Review*, 1988.

P. Roberts, "The Empire Strikes Back," *Fast Company,* February-March, 1999.

P. R Lawrence and J. Lorsch, *Organization and Environment*, Boston: Harvard University Press, 1967.

R. Craver, "Dell Thinning Out List of Job Candidates," *Winston-Salem Journal,* April, 2005.

R. Rosmarin, "Your Custom Car Is Ready at Toyota," *Business 2. 0,* October, 2004.

R. Teichroeb, "End to Forced Busing Creates New Problems for Seattle's Schools," *Seattle Post Intelligencer,* June, 1999.

R. E. Quinn and N. T. Snyder, "Advance Change Theory: Culture Change at Whirlpool Corporation," in *The Leader s Change Handbook,* ed. J. A. Conger, G. M. Spreitzer, and E. E. Lawler III, San Francisco: Jossey-Bass, 1999.

R. S. Kaplan and D. P. Norton, *The Balanced Scorecard: Translating*

Strategy into Action, Boston: Harvard Business School Press, 1996.

S. Chambers and R. Johnston, "Experience Curves in Services," *International Journal of Operations and Production Management*, 2000.

S. Kotha, "Mass Customization: Implementing the Emerging Paradigm for Competitive Advantage," *Strategic Management Journal*, 1995.

S. Sackmann, "Culture and Subcultures: An Analysis of Organizational Knowledge," *Administrative Science Quarterly*, 1992.

S. Thomas and L. S. D'Annunizo, "Challenges and Strategies of Matrix Organizations," *HR Human Resource Planning,* 2005.

S. A. Snell, "Control Theory in Human Resource Management," *Academy of Management Review*, 1992.

S. F. Jablonsky and N. P. Barsky, *The Manager's Guide to Financial Statement Analysis*, New York: Wiley, 2001.

S. G. Green and M. A. Welsh, "Cybernetics and Dependence: Reframing the Control Concept," *Academy of Management Review*, 1988.

S. G. Harris, "Organizational Culture and Individual Sensemaking: A Schema-Based Perspective," *Organization Science*, 1994.

S. M. Davis, "Managing and Organizing Multinational Corporations,' in *Transnational Management,* ed. C. A. Bartlett and S. Ghoshal, Homewood, IU: Richard D. Irwin, 1992.

S. P. Seith, "The Impact of Flexible Automation on Business Strategy and Organizational Structure," *Academy of Management Review*, 1992.

T. Copeland, T. Koller, and J. Murrin, *Valuation: Measuring and Managing the Value of Companies*, New York: Wiley, 1996.

T. Hamilton, "RIM on a Roll," *Toronto Star,* February, 2004.

T. Parker-Pope, "New CEO Preaches Rebellion for P&G's 'Cult," *The Wall Street Journal,* December, 1998;

V. S. Borland, "Global Technology in the Twenty-First Century," *Textile World,* January 2003.

W. G. Ouchi, "Markets, Bureaucracies, and Clans," *Administrative Science Quarterly*, 1980.

Wolf and W. G. Egelhoff, "A Reexamination and Extension of International Strategy-Structure Theory," *Strategic Management Journal*, 2002.

Index

219, 220, 224, 225, 227, 228,